SEARCHING
FOR
BOBBY
FISCHER

SEARCHING
FOR
BOBBY
FISCHER

THE WORLD OF CHESS,
OBSERVED BY THE FATHER OF
A CHILD PRODIGY

FRED WAITZKIN

RANDOM HOUSE  NEW YORK

Portions of this work have appeared in *New York* magazine.

Grateful acknowledgment is made to *The New York Times* for permission to
reprint an article entitled "Fathering a Chess Prodigy," by Fred Waitzkin,
which appeared the July 21, 1985, issue of *The New York Times*. Copyright ©
1985 by The New York Times Company. Reprinted by permission.

Library of Congress Cataloging-in-Publication Data
Waitzkin, Fred.
Searching for Bobby Fischer.
1. Waitzkin, Josh.   2. Chess players—United States—
Biography.   3. Fathers and sons—United States—Case
studies.   4. Fischer, Bobby, 1943–   . I. Title.
GV1439.W35W35   1988   794.1′092′4 [B]   88-42657
ISBN 0-394-54455-2

Manufactured in the United States of America
24689753
First Edition

For Bonnie,
without whose love and ideas this book
could not have been written,
and for Katya and Josh

CONTENTS

1. Fathering a Chess Prodigy   3
2. Fischer's Legacy   11
3. Washington Square   17
4. Bruce Pandolfini   26
5. The Greater New York Open   33
6. Training for Moscow   38
7. The Hall of Columns   45
8. Mark Dvoretsky   56
9. Volodja   64
10. The Pressroom   75
11. Not Closed for Repairs   84
12. Boris Gulko   90
13. The Chess Shop   100
14. Josh and Bruce   104
15. Playing for the Title   114
16. The Championship of Bimini   119
17. Losing It   132
18. A Chess Fan's Notes   145
19. Chess Parents   155
20. Roman   169
21. Searching for Bobby Fischer   175
22. The Nationals   201
    Epilogue   223

SEARCHING
FOR
BOBBY
FISCHER

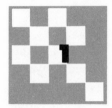

FATHERING
A
CHESS
PRODIGY

In the spring of 1984, at the National Elementary Chess Championship in Syracuse, New York, a distraught father began to whisper moves to his son. Across the gymnasium floor, scores of other parents crowded close to the chessboards and nervously discussed the games within earshot of the players. Some of the six-, seven- and eight-year-old children asked the parents to be quiet and to give them room to play. Two frustrated fathers began shoving each other, and one took a swing. Eventually the irate tournament director ordered all parents out of the playing room. Soon more than a hundred fathers and mothers were pacing in the hall outside. The absence of desperate parents was a relief to the kids, no doubt, but being locked out heightened the already feverish anxiety of these poor people. Once in a while the tournament director would open the door a crack so the children could have some air. Instantly, scores of parents would scramble for a hand-in-your-face glimpse of their kid's game. I was among them.

When Josh was a baby, I fantasized that he would grow up to be a star basketball player, with me cheering from the stands. Together we would stay in shape, jogging like Joe and his father in Ernest Hemingway's story "My Old Man." Instead my son is a chess player. Since he began playing in tournaments at the age of seven, he has frequently been the highest-rated player for his age in the United States. Our home has become cluttered with gaudy trophies, chess sets, chess clocks, score books, computers and chess literature in different languages. His precocious ability for this board game has seized control of my imagination. I used to worry about my career, my health, my marriage, my friends, my mother. Now I mostly worry about Joshua's chess. I worry about his rating and whether he's done his chess homework. There are tournaments to be concerned about. Has he practiced enough? Too much? In years past, while I sat at my desk struggling to write, I often daydreamed about the Knicks or about going fishing. Now in my mind I play over my son's chess games; his sedentary activity has displaced many priorities in my life.

Josh is very athletic, and at chess tournaments he is eager to play ball between rounds. While I gather up his chess pieces and pencils, it's my job to say, "No, Josh. You don't want to knock yourself out. Why not go over your openings?" Usually at scholastic tournaments he is seated at the number-one board, and other little kids sometimes get sick to their stomachs because they have to play against my little kid. Their parents treat me deferentially, as if I had done something myself. It's an odd position for a father to be caddy and coach for his three-and-a-half-foot, sitting, brooding son.

Josh and I played our first chess games on a squat coffee table in the living room when he was six years old. He sat on the floor, his face cupped in his hands, his eyes at the level of the wooden pieces as if he were peering into a dangerous but alluring forest. By trial and error, more than by my instruction, which he staunchly resisted, he found tricky ways to trap my pieces. He unearthed standard chess strategies and tactics that players have used for centuries. He was good at this new game.

So good that I kept forgetting how old he was. Often I became caught up in the intrigues of combat and found myself trying to take my son's head off. I batted aside his little attacks like Rommel—I crushed him. Josh would come back shaking his fist at me and grimacing. "I must win, I must win," he'd mutter to himself while setting up the pieces. It must have been profoundly confusing for him that I was able to defeat his best ideas. A couple of times I offered him the handicap of knight odds and he cried at my impudence, as if I'd tried to humiliate him. Already he seemed to know that his old man was a hack, what chess players call a patzer.

While I tried to slaughter Josh, I rooted for him to win. The game became a quicksand of passion for us. After an emotional loss, he would pretend not to care, but his lower lip would tremble. Dejected, he'd go off to his room and my heart would be broken. My carefully crafted victories felt like defeats. The next day he would refuse to play me again, not even for a new toy car—not even for candy. I would feel panicky. Maybe during my last blistering attack I'd killed off his baby dream of being the world champion. Or maybe it was my dream, not his. Such distinctions are ambiguous between a father and a little son. This is how fathers mess up their kids, I'd lecture myself. Would you throw a slider to a six-year-old just learning to hit? Or smack him in the belly with a hard spiral? Still, a few days later we'd be at it again. Once after I'd sprung a trap on his queen, Josh announced that he didn't want to become a grandmaster; "it's too hard," he said. Feeling bad, I asked what he would do instead. He announced soberly that he would work in a pizza shop that had a Pac Man machine (he knew how much I hate video games).

In retrospect I suppose that Josh was just beginning to exercise his muscles as a chess psychologist, trying to soften me up, because the following afternoon he was squirming with pluck and purpose, knocking down pieces each time he reached his short arm across the board to take one of my pawns. That day I was feeling like Karpov, carefully building an insurmountable attack. The game took a long time, and while he was considering the position, I took a break for a shower. I was toweling off when Josh called me, beside himself with impatience. I grabbed a beer, checked the position and made my move. Josh smiled, slid his rook over and announced, "Mate in two."

"I doubt it," I said smugly, but every move was a vise. He had me. I hugged him and we rolled on the floor laughing. It was the first time he'd ever beaten me.

A FEW MONTHS later, to find Josh stronger opponents we took him to the Marshall Chess Club on 10th Street, which was within walking distance of our apartment. In the Marshall, the worn Victorian furniture, the unpolished parquet floors, even the dust resonated with brilliant chess games from the past. But in the shadows of late afternoon the tangible presence of chess history made no impression on six-year-old Josh, who picked red gummy bears out of a plastic bag while he observed two chess masters playing speed chess, which is called blitz. While my wife and I chatted with the manager, our son giggled as the players moved the pieces at sleight-of-hand speed and took turns ferociously slamming the time clock after each move.

We were politely informed by the manager that there had never been a six-year-old member of the Marshall, and that it would make more sense to bring him back in six or seven years, after he had learned more about the game and was old enough to read chess books. By now Josh had sauntered to a far corner of the room where a young man with a sallow complexion sat in front of an inlaid oak-and-mahogany chess table and played from a book of Russian openings, silently moving the pieces for both black and white, a mime of chess. Josh didn't know what to make of this; maybe the man was pretending, like playing with dragons and superheroes. After a moment, he asked exuberantly, "Wanna play?" and the young man looked up with a dazed expression.

A few minutes later my little boy was sitting on a telephone book so that he could see over his chess pieces, and as he plunked his men down he chewed gummy bears. Surprisingly, the game went on and on, into the second hour; by then half a dozen members of the club were clustered around the table watching. Down only a pawn, Josh moved almost instantly, parrying attacks, then fidgeting, looking out the window and making faces at his embarrassed and proud parents while waiting for his opponent to move. The young man played the game in a vacuum; he seemed to sift through history before making each decision and never glanced at his miniature opponent.

"Trick or treat," Josh announced finally as he pushed a pawn forward. The young man was perplexed for a moment, then flushed as if he'd been slapped. One of the members couldn't contain his excitement and whispered, "He's won the rook!" The pawn had sprung a discovered attack. Josh's bishop was checking the king, and when it moved away, he'd take the rook.

The young man ran his fingers through his hair, his expression anguished. After five minutes of considering he reached across the table and offered Josh his hand. My son was confused by this gesture; he had not yet learned about resigning.

BY THE TIME Josh was seven, he was clearly a stronger player than his father, and his United States Chess Federation rating was higher than those of half the tournament players in the country. Sometimes my friends would watch while he took me apart. They'd shake their heads, and I'd beam with parental pride. But later that night I'd be studying chess books for a new opening to use against him. Excited as I was by his burgeoning and inexplicable chess talent, I found it unsettling that he could calculate exchanges more accurately and three times faster than I could. He beat me game after game. Losing to him made me feel old and dull. The first time he offered me knight odds I became furious, as if he'd been egregiously disrespectful. There were times when he was so blithely trapping my pieces that I'd want to wrestle him to the ground and pin his arms.

Long before he turned eight Josh knew that he was in a different class than his old man and in our games he stopped trying. While I carefully appraised the possibilities for each piece, he thumbed through books, looked out the window, chewed gum, chatted with his mother, cracked jokes, tapped his foot, sighed. Usually when he played in this indifferent manner he lost. I took his neglected knights and bishops. He yawned when I snatched his unprotected queen: so what, big deal. It made me furious. With a chess player's reasoning and guile he pointed out that he was allowed to lose to me; he was only seven. Sometimes, after he'd carelessly lost a piece, I'd get impatient with him and sweep the chessmen from the board. I yearned to be beaten, but Josh would have no part of it. Once, after a particularly frustrating encounter, my wife, who frequently reminded us that there is life after chess, said, "Don't you understand? He really doesn't want to beat his daddy." The remark stopped me in my tracks. In the heat of our competitions it had never occurred to me that my son might feel uncomfortable snuffing out his old man like an ant.

After that, Josh and I rarely played chess. Instead, I watched his chess lessons or took him to play stronger opponents in Washington Square Park and in tournaments. In my new role as chess coach and fan I've come to feel compassion, if not grudging respect, for John McEnroe's father and for other fathers and mothers like us, a beleaguered fraternity of watchers and worriers who have been unexpectedly sucked into a world in which we are not proficient.

Josh is a rough-and-tumble kid, handsome, with thick brown hair, his mother's brown eyes and a sturdy body. Since the age of three he has called me Fred, though I would have preferred Daddy, and has waited impatiently for me to finish work in the evenings, as if my raison d'être were to throw him passes beneath the streetlights in front of our apartment building. After dinner he badgers me to wrestle with him on the living-room floor and argues to the last instant about how much more time remains before bed. To his schoolmates he is a basketball and football kid, a big eater, a good math student, but more conspicuously a cutup in class, often testing his teachers' patience with tardy or sloppy homework and boisterous practical jokes. They know him as a vicious kickball player, a teaser, a candy maniac, crazy about the Hardy Boys but a scaredy-cat about horror and kung fu movies. To them his chess playing is a vague activity which results in big trophies. One afternoon during a conference with his second-grade teacher, Bonnie and I tried to explain that Josh had a special talent for the game. As we spoke the woman tapped her foot, as if we were describing a different boy from the one who couldn't sit still in his chair and was struggling with reading and writing. We urged her to come to the park to watch him play; he just doesn't seem like a chess player until you see him settle in front of the board, his body stiffening a little, his face becoming serene and ageless, the little boy taking leave for a time while Josh muses over ancient, difficult ideas.

OUTSIDE CHESS CIRCLES, my involvement with Joshua's chess is often perceived as a kind of quirky self-indulgence. I watch the parents of his friends make harsh, silent judgments when I try to explain that he is living a well-rounded life, but that there is simply no time for Little League. "What're you doing with that boy? Chess? He should be taking piano and tennis lessons, playing stick-

ball, going to more Yankee games. And what about his religious
education? You mean you're keeping him out of Hebrew school
because of tournaments?" Such disapproving messages confuse me
and make me feel guilty. Perhaps Josh doesn't really like chess, I
tell myself. Maybe I'm forcing it on him. When I ask him how he
feels about the game he shrugs in a way that suggests he likes video
games more. Then I have to wonder if you can really trust what
an eight-year-old says he likes. I'm the parent; I must decide what's
best for him. But what is best? Many afternoons Josh sits at the
chessboard shielding his ears from the siren song of little boys
riding their bikes on the sidewalk below our window. When I was
seven, I'd have cried if my father had made such a demand. But
my father didn't make a little John McEnroe.

ONCE OR TWICE a week, Joshua's chess teacher, Bruce Pandolfini,
arrives at our apartment at six-thirty in the morning, and our son
stumbles out of bed in pj's wearing a face as dreamy as his infant
sister's. But within a few seconds he has assumed the position—
two hands under his chin—and is staring bullets at the chessboard.
My little Karpov. Watching him sit at the board concentrating like
a miniature master has become more exciting to me than watching
Michael Jordan whirl 360 degrees and jam. But maybe Josh will
hate me when he grows up. Will he spend years talking to a psy-
chiatrist about the trip I laid on him at seven, when he stopped
concentrating during a speed game with his eight-year-old friend
Nicky Silvers?

WHENEVER JOSH IS about to play in a tournament I'm haunted by
the possibility that he isn't any good, that his supposed talent is a
house of cards manufactured by a father who thrives on fantasy. I
bring a book or the Sunday Times to read while he plays his games.
Hours pass with the paper on my knee but I haven't read a paragraph. I'm preoccupied with his game. The last time I looked he
was down a pawn. Did he get it back? Is he concentrating? Has
he had too little to eat? Too much Coca-Cola? Other parents also
pretend to read the Sunday paper while they worry. The kids sit
monkishly in front of their chessboards, a roomful of miniature
Erasmuses assiduously inscribing moves on score sheets. When

the games end, they offer their hands in congratulation like courtly gentlemen. But for the parents the tension is often too great and the veneer of nonchalance cracks. Mothers and fathers wring their hands, feel nauseous and shake. Veins in their foreheads pulse with tension. Sometimes they snap at one another or at the tournament director.

When he was eight, in the final round of the 1984 New York City Primary Championship, my son played against a boy also named Josh. A group of fifteen or twenty parents and children crowded around the game, which would decide the city championship for kids between the ages of six and nine. I was too nervous to watch and stood in the stairwell of the Manhattan Chess Club with a couple of mothers who were nursing babies. Someone asked me why I wasn't watching. "I don't want to make him nervous," I lied. "The position is dead even," someone called hastily from the door. "Josh is using too much time." Which Josh?

At one point I caught the eye of the other Josh's father, an intelligent, gentle man, and we nodded at one another, a little sad that it had come down to this: both of us rooting for an eight-year-old kid named Josh to crack under the tension and make a heart-breaking blunder. This father had been a star running back in college, and it occurred to me that he had probably never felt more pressure on the football field than he did right now, all of those bone-crunching games toughening him up for an afternoon like this, watching his son trying to outthink another kid.

"Josh is running out of time," someone whispered loudly. "Josh is crying," another boy said. Which Josh?

Finally I couldn't bear the stairwell and went outside to walk around the block. When I returned twenty minutes later, it was all over. The awards ceremony was finished, and my Josh was joking and playing speed chess with another boy. They were having a good time, in between moves making plans to get together. The tournament was old news. When Josh caught my eye and lifted up the big first-place trophy, I made a gaudy high five from across the room. My son was a little embarrassed, but it was impossible for me to be casual. At such a moment, a parent is truly the child, giddy and dancing like a fool with fantasies of glory and immortality that he will carry to his grave.

FISCHER'S
LEGACY

As a young man, I thought of chess as cerebral and boring, and I had no interest in learning to play. But on many summer afternoons in 1972, when Bobby Fischer played Boris Spassky for the world championship, I found myself sitting in front of a television set with a few friends, rooting and even screaming at an outsized chessboard as if it were a basketball court rather than the evolving chess positions of two men sitting motionless thousands of miles away. At the beginning of the match I didn't even know how the pieces moved, and yet these slow-moving esoteric battles filled me with passion and a yearning that at first I didn't understand. I imagined the pressure the champion and the challenger must have felt as they tried to outwit each other, searching for the most intricate and subtle nuances of advantage while millions looked over their shoulders and second-guessed them. It must have been like trying to compose a sonnet with a guillotine blade poised to fall if the verse didn't come up to Shakespeare's. Each man bore the responsibility for his country's national honor. Spassky would be Russia's greatest hero if he won, and would fall into disgrace and lose his privileges if he didn't. Fischer wanted to annihilate the Russians, whom he had hated since he had decided as a teenager that they cheated in international tournaments. If he won he would instantly become a legend; if he lost he would be dismissed by many people as a crackpot. Henry Kissinger gave his moral support to Fischer, and Brezhnev nervously awaited the results of each game. For many viewers, communism and capitalism were fighting it out on afternoon television. Fischer's precise style of chess was charged with innuendos of violence and irrationality; like a Rambo of the mind he talked of crushing his opponent's ego. Spassky, on the other hand, was urbane, ironic, intellectual, an aesthete and an exquisite foil for Fischer's crude excesses. That summer of 1972, chess became monumental, a game unlike any other, and everyone wanted to play.

I HAVE ALWAYS loved sports even though I was never exceptionally good at them. But in 1972, along with millions of other Americans, I discovered the sport of thinking. It seemed tailor-made for me. I have patience and good reasoning ability and am happy sitting for hours working on a paragraph or turning over an idea. In the flush of Bobby's winning, I decided that chess might be my sport. During the course of the match I learned the moves and a few simple tactics. I bought elegant wooden pieces and began to play games against my friends. I watched how slowly the moves came in from Reykjavik, Iceland, and at least to that extent I patterned my games after those of the championship contenders. I thought about each move for a long time, sometimes for half an hour, like Fischer and Spassky, which drove my friends to distraction. They urged me to move faster, made fun of me, threatened to quit, but I tried to ignore their ill humor and to concentrate on the position. I recalled what Bobby had said: "I don't think about the man, only about good moves."

Each game I listened attentively to National Master Shelby Lyman and to Bruce Pandolfini, another master who appeared regularly on the show, and tried to guess the next move from Reykjavik. Spassky might have played your move, Lyman suggested hundreds of times, he might have played mine, but he chose something else, not necessarily stronger. Sometimes I was smugly convinced that my idea was better than the one selected by the grandmaster. Lyman was young and charming, with a gift for democratizing chess, for clouding distinctions between ability and ineptitude. Riding the coattails of Bobby's charisma, he became a celebrity overnight, the Johnny Appleseed of chess. Without actually saying so, he was persuading the United States that chess genius was within reach of all of us; it was a tour de force of showmanship. By the end of the match, I still understood virtually nothing about the game, but I could feel it welling up in me like a calling.

When Lyman went off the air, I decided that it was time to get serious. I bought chess books and memorized a few openings. I went over the game that thirteen-year-old Fischer had played against Donald Byrne, in which he had sacrificed his queen to win twenty-four moves later, and I wondered how many more weeks it would take before I would be making such moves. I pestered my friends to play, and to my delight, I won more than I lost. My style was the waiting game. I took a long time to move and never attacked, always looking for safe, protected harbors for my pieces. The longer I took to make my passive decisions, the faster my friends responded, as if to say, "Look, you're killing the game and boring me to death; play faster." Usually, moving quickly and petulantly, they blundered, and slowly I would grind out a win. Despite my meager experience, when friends who had played the game since high school decided they didn't want to play me anymore, I concluded that I must be too good.

ONE DAY IN 1972 I discovered the chess coffee shop on Thompson Street in Greenwich Village, where years later on winter afternoons I would take Josh to play. On that first occasion, I played against a pimply adolescent who after twenty minutes caught on to my methodical bob-and-weave style and began to read a newspaper. I was annoyed by his lack of concern, then astounded when he mated me, barely looking away from his reading.

During the second game, he read from the beginning, but this time it lasted longer. After a couple of hours I was muddled. The more I looked, the less I saw. All of his pieces were attacking, and soon I was out of safe hiding squares. I was sweating and feeling humiliated while he read and glanced at other games. I would have to engage, but I knew I'd be crushed. I moved a piece ahead, half-expecting him to laugh in my face; instead, he put down the paper, stared at the position with concern and then knocked over his king and put out his hand. Even after he left the table and I had studied the position, I could see no possible reason why he should have resigned. Finally I asked another player, who briskly demonstrated that I had forced mate in three. He had to show it to me twice before I could follow the moves.

After this victory I walked home, packed my Staunton pieces in their wooden box and shoved it to the back of a shelf, where it remained without interruption for the next ten years until six-year-old Josh begged me to take it down. That day in the chess shop I had realized that just as surely as I lacked the running and leaping ability for professional basketball, I didn't have what it takes to be a good chess player.

Still, the game was in my blood, and over the years Bobby Fischer has occupied much time in my fantasy life. Like many fans of the Fischer-Spassky match, I have wondered what happened to Fischer after winning the championship, and often I have had shivery daydreams about his comeback, his blustery late entrance on stage, barely noticing Karpov or Kasparov as he sprawls into his swivel chair and contemptuously pushes ahead the king pawn. I have waited for Bobby as if his disappearance were no more than a tease, to be followed by greater victories than anyone had ever dreamed possible.

CHESS CLUBS PROLIFERATED during the early seventies, inspired by Bobby's success and charisma. Mothers pulled their sons out of Little League and ferried them to chess lessons. Talented young players with dreams of Fischer, television immortality and big chess money spurned college and conventional career choices to turn professional. For a brief time shy, introverted chess players basked in national glory, along with running backs and rock stars.

"There were even chess groupies," recalls Bruce Pandolfini. "The chess world has always been essentially sexless, but these girls studied the U.S. Chess Federation rating chart and began working their way up. They were playing their own kind of chess game. They seduced the most ascetic grandmasters. They all wanted Fischer."

In 1972, before Shelby Lyman put him on television, Pandolfini was an impoverished tournament player who subsisted on a variety of part-time jobs. "One week I was sorting mail at the post office and the next I was on television. A few days after the show began, I was walking along Sixth Avenue when suddenly a big limousine screeched to a halt. A beautiful woman whom I had never seen before stepped out. She shouted, 'Bruce! Bruce Pandolfini! Oh, wow!' "

Overnight this cerebral, slow-moving board game became supercharged with American glitz. Fischer was on the cover of *Sports Illustrated, Life, Time* and *Newsweek*; he appeared on the Dick Cavett and Johnny Carson shows. "Chess is like war on a board," he told us. "The object is to crush the other man's mind. . . . I like to see 'em squirm." It was as if he had invented a new game.

Chess sets became a best seller at Brentano's. Fischer's two books on chess sold hundreds of thousands of copies, and his good fortune trickled down to other chess professionals. Pandolfini said, "I began charging up to a hundred and fifty dollars an hour for private lessons. Some of the Wall Street lawyers and rich doctors I taught were just terrible. They had no talent or appreciation for the game. Sometimes I fell asleep during lessons, but it didn't matter. They thought they'd catch chess genius just being around the guy who'd talked about Fischer on television."

BOBBY FISCHER WAS born in 1943. From the time he was a six-year-old living in Brooklyn until he won the world championship at twenty-nine, he was totally preoccupied with chess. At the age of fourteen, he won the United States championship, an unparalleled feat. But he was already becoming bitter about the shabby treatment of chess in the United States. He was incensed, for example, that while the Russians spent lavishly to field a well-coached team for the Olympiad, Americans were hard pressed to raise the airfare to compete. In his biography of Fischer, Frank Brady suggests that the reason for Bobby's grandiose financial demands after his rise to fame was as much the desire to give chess in the United States recognition and stature as the wish for personal enrichment.*

* Frank Brady, *Profile of a Prodigy* (New York: David McKay, 1973), p. 211.

In 1977, Bobby Fischer was offered a quarter of a million dollars to play a single game at Caesars Palace but turned it down: it was not enough money. President Marcos offered to sponsor a three-million-dollar championship match in the Philippines, and Bobby was said to have ten million lined up in commercial offers. Then, turning his back on fame unprecedented for a chess player and tremendous potential wealth, he surprised his fans by retiring from the game and becoming a recluse. He has not been seen in public for years.

With his disappearance, Fischer created a chess wasteland. The new clubs of the seventies disappeared along with him, and many of the old ones withered in membership and grew shabby. For example, the Marshall Chess Club has become badly run-down and is so financially depleted that frequently there are no chess pieces available for its members. It is empty most of the day, except for a few old men who snore in their armchairs, and its membership has shrunk from more than seven hundred in 1974 to only about two hundred today. Directors of both the Marshall and Manhattan chess clubs have speculated that without an unexpected infusion of money and interest in chess soon—perhaps the reemergence of Bobby or the coming of a new Fischer—New York City may not be able to support a clean and respectable chess club.

During the past fifteen years, the parents of some of America's strongest young players have forbidden them to pursue the game lest it become a dead-end preoccupation. Noted chess teachers have become computer programmers, art dealers and bookies. To survive as weekend players, some of the talented young men who were lured to chess by Fischer fifteen years ago now drive cabs, unload trucks or hustle chess in the parks. One international master who for many years has supported himself by working at menial jobs says, "I can't make a living from chess, but I've devoted so much time to the game that I have no other marketable skill. Sometimes when I look back, I wish I hadn't seen Shelby Lyman on television. I would have done something else with my life."

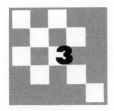

WASHINGTON
SQUARE

The crooning of a saxophone mixed with the uneven click of plastic chess pieces on marble chess tables in the southwest corner of Washington Square Park. Vinnie, a thirty-four-year-old black man, sat at one of the tables, nursing a paper cup of coffee. He was wearing a torn maroon sweater, soiled corduroy pants and unmatched socks rolled at the ankles. Seated beside him was a junkie, mumbling and swaying. In front of Vinnie, on a table stained with Coke and dried pizza sauce, chess pieces stood poised. A young man approached. He had a strong athletic build, which drew attention to the sickly pallor of his boyish face. In a tremulous voice, he asked if Vinnie wanted to play for a dollar a game. Vinnie tried to hide his smile as he reached into a shopping bag for his chess clock. He'd found a fish and was already tasting the Chinese dinner he'd eat that night. Vinnie is a master-level player, but he's often short of change for a subway token.

The young man sat on a green park bench, and almost immediately the two players were surrounded by a crowd of kibitzers. Among them was my six-year-old son, chewing bubble gum and leaning familiarly on Vinnie's arm. Although Josh could barely read, he sometimes beat some of the adults here and watched intricate speed-chess games by the hour with the same pleased expression as when he looked at cartoons on television.

"Two minutes a game?" the young man asked in a Germanic accent, suddenly confident and contemptuous.

Playing at this speed, the men raced through this most deliberate and cerebral game as if it were pinball. Paced by the nerve-racking snap of the clock, chessmen flowed into lines of attack. Captures were made with a snatch, and sometimes, during last-second flurries, knights and bishops were knocked to the ground. Vinnie talked while he played. "To kill a vampire you gotta put a stake into his heart. Josh, I said you gotta put a stake in his heart. Remember that," Vinnie repeated, playing to the crowd with operatic bravado. Then he announced, "Mate in three."

Speed chess is thrilling to watch, and the onlookers were as tense and giddy with excitement as a fight crowd. Someone whispered that the pale young man was a grandmaster named Eric Lobron, one of the top chess players in the world. Vinnie the hustler was being hustled. Lobron blushed at being recognized and for a moment tried to pretend he was someone else.

"Let's see what you know, Mr. Grandmaster," Vinnie taunted while they set up the pieces for the next game. "What d'ya know, Grandmaster?" he chanted after each move, using his rap like an extra rook. "Whad they teach ya in Germany, Grandmaster. You wanna exchange queens? Okay, let's go." BAM. BAM. The pieces snapped against the marble table like caps. Lobron, who was used to playing in the sacred quiet of international tournaments, was disconcerted by Vinnie's mouth and couldn't play up to his strength. "Ya got nuthin', Grandmaster. I said you got nuthin'. What you think you're gonna do to my black ass? You think you're gonna come into my office and take my money? Get outta here."

Like Vinnie, Lobron had come to the park to hustle a few dollars for his dinner. As it turned out, each player won three games, and no one made a nickel.

JOSH DISCOVERED CHESS in Washington Square Park when he was six years old. It was a cold March afternoon, with dirty clumps of snow on the ground. We paused to watch two men who were sitting at one of the tables. One of them was rocking back and forth as if he were reciting the Kaddish. The other man wore only a light nylon jacket and from time to time shivered violently. He was concentrating so hard on his game that he didn't seem to notice how cold he was. It was hard for me to pull Josh away. The next day he asked a teacher in his after-school play group to show him how the pieces moved.

Several weeks later on a sunny Sunday morning, while crossing the chess corner on the way to the swings on the other side of the park, Josh broke away from his mother and ran up to a distinguished-looking man with a beard and asked if he could play. The man, David Hechtlinger, who was waiting for a friend, was willing to give him a game. He was fond of children who want to play chess because his son had been a young master, and he had often wondered how good his son might have become if he had continued to work at it. After the game was over, he explained to Bonnie that Josh had used pieces in combination to launch an attack, a sign of chess talent in a beginner. Hechtlinger wrote Josh's name on the masthead of his newspaper. "I'll look for your name someday," he told our son. After that game, Josh began to pester his mother to take him to watch the men in the park after school. He said he liked the way the chess pieces looked.

WASHINGTON SQUARE IS six blocks from our apartment, and now it became Joshua's chess playground. Many afternoons after school, while other little boys played touch football under the trees or jumped bicycles over the nearby asphalt mounds, he played chess with school dropouts, retired workers, talented winos and down-and-out masters. Some days he'd look up mournfully at the kids on their bikes and lose his concentration, but mostly he didn't seem to notice them and would surprise adults by winning a few games.

Chess players greet each new young talent with curiosity and expectation; it's almost as if they are waiting for the messiah. Josh was affectionately referred to as "young Fischer" by some of the old-timers, who recalled the games Bobby played in Washington Square as a little boy in the fifties.

If Josh ever becomes a grandmaster, he'll owe a lot to the guys in the park who helped him. These early teachers couldn't have been more caring, enthusiastic or perceptive. For example, Jerry, a short black man who wore a bandana and played without a shirt whenever it was warmer than fifty degrees, pestered Josh to be an aggressive player, reminded him not to make passive moves and emphasized that even when his position was difficult he should try to attack and defend at the same time.

Jerry worried about Joshua's chess and Josh worried about Jerry. He was a strong A player* with sweet chess tactics, but he was also a thirty-eight-year-old alcoholic. Ten years ago he had been an auto mechanic. That part of his life ended one night when he had a fight with his wife and she put five bullets in his back. Jerry said it had been his fault but never explained why. After he got out of the hospital he began living in flophouses and playing chess in the park.

Jerry had a way of helping Josh without patronizing him. "You lost because you didn't castle, Josh, and you're gonna keep losing until you castle." He always played his hardest against Josh and beat him game after game, all the while showing him that he hadn't developed his pieces or had split his pawns so that they were vulnerable to attack, or pointing out the mates Josh had missed. When occasionally Josh beat Jerry he felt he'd accomplished something special—unless Jerry was drunk or high. Then it didn't mean anything; Jerry would stumble all over the park and couldn't beat a patzer.

When Josh turned seven and began playing in a few scholastic tournaments, it made Jerry nervous. He had never been good in tournaments himself. He said it was too much pressure for a kid, and he was always relieved when the weekend children's competitions were over and Josh was back playing in the park after school. In turn, Josh was afraid that Jerry would starve to death, and he brought food to the park almost every day for six months. He was particularly concerned on rainy nights when Jerry didn't have the money for a room and had to sleep on a bench.

One summer before we left for vacation, things were looking up for Jerry. He'd been on the wagon for nearly two months. Financed by the Veterans Administration, he was about to begin a six-month course as a computer repairman. He showed us the brochure; it

* The United States Chess Federation categorizes players by rating—as Class E, D, C, B, A, Expert, Master, or Senior Master. An A player has a rating between 1800 and 1999 and is among the top 17 percent of all tournament players. Numerical ratings are estimates of chess skill based on tournament results. Rating points are awarded or subtracted for winning or losing games in recognized tournaments. More points are gained for beating stronger opponents or lost for losing to weaker ones.

was a new chance, he said, and he wouldn't mess it up by starting to drink again. The V.A. was giving Jerry a set of tools worth five hundred dollars. In the afternoon after school he was going to study his manuals under the trees behind the chess tables, but maybe in the evening there would be time for a couple of games. Josh, Jerry and I all agreed that computer repair was more important than chess.

One afternoon Jerry proudly showed his new red toolbox to Josh, and as the two of them sat on the grass, Josh tutored his friend on the multiplication table, which was part of the course requirement. At night Jerry slept on a bench with his hand slung over the toolbox so that it wouldn't be stolen.

When we returned to the park after the summer vacation, Josh couldn't find Jerry, and none of the guys knew where he was. A couple of weeks later, he showed up with his face bruised and cut. He had been in the hospital and said there was something wrong with his chest. He'd been beaten up by three guys and his tools had been stolen. He was very angry. He said the cops wouldn't help and had treated him like a criminal because he was poor and black. He said he was going to be away for a while and wouldn't have time for chess, and he forced his copy of *My System* by Aron Nimzovich on Josh. He had bought a gun and said he had to do some things.

We never saw Jerry again.

ANOTHER CHESS HUSTLER in the park was Israel Zilber. At some fifty years of age, he was emaciated, his face so creased and weather-beaten that he could easily have passed for seventy-five. He wore a scuffed leather jacket and a naval cap decorated with a large sheriff's badge. Each of his fingers was weighted with garish costume jewelry, and he had the look of a tattered Hell's Angel. Zilber was an international master and one of the best in the country at blitz*—games that last anywhere from one to ten minutes. Thirty

---

* In speed chess, or blitz, each player is allotted a short time, usually one to ten minutes, on the clock. A chess clock is actually two stop clocks, mounted together. When a player moves he presses a button which stops his clock and engages his opponent's. If either player runs out of time before resignation or checkmate, the flag on his clock falls and he loses, even if his position on the board is favorable.

years ago, Zilber had beaten the brilliant Mikhail Tal, who would
soon become world champion, for the championship of Latvia, and
some of his games appear in evergreen collections of great chess
games. But these days in the park, he offered chess players and
tourists a choice: for a dollar he would pose for a photograph or
play you a game of chess. Each game he played, no matter how
powerful or pitiful the opposition, he scribbled in Russian notation
on a napkin or an old envelope. At night he slept on a bench, his
most valued possessions stuffed under his shirt and a few dollars
rolled into a sock or an empty cigarette box.

When Josh first played Zilber at the age of six, the master would
make wonderful wild sacrifices, like Tal, his old rival, and crush
my son in twelve or fourteen moves. I asked Josh if it upset him
to lose every game to Zilber, and he answered, "I try to look like
I don't care, but inside I'm very angry." Two years later, the games
generally lasted for thirty or forty moves and Josh would lose in
the endgame, the phase of play when there are few pieces on the
board. Usually, while my son was thinking, Zilber would stare up
at the trees and sing in Russian to the squirrels. But he had an eye
like an eagle, never missed a trap and wagged a harsh finger if a
tourist tried to snap his picture without first paying a dollar.

One winter night during a driving snowstorm, I passed through
the park and saw Zilber asleep on a bench partially sheltered by
his chess table. I wondered if he would make it through the night.
A few days later, as we walked through the chess corner, he was
sitting alone at his table talking to the trees and taking notes. "I
hope Zilber doesn't die in the winter," Josh said as we hurried
home for dinner. "Why is there no money for such a great player?"

Whenever I happened to run into Zilber walking with his suit-
cases on the street or sitting alone in the park, I offered to buy
him food or to give him money, but he always shook his head
relentlessly. He had beaten Tal two out of three and had no need
of my nickels and dimes.

ZILBER WAS BY far the strongest player in Washington Square, but
each year the other players predicted that living outdoors in the
winter would take a toll on his game. It was wishful thinking.
Despite his fulminating madness and the ravages of the weather,

his play remained sharp and clear, and masters throughout the city continued to come to Washington Square to practice against him. In the spring of 1986, the strongest woman player in the world, the Hungarian Susan Polgar, sixteen years old, serious and pretty in a sturdy way, came to play against the Latvian, who reeked of urine and raged at the voices in his head while he and she created brilliant games. "He's a great player," she said afterwards.

Vinnie the hustler calls Zilber the Sheriff. Everyone wants to beat the Sheriff. For a month or so in the spring of 1986, a twenty-three-year-old black chess hustler was playing him nearly even, and kibitzers weren't sure if winters on the street were finally finishing Zilber off, or if the young man's game had taken a fantastic leap. But then the black man started doing too much crack, his game fell apart, and soon he was in jail for armed robbery; he'd had to steal to support his habit. He had learned the game on the street, and for him it wasn't an art form, it was just a way to earn a few dollars. What a great player this young hustler might have been with the right motivation and encouragement, with a master-level chess teacher. But then, perhaps Zilber could have become U.S. champion if he hadn't gone to pieces.

Each spring the guys in the park look to see whose game is slipping. By the spring of 1986 people were saying that Vinnie's game had fallen off too, but to me he still looked strong. Maybe he was hustling a few of the guys, dropping games so that he could raise the ante; with a great hustler you never know for sure. The better players in the park are always testing one another. A chess game between two park hustlers is a litmus test of a man's worth. "Everyone wants to be the Sheriff," says Vinnie. When Zilber is off sleeping somewhere else, Vinnie is the Sheriff, the fastest draw in the park, the one to beat.

ONE AFTERNOON I was crossing the park when a friend of Joshua's, a clean-cut thirty-year-old graduate student who worked long hours to put himself through school, began to play for five dollars a game against a third-rate hustler. In the evening I passed through the park again and they were still at it. Joshua's friend, a kind, good-humored man, was chain-smoking and moving too quickly. His shirt and jacket were disheveled. The hustler was shouting at him after each move: "You're nothing. You're a fish." The student was coming apart. "You're the dog of the world." By ten P.M. he was playing like a beginner, hanging pieces in almost every game. The two men were of approximately the same playing strength, but the hustler had convinced Joshua's friend that he was a loser.

At midnight they were still at it beneath a streetlight. A few kibitzers were hanging around, watching and passing a bottle of wine. It was a bad moment for the student; he wasn't going to have the money to pay the rent. He had played so many encouraging games against my son that I felt embarrassed to be watching his humiliation, but I couldn't leave.

The hustler was doing very dark work. He had started this twelve-hour session with ten dollars in his pocket and would leave the table with almost seven hundred. The next day all the players would be talking about it. The hustler would go to sleep tonight in a flophouse, convinced that he could beat Zilber.

During their last half-dozen games, the graduate student moved the pieces instantly, without thinking. His jaw was set and sometimes he shook his head. He threw the last of his month's wages on the board as if he were trying to get rid of a part of himself that he despised.

I never thought he would return to the park, but a few days later, he was sitting there at lunchtime with a sheepish smile on his face, watching two of the guys play a five-minute game. He asked me when Josh would be coming to the park to play with him.

SPRING AND FALL are the best times in Washington Square. When it's a little cool or there's a breeze, the guys play more sharply, with renewed promise. Although they rarely look up from the board, they sometimes talk as if they are outdoorsmen.

"I love the weather today, the breeze. It's beautiful," said one bald player without taking his eyes off the board. He had a winning position and wanted to savor it while his opponent, generally a stronger player and a braggart, squirmed. In point of fact, the park was shrouded in the dark gray clouds of an impending storm, and the air was thick.

"I feel some rain," said the stronger player, who shook a little from the chill of the storm, or perhaps from the inevitability of defeat.

"No, you're wrong. It's great today. Not too hot."

"I tell you, Stanley, I felt a drop."

"Maybe, maybe, but maybe not. If it's anything, it's passing," said Stanley as if he were analyzing an impenetrable Alekhine position. By now the wind was blowing about twenty miles an hour. A yachtsman would have raced for shelter, but neither player looked up.

"I feel some rain, you fishcake," said the stronger player, who was trying to find some final resource to salvage the win. Maybe Stanley would become distracted and lose on time.

"I love this weather."

"I felt rain," said the bully, eyes flashing over his dwindling pieces. He hadn't noticed that the wind had blown a leaf into his thinning hair.

"It's only moisture off a tree," insisted Stanley as he made the decisive move. "It isn't rain."

BECAUSE JOSH WAS so young, whenever he played in the park people watched his games. He liked being on stage and concentrated better when kibitzers were standing around his table, but he didn't understand what all the fuss was about. Before he began serious study, chess to him was only another game like Monopoly, Pac Man or gin rummy. But for some of his adult opponents, games against him were grim, no-win contests. An experienced adult player is expected to beat a little kid but is considered a bit of a bully for beating a child badly and can't help feeling humiliated and ridiculous if he loses. When Josh was eight, he played a long game in the park against a short, bearded man, who scrutinized the pieces with almost desperate intensity. Josh was down a couple of pawns when he sacrificed a rook, which forced mate in three. His opponent, a master, was so upset that he looked at the position for fifteen minutes and kept repeating, "There must be a way out of this." A week later, we ran into the master again, and when Josh said something about their game, the man looked at him blankly. "I've never played you," he said to Josh in front of Jerry and a few of the other guys who had watched his defeat. Josh didn't know what to say. I don't believe the man was lying; he had simply erased the game from his mind.

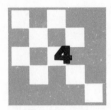

BRUCE
PANDOLFINI

One afternoon as Josh was playing in the park when he was six, I noticed a tall man with an overstuffed, badly worn briefcase watching his games. He introduced himself as Bruce Pandolfini, chess teacher and manager of the Manhattan Chess Club. He was excited by Joshua's play and with some urgency insisted that our son should have formal chess instruction. He gave me his card, and two weeks later I called and left a message on his answering machine. Pandolfini didn't call back, even though during the next few weeks I tried to reach him several more times. This was the unlikely beginning of Joshua's most important chess relationship.

I think of Pandolfini as the prince of chess. He is a handsome man with curly brown hair and a generous, caring manner. He is very visible on the New York chess scene, usually in attendance at chess exhibitions, at the lectures of top international masters and at organizational meetings for citywide and national chess programs. More often than not, when a chess personality is asked about the latest Karpov-Kasparov match or about the whereabouts of Bobby Fischer or is quoted in the *Times* about the potential of an up-and-coming chess prodigy, it is Pandolfini who is being interviewed.

Even when he is broke and consumed by financial concerns, Pandolfini, like a ruined aristocrat, has the carriage of success and money. In the park I've seen him share his meager pocket money with a hungry player. Pandolfini needs to be needed, and sometimes he gets carried away and promises too many people too much. One morning he was teaching Josh in his cramped little bedroom, where there is hardly room for Pandolfini's lanky legs and elbows. At the end of the lesson, Josh wished plaintively that his room were a little larger. It had been an inspired lesson; all of the infinite permutations of chess seemed to fall into place during their hour and a half together. Feeling ebullient, Pandolfini answered wildly, "We can do something about that also, Tiger."

WHEN PANDOLFINI SHOWS up at a small local tournament, players greet him like a long-lost friend. He is unctuously received by the smiling director, who explains how special the smoky gathering of a few dozen men is: "Look who's come all the way up from Pennsylvania for the Greater February Open," he says, pointing Pandolfini in the direction of a heavily perspiring fellow cramped over a chessboard with his fingers jammed into his ears to block out the noise. The director is hoping that Pandolfini will mention the gala event in his popular column in *Chess Life* magazine.

In private, some impoverished players speak of Pandolfini with a trace of anger as the ultimate chess hustler—an ordinary master who wheels and deals inside and outside the chess world in order to make money from the game. The unspoken implication is that one ought not to make money from chess. Many players assume that he has become wealthy from the game, which is not true. For most of his adult life, working chaotically sixty or more hours a week at fifteen or twenty different projects, Pandolfini has managed a modest living. This is no small accomplishment in a land where chess is considered an esoteric hobby—when it is considered at all—rather than an art or a profession, and where even top grandmasters are unable to support themselves.

In the first twenty minutes of his visit to a tournament, half a dozen players are likely to ask Pandolfini favors:

"Bruce, can you get me any students?"

"Bruce, can you help me find a publisher for my collected games?"

"Pandolfini, would you see if you could get me a discount on the new Fidelity chess computer?"

"Bruce, my last published rating in *Chess Life* was eight points too low. How could they do that to me? Would you check with the Federation?"

His brown eyes soft with regal beneficence, Pandolfini says yes to everyone. He has every intention of coming through and feels glad to have been asked, but in many cases he forgets. His forgetfulness is entirely democratic: he neglects to return the phone calls of grandmasters and patzers alike. He is as likely to come late to the lesson of a movie star as to that of a telephone operator. It is a quirk of nature that this man, who can play ten simultaneous chess games blindfolded and has total recall of tens of thousands of chess positions, has such difficulty remembering appointments, publication dates and the departure times of airline flights.

Pandolfini's students are in love with him and gladly put up with late or broken appointments and midnight lessons in a cafeteria, on a bench in the park or on a sofa at the New School. When a lesson is going well, Bruce sometimes continues for hours, oblivious to who or what is scheduled next.

Students who manage to get his home number call Pandolfini day and night, as if it were their right. He is polite, even if he was asleep. For several months, one little brunette who cut and curled her hair to look like his called him four or five times a day. She was a bulldog, and whether he was sleeping, giving a lesson or presiding over a board of directors meeting at the Manhattan Chess Club, she refused to hang up until he gave her a jewel of chess insight.

Since the Fischer-Spassky match in 1972, when he appeared daily as a master analyst on Shelby Lyman's televised coverage, Pandolfini's reputation as a chess teacher has grown steadily. Even when most chess teachers are starving for work, prospective students contact him regularly. He has no time, but he can't bear to say no. Instead he matches disappointment with heartfelt regret: "I'll call you as soon as I have an opening. Don't worry, it will work out." If there is a hint of irritation or unhappiness on the other end he keeps talking. Only when he senses that his caller is appeased will Bruce hang up and peacefully forget. He is by nature a great confidence builder—one aspect of his gift for teaching.

*   *   *

PANDOLFINI WAS THE manager of the Manhattan Chess Club from 1983 to 1986, and one afternoon while Josh played chess for a couple of hours before his lesson, I watched him perform his managerial duties. He came through the door three quarters of an hour late with a guilty smile that coaxed forgiveness (I knew it well), long arms swinging like Ichabod Crane's. In passing, he gave a crisp executive "Good afternoon" to half a dozen club regulars while moving to the phone in his office, which had been ringing for some time. "Hello, Bruce Pandolfini, Manhattan Chess Club." It was a journalist from *Newsweek* demanding to know where Bobby Fischer was hiding out; he had been calling every day for the past week. "I can't speak about this right now," Bruce said conspiratorially, as if Fischer's sister were standing next to him. "Can you get back to me?" The phone rang again. It was U.S. Champion Grandmaster Lev Alburt calling to discuss a lecture series he and Pandolfini were planning to give on the upcoming Karpov-Kasparov championship match in Moscow. "I'll have to get back to you," Bruce said officiously, sipping his coffee and shuffling through his mail. He was in full stride now but had forgotten to take off his scarf, which made him appear disheveled and daft. The phone rang again while two club regulars stood outside the door to his office, cursing one another at the top of their lungs. "Keep it down out there," Bruce called, which only fanned their fury. The caller represented a Hadassah chapter in Staten Island and wanted Bruce to give a lecture on the history of chess and the psychology of the chess player, followed by an exhibition of blindfold play. "We're willing to pay you thirty dollars," the man on the phone said as if he were making an unusually attractive offer.

"You're a liar," one of the men outside the door was bellowing, his face purple with rage.

"You took your hand off the piece," said the other, who had been having arguments at the club nearly every afternoon for the past eighteen years.

"I did not take my hand off the piece."

"You're trying to steal the game! I had a won game!"

"Touch move! Touch move!"

"I know the kind of guy you are. You're the kind of guy when you were a kid you stole from your mother's wallet. I'm not going to let you get away with it."

"Bruce! Bruce!" By now everyone in the club was roaring at the two men to shut up, and Pandolfini was on the phone again.

Later he scrubbed the toilet, one of the manager's jobs at the Manhattan Chess Club. Then he did the books, cleaned the ashtrays and filled the Coke machine. These days he was especially careful not to forget the Coke machine because at the last board meeting the president of the club had been outraged that Coke sales were down four hundred dollars from the previous fiscal year.

Beside running the Manhattan Chess Club, teaching private lessons until twelve or one in the morning and writing for *Chess Life*, Pandolfini lectured at the New School and ran the chess programs at Trinity, Browning and the Little Red School House. He had recently signed a contract with Simon and Schuster to write a comprehensive series of instructional chess books, which in all likelihood will make him the most widely read American chess writer of the twentieth century. By 1989 he will have written eleven full-length chess books in four years.

But teaching chess to children is what Pandolfini considers his art form. He leads his kids laughing through deserts of tedium. He'll spice up a technical rook-and-pawn endgame exercise with basketball analogies, dares, popcorn, cupcakes and soft threats. He carries a briefcase full of superhero and dinosaur stickers to reward discovered checks and passed pawns, and when his little students win a tournament or discover a mate in five they earn mysteriously powerful master-class points. If they achieve enough master-class points in a month they are ceremoniously rewarded with a master-class certificate that has the authoritative look of the Declaration of Independence. His little kids think Pandolfini's magical rewards are far more significant than weak squares and maintaining the opposition; these concepts they learn almost in passing.

DURING THEIR FIRST lessons, Josh refused to accept instruction from Pandolfini. When he was six, his chess ideas were like pieces of his body and he could not give them up. For example, he simply could not cope with being told not to bring out his queen early in the game. Why shouldn't he? In games against his father or in Washington Square he had often won with an early attack using his bishop and queen. Why was this suddenly wrong? Bruce seemed to understand immediately and declared that Joshua's obstinacy was an aspect of his talent and passion for the game. Their first lessons consisted of scores of riotous clock-banging speed games during which Bruce joked with him, and at the same time nudged his pupil in the direction of time-honored fundamentals by dint of repeated good-natured beatings and the awarding of dinosaur stickers and master-class points when Josh experimented with a "master-class move." He chased our son's brazenly forward queen with pawns and knights until she learned to stay on the back rank waiting for a more prudent time to attack. Gradually Josh learned more orthodox openings and maneuvers without fully realizing that they weren't entirely of his own design.

PANDOLFINI IS CONTENT playing the pied piper, but when he emerges again into the adult world he often feels pressured and frantic. "I'm doing terribly," he will answer frequently to a friend's question. He is frazzled by too much work and too little sleep and nagged by guilt and confusion about his life choices. "Certainly in the traditional sense I'm a failure," he said one harried afternoon at the Manhattan Chess Club. "In our society a chess teacher is not considered in the same league as a professor of chemistry or mathematics. I could have made a lot more money in the commercial world. My mother still asks me when I'm going to get a serious job. The worst time is holiday dinners with the family, when I have to explain that I'm still giving chess lessons." He gestured out the door toward rows of club regulars who were eating cheap Danish, snapping time clocks and bickering. "Let's face it, we're not exactly saving humanity up here at the Manhattan Chess Club," he said wryly.

OVER THE YEARS, the parents of some of Pandolfini's most gifted young students have guided them away from chess. This is true for other teachers as well. It's hard to blame the parents. In our culture there is virtually no respect or payoff for chess players. Sometimes at a scholastic tournament a couple of teachers of chil-

dren shake their heads and talk nostalgically about the great ones
who are now long retired. It is like Red Holzman and Red Auerbach
remembering Cousy, Guerin, Pettit and Arizin—except that the
chess teachers are talking about players who retired at nine or ten
years of age. Today some of these brilliant kids, who left the game
at the top of the rating list years ago, are completing Ivy League
educations, and others are already making big salaries in conventional careers, but from the point of view of their impoverished
chess teachers, it is a tragic loss.

It is upsetting to me when Pandolfini confesses his self-doubts.
Why are we working so hard at chess? I wonder. Some of the men
outside his door have given up families and careers to spend their
afternoons and evenings pushing wood at the Manhattan Chess
Club. What for? Why should it mean so much to me when Josh
wins a children's tournament or even a casual game? Why am I
bringing my seven-year-old son for chess lessons twice a week and
waiting in a rage when Pandolfini is late? Sometimes I think that
Josh and I are on a thrilling, precipitous slide, with certain doom
and failure at the bottom.

ONE AFTERNOON I was leaving the club with Josh when an old
woman, a club regular for almost fifty years, approached. I was
prepared for a pat on Joshua's head and a warm greeting from this
woman, whose quaint smile and thinning gray hair reminded me
of my grandmother. "So you're here again with your seven-year-
old son," she said with a sad smile. "Dragging him in to this smoke-
filled place to play chess. Don't you know you're making him an
addict? You're trying to make up for all the things you couldn't do
with your own life."

SOMETIMES I WATCH Joshua's chess lesson. During the course of
their hour and a half or two hours together, Pandolfini is upset or
delighted with Joshua's work, and my emotions trail along behind
his. Later, thinking about the lesson, I realize that I haven't been
following what they've been talking about; I've been dreaming
about championships—his, my own. They are the same. The old
woman is right, of course.

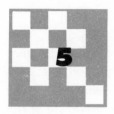

THE
GREATER
NEW YORK
OPEN

Soon after Josh began to study chess I went to a tournament to see the professionals. The players in Washington Square directed me to a game room called Bar Point on the corner of 14th Street and Sixth Avenue, which was where most master-level chess tournaments in the New York area were held at that time.

I arrived at a shattered glass door, labeled "Bar Point: House of Backgammon," that was flanked by a couple of reeling drunks. Inside were two flights of stairs, littered with cigarette butts and reeking of urine.

It was the weekend of the 1984 Greater New York Open, and the rooms inside were packed. The congregation of talent at this tournament made it one of the strongest in the United States that year, according to promoter Bill Goichberg, the Don King of chess. Scores of chess players were sitting across from one another at cafeteria tables, sighing, saying "Shhh," moving a piece, pushing a time clock, writing on a score sheet, but mostly just sitting on hard plastic chairs and thinking. Beyond a door padded against slamming with wads of newspaper and silver duct tape, the best players were in a sorrowful front room over a pizza parlor, with discolored wall paneling, peeling paint, torn rugs and electrical wires dangling from holes in the ceiling. From time to time Goichberg's voice boomed from the back room, "Keep it down!"

Most of the players with international titles—the stars—sat at a table near a row of curtained windows, closest to the din of buses, trucks and ghetto blasters cruising up Sixth Avenue. Grandmaster Dmitry Gurevich, the tenth-ranked player in the country, was playing against Asa Hoffmann. Gurevich, a short, handsome man, had a finger jammed into each of his ears and flinched at noises as if he were being stung by wasps. Hoffmann, ranked ninetieth at the time, is a tall, thin man with black hair and a weary, acne-scarred face. He played more casually than Gurevich and didn't take nearly as much time between moves; he didn't seem to care as much.

Next to Hoffmann sat Joel Benjamin, twenty, who had just finished his junior year at Yale. Many in the chess world feel that Benjamin is the most talented young chess player in America, a potential world champion. While he studied the board, his pale boyish face was calm and cheerful, and he waved casually when he noticed a friend enter the room. He sat on folded legs as if he were doing yoga, but his fingers moved with a will of their own. They were in his mouth or wrapped around one another or quivering indecisively above a rook or a bishop.

For many minutes, sometimes for an hour or more, players analyzed the positions on their boards. At times they seemed to be meditating or daydreaming. In fact, as a player explained, "They're boiling inside with attacks and counterattacks. Emotionally, it's a battle of life and death. You enter into someone else's head and battle against his ideas."

When played beautifully, chess goes on, hour after hour, with the tension of a baseball game tied in extra innings. But unlike baseball, the tactics involve such complicated ploys and feints, the crafting of such devious illusions, that what appears to be a tie is often no such thing. In even the sleepiest of games, the player must consider the possibility that what looks like a draw may be the artful precursor of a decisive, crushing attack. After minutes of painful stillness, he will move a piece, then bound from the board as if suddenly unchained. During one such break, Asa Hoffmann chatted with friends. "I've got him thinking," he said referring to Gurevich, who had been agonizing over his move for more than an hour. "Maybe I'm gonna win a pawn."

Hoffmann, the son of two lawyers, grew up on Park Avenue,

went to Horace Mann and then to Columbia until he dropped out "because I became a chess fanatic." He is one of the most active tournament players in the country, participating in about two hundred tournament games a year and earning a consistent two thousand dollars annually from all these competitions. "My family would be real proud of me if I were a baseball player and made a couple of hundred thousand a year," he said, "but they're ashamed of me because I'm a chess player. I'm forty-one, and they're still asking me, 'When are you going to get a job?' "

To make ends meet, Hoffmann hustles chess games for a couple of dollars each. "The chess-hustling business is bad. It's down with the economy, and O.T.B. and Lotto have hurt." He is a great speed player, generally thought to be the most savvy and successful of the chess hustlers, and makes about one hundred dollars a week this way. "It's not a good game for a gambler," he explained, "because chess players are too rational and conservative. You have to find a true compulsive who happens to play chess—someone who's essentially masochistic and enjoys being humiliated. One of my best customers was a rabbi. He would come in to play me wearing a yarmulke and would say a prayer in Yiddish. While I beat him, he cursed and screamed, begging me to have mercy on him. I'd tell him, 'What a fish you are. I'm gonna crush you.' I took a lot of money from him. Unfortunately, he's dead now."

A few minutes later, Gurevich resigned and walked quickly from the front room. "I wasted him," Hoffmann said matter-of-factly. "It was a classic psych job. Before we started playing, I said something about his old girlfriend. I set him up."

At the next table Joel Benjamin moved the white queen forward three squares, and after considering for a moment, his opponent reached a hand across the board to resign. The position seemed much the same as it had an hour before. The pieces were all engaged and balanced against one another, but both players knew that in six or eight moves something terrible would happen to black; it was inevitable.

Immediately the two men began to analyze. "If only you hadn't put the bishop on e7," Benjamin said sympathetically. "I think you had winning chances." "Yes," the loser answered softly. For young players particularly, losing is terrible—a chaotic, vulnerable moment, a glimpse of ultimate limitations.

"I used to play against Bobby Fischer all the time," said Asa Hoffmann, taking a break from a backgammon game. "I lost hundreds of games against him for two dollars. I was Fischer's fish."

BOBBY FISCHER MOVED like a phantom through the broken-down rooms. Everyone had a Fischer story. One player said he'd gotten a letter from Fischer three weeks ago but wouldn't let anyone read it. A grandmaster who played in the front room was supposed to have just returned from a two-month visit with Fischer in California, but he walked away without a word when asked about it. Bobby is the libido of the game, a chess player who could call a press conference tomorrow and play a game for a million dollars.

"During the Fischer period, it wasn't chess that turned people on," said Joel Benjamin. "It was Fischer. He was a lunatic, and at the same time such a great player that he could beat the Russians single-handedly."

Slightly built and wearing gold-rimmed glasses, Benjamin has the look of a young librarian, but his speech is full of willfulness, sharp judgments and more than a few Fischerisms: "Sometimes during a match you get a bad feeling about a person. Mannerisms affect you. The way someone moves a piece is important. If a player bangs down the pieces, I know he's an idiot and it makes me want to tear his head off."

Benjamin, who learned how to move the pieces when he was eight while watching the Fischer-Spassky match on television, acknowledged that if the economic realities for chess players were different, he probably wouldn't have bothered going to college. "It worries me that chess players in this country can't make it," he said. Still, when he graduated from Yale, he devoted himself to the game, winning the U.S. championship in 1987. "My goal is to be world champion someday," he said, just as Fischer had said thirty years ago in Washington Square. "I dream about it."

AT ELEVEN O'CLOCK on the last night of the Greater New York Open, all but the final game was finished. The winner of this one, which was in its sixth hour, would take the four-hundred-dollar first prize.

Joel's father sat waiting while Bill Goichberg tallied the results. His son's biggest fan, Alan Benjamin is the chess coach at Madison High School in Brooklyn, where he is also a history teacher. When Goichberg finished, Benjamin would drive Joel back to New Haven; he had been driving his son to and from chess tournaments since Joel was a young boy.

Joel ended up with two wins and two draws, which tied him for third place, but because he had to share the one-hundred-fifty-dollar purse with four others, he ended up losing money after paying his entry fee and expenses for the weekend.

"This was a special tournament," said Goichberg. "Normally I can't afford to pay prizes like this. It's been nearly a year since we've had a four-hundred-dollar first prize here. New York doesn't seem to support chess."

Meanwhile there had been a mishap in the dimly lit back room where Joel was analyzing a game with several other masters. The single working toilet at Bar Point had finally given out, and the floor was awash; Coke cans, broken glass, soggy candy wrappers and wads of toilet paper floated on the putrid rug. A young woman in shorts tiptoed across the room, ineffectually spreading newspapers over the mess.

A brilliant Russian emigré grandmaster sat with Joel and two other masters at a nearby table, demonstrating an original opening variation he'd just used in a game. He talked theatrically with sweeping gestures, as if he were lecturing at Moscow University. Soon Joel began shuffling the pieces, trying to decide if there was a line he liked better. The men took turns, and the chess pieces skidded and darted as if they were on ball bearings. The four men had been playing chess for two days, but they couldn't stop. Their eyes flashed and blinked, looking for new combinations and possibilities. No one seemed to mind, or even to notice, the plaster falling off the walls or the slop underfoot.

TRAINING
FOR
MOSCOW

During the summer of 1984, be-
fore the first Karpov-Kasparov championship marathon, Josh and
I had our own titanic struggle. We were away from New York, and
I was his only available opponent. I was planning to leave for
Moscow in September to write about the match and to visit Russian
chess schools with Josh, so I wanted him to be in top playing form.
But he greeted my daily suggestions for games with a preference
for fishing or spearing crabs. I was a persistent nag and occasionally
justified myself by playing through testy dialogues that might have
taken place between Chris Evert and her father when she was a
young girl and didn't want to practice. But after hundreds of games
that he didn't want to play, Josh fell into a state of sullen torpor.
Time and again his king stood languidly on the back rank, indifferent to the march of my passed pawns.

By the time we had received our visas for the Soviet Union, I
had lost all confidence in Joshua's ability to play chess at all. A visit
to Washington Square Park confirmed my fears. Josh took on all
comers while looking at the pigeons and squirrels. He lost his pieces
with a melancholy smile, as if thinking, What does the loss of a
bishop mean in the larger scheme of things?

I was feeling nervous about the trip to the Soviet Union for a
variety of reasons. Josh had never been away from his mother
before, and after the past summer he and I were angry at one
another. In the days before we left, Bonnie reminded me so often
to take care of him that I was beginning to doubt that I could. How

was I going to interview Russian grandmasters and at the same time keep track of his toy cars and make sure he was drinking enough milk? Besides covering the championship match for *Chess Life*, Bruce Pandolfini, who was going to travel with us, and I were planning to meet Russian chess teachers and to arrange games between Josh and talented Russian children. But our player was suffering from ennui. Russian chess educators would be scrutinizing my kid while he looked out the window.

AS THE DC-8 shook and roared down the runway to begin the first leg of our flight, Josh looked up from his Snoopy book and announced, "Off to Russia." He had no idea where Russia was; it might have been Philadelphia. At the time, he didn't seem to understand the difference between a country and a city.

Bruce suggested a game on his pocket set. Josh shrugged; he wasn't interested. Soon the stewardess gave him a puzzle book in which numbered dots created figures, and he immediately tried to talk Pandolfini into tracing dots with him.

I began to read a chapter of David Shipler's book about the Soviet Union, *Russia: Broken Idols, Solemn Dreams*,* dealing with what he perceived to be the illusion of collectivism throughout the society. I had trouble concentrating; it was difficult to relate Shipler's drab Russian factories and schools to my fantasy of Russia. Like many other Americans', my impressions of the Soviet Union had been manufactured from such diverse sources as Tolstoy's novels, James Bond movies and endless foreboding articles in the *New York Times*. Russia was catchwords such as "Cold War," "Raskolnikov," "vodka," "Kremlin," "Bolshoi," "KGB," "Anna Karenina," "Iron Curtain," "gulag." I was half expecting to see forests of missiles and peasants driving horse-drawn sleighs.

IN THE WEEKS preceding our departure I had spoken to Russian defectors with harrowing stories and sad, urgent requests that I try to track down relatives and friends. In certain instances I would have to make these contacts surreptitiously from phone booths on

* New York: Times Books, 1983.

the street because the hotel phone would be bugged, and use a code name for the American defector so that I didn't compromise his mother or girlfriend. I got the impression that a third of the Soviet population must be employed to listen in on phone calls or to open mail. Although very poor, some of these men had brought expensive gifts for me to smuggle to their relatives and friends—presents conveying the fatuous message that life in the United States was all leisure and luxury: fancy tape recorders, radios, cameras, digital watches, pens with digital watches, computers. Had a customs man searched through my underwear he might have decided that I was a secret agent for Crazy Eddie. There was something sad and distasteful about my baggage of high-tech trinkets.

I WAS ASKED by one Soviet defector to try to locate a Jewish friend, Soviet chess champion Boris Gulko. I was told that Gulko would be willing to discuss the politics of Soviet chess, as well as the problems of Jewish chess players in the Soviet Union. It was rumored that Gulko and his wife, a Soviet women's champion, were being held under house arrest. "To find Gulko, you'll need to contact a man I know who is a well-known grandmaster, an expert in the endgame," said the Russian American, who gave me a name and a Moscow phone number. "He is also a KGB agent, but don't worry, he is totally corrupt. The first day you meet him, give him a present worth fifteen or twenty dollars—a digital watch, maybe. Don't expect him to speak candidly at first. Most likely he'll seem apathetic. But I know this man, and you'll have aroused his curiosity. He will suggest dinner. During this meal present him with pornographic books and magazines; then the chances are he will arrange for you to meet Gulko."

In case this approach didn't work, the man gave me the name of a second grandmaster to bribe with a few digital pens; he wouldn't be as expensive. He cautioned that I must never mention the name of the second grandmaster to the KGB grandmaster because they were enemies.

LEV ALBURT, A top Soviet grandmaster who defected to the United States in 1979 and became the highest-rated player here the fol-

lowing year, described the politics of Soviet chess to me. Alburt
is an engaging conversationalist who, like the great European players of the nineteenth century, combines his genius for the royal
game with aristocratic taste and manners. He is a charming, urbane
man with an appetite for fine food, history and world politics as
well as for chess. From across the room he could pass for a youthful
Charles Boyer.

"In the Soviet Union," Alburt said, "chess is supported by the
government, and since Stalin's time they have used victories in
international chess tournaments to propagandize the notion that
the best minds flourish under the Communist system." Alburt
speaks so quietly that I found myself leaning closer to him. Talking
about Soviet chess with him was at once intimate and unsettling—
a little like falling into a John le Carré novel. "They will go to great
lengths to get the most from their players," he continued. "For
example, sometimes during my matches I was wired and tested
for blood pressure, heart rate, galvanic skin response and other
things. I was given amphetamines and tranquilizers on the days of
important tournaments. Perhaps you don't realize that when Karpov plays in a big tournament he has the help of forty, sometimes
fifty, aides. They do everything from analyzing positions and per-
forming physical therapy to providing sophisticated psychological
profiles of opponents. Karpov has a doctor on hand to regulate his
medications. During the match against Korchnoi he was so exhausted that they had to give him high dosages of amphetamines,
which saved him in the end. Karpov has used hypnotists to try to
distract his opponents. He has the use of a computer in Moscow
that can calculate endgame positions more accurately than any
grandmaster who ever lived. Without the advantages of his political
connections, I doubt that Karpov would be a stronger player than,
say, Joel Benjamin."

Alburt's conversational style is at the same time eloquent and
understated. While he talks he occasionally puts his hand on your
shoulder or arm in the manner of a reassuring older relative. When
he senses that his remarks have caused surprise, he lifts an eyebrow, then continues in a quiet melodious voice. "In the Soviet
Union I was often asked to draw games in important international
tournaments, and even famous players such as Tal and Bronstein

were occasionally asked to lose games. When they organize a tournament in the Soviet Union, they have a plan. If they want to make a new grandmaster, they will tell the stronger players that they must lose to him. Occasionally you can refuse, but it depends on who's asking. If it's someone important, you can be punished severely and lose your source of income. Being asked to draw and lose games is so natural on the lowest level that when you play in an international tournament and an official says, 'You must lose; the prestige of the Soviet Union is at stake,' you have already learned to obey. To refuse would be a hard crime against the state."

For the past several months, the upcoming championship match in Moscow had dominated the daily conversation of chess players in New York City, but when the subject was raised with Alburt, he seemed sad and slightly bored. "Today Kasparov would be the favorite," he said, "but changes could take place in the highest reaches of the Soviet government that would make the match a fiction. For years, Karpov had a benefactor in the government. Through his connection with this man, Karpov gained more political power and material privileges than any other Soviet chess player in history. Then, during the time of the Korchnoi match, he became a favorite of Brezhnev. But after Brezhnev's death, Andropov removed Karpov's patron from his high government position and sent him to Hungary on the pretext that he was a homosexual. This weakened Karpov's position, even though he was still world champion.

"At about the same time, Andropov brought in a man named Aliev, who rapidly became one of the most powerful men in the Soviet Union. He was Kasparov's benefactor, and Kasparov became as powerful as Karpov—maybe even more so. Now, with Andropov's death and Chernenko's coming to power, nobody knows what will happen. Kasparov, who is half-Jewish and half-Armenian, is not the ideal Soviet hero. If Aliev were to lose his job in the Politburo before September tenth, I would bet ten to one that Kasparov will lose the match."

THIS CYNICAL VIEW of the Soviet chess establishment was titillating but hard to believe. It sounded more like a description of a covert CIA operation than like my kid's favorite game. Vitaly Zaltzman,

Igor Ivanov, Lev Alburt and Victor Korchnoi all told the same extravagant story: "Karpov would have Kasparov poisoned if he could get away with it." "Watch to see if Kasparov becomes ill." "Karpov will use germ warfare. They'll do anything." "When Russian chess players travel abroad they carry out espionage assignments." "They play by their own rules." "Chess is entirely political in the Soviet Union." But was it true? Many American chess players, like Joel Benjamin, whom Alburt admires, dismissed his observations and those of other Russian defectors as influenced by political bias and personal bitterness. "I always take Lev with a grain of salt," Benjamin said.

Traveling to Moscow to watch the world championship and perhaps to track down Boris Gulko and other dissidents, using watches and pornographic books as bait, had seemed like a great adventure before we left New York. But now, flying through the night with my seven-year-old son asleep on Pandolfini's shoulder while I read David Shipler's accounts of KGB agents setting up journalists, our plans seemed naïve, even stupid. I'd been warned not to bring books critical of the Soviet Union into the country and so I decided to leave Shipler's book in Helsinki, although it seemed like a sneaky way to begin the trip.

Six hours later, as the plane approached Finland, Bruce and Josh were playing chess. "Josh, you've hung your knight. You're not concentrating," Bruce said with an edge of impatience as I tried to doze. "Why aren't you looking at the board, Tiger?" Joshua's bad moves felt like little stings.

THE TERMINAL IN Helsinki was cheerful and attractive. In front of the duty-free shops little boys wearing penny loafers skated across slick floors, and fashionable ladies in high heels clicked past carrying clear plastic bags crammed with reindeer skins, vodka and mohair shawls. There were elegant well-lighted delis with hams, fat sausages and smoked fish, and a kiosk where boys ogled toy trucks and Eastern European men furtively glanced through girlie magazines selling for four times their price in the States. I considered buying a few magazines for the KGB grandmaster who might lead us to Boris Gulko but decided not to.

As we walked toward Immigration at a distant end of the airport,

Bruce and I joked about crossing the Iron Curtain, but we were both a little nervous. Apparently all those years of bad television movies in which the good guys got shot down a few feet from freedom had left a mark. "What's the Iron Curtain?" Josh asked.

"Shh."

"Is it tall? Will we see it from the plane?"

"Shh."

At the far end of the airport the terminal was quiet. While we sat waiting for our flight to Moscow, Josh played with his miniature racing cars, and his little imitations of their sounds seemed brassy and inappropriate. I turned to Bruce to whisper something, then stopped myself. Josh began to tell a joke and Bruce barked at him, "No more, Josh, not until we get there." Like everyone else at this end of the terminal, we were uneasy and humorless.

7

THE
HALL
OF
COLUMNS

The world championship stirred the passion and patriotic pride of millions of Soviet chess players and fans. Throughout September 3, the first day of the match, there were television programs and updates about it. Taxi drivers in austere black Volgas waiting outside our hotel and old ladies sweeping majestic subways with Mother Hubbard brooms talked about Karpov and Kasparov.

Early in the morning, Pandolfini, Josh and I took a taxi from the Cosmos Hotel to the Central Chess Club to pick up our press credentials. Behind heavy, ornate wooden doors we climbed wide staircases flanked by rows of austere portraits of great Russian players. This sprawling building had the worn, formal look of a state assembly that had seen better days. The rugs were colorless and the furniture was old and musty. There were scores of dusty offices devoted to chess management, but it was impossible to guess exactly what happened in them. Many of the offices were empty; others were occupied by a few men who seemed to sit idly at desks or to look out windows. In the halls were chess tables but no pieces were set up. We had expected rooms with rows of chess players such as we would find at the Manhattan Chess Club. Although Josh was exhausted by jet lag, he was looking forward to his first game in Russia, but in this whole large building not a single game was in progress.

A GROUP OF fifty or sixty journalists waited on line in the hall outside one of the offices to get their press passes. Everyone was caught up in the excitement of the match, which was being touted in chess circles as one of the greatest of the century. But some writers were apprehensive; stories were circulating that the Russians were being difficult about allowing newsmen into the Hall of Columns. Someone said that Harold Schonberg and Robert Byrne from the *New York Times* hadn't come because they had been denied visas (eventually Schonberg did arrive). A Russian chess writer came out of the room livid; for some reason he had been refused credentials. "What am I to do?" he asked us in English. "I'm suppose to write about the match but I can't get in."

One European journalist, who was also an international chess master, came out of the room wearing his plastic press identification and recognized Bruce from the photograph above his column in *Chess Life*. He introduced himself and said that he looked forward to playing chess with Bruce in the evenings after the championship match had adjourned for the day. Pandolfini nodded and smiled thinly.

By the time it was our turn we had been standing on line for an hour and a half and Josh was asleep in a chair. I guided him into an office where several men sat behind a long table. Josh opened his eyes and whimpered that he was thirsty. At the far end of the room there was a Polaroid camera mounted on a pedestal. The first sophisticated piece of equipment we had seen in the Soviet Union was American-made.

Pandolfini and I pronounced our names, and a man who spoke no English thumbed through a list. After a few minutes he smiled and shook his head; we were not on the list. He shrugged and gestured for the next man to enter. I tried to explain that we were journalists and that we had written ahead for press credentials, but again he pointed to the list and invited me to look. It was a simple problem: we were not on the list and would not be able to attend the match.

Next on line was a tall, dashingly handsome middle-aged man from Yugoslavia, Dimitrije Bjelica, who I later learned is a television celebrity and the most widely read chess journalist in Eastern Europe. He was on the list, and the Russians treated him like Karpov. Bjelica began handing out copies of his newest book to the men working in the office. Feeling helpless and foolish, I pulled a letter of reference from my passport case and said, "Random House. Big book publisher." I gestured widely with my arms, picked up a bulging folder from a desk, trying to demonstrate that I had come to write a book. Again the bureaucrat pointed to the list of names and shook his head.

Bjelica was the last of the journalists waiting for credentials. Posing for his Polaroid snapshot, he looked suntanned and ecstatic, like a movie star with the cameras rolling. Soon the photographer was taking the camera off its tripod. The Russian office workers were winding down from their morning's work, joking and chatting with Bjelica, who titillated them with tidbits about Fischer, whom he had known since Bobby was a teenager. "Maybe Thursday you will be on the list," the photographer said to us in broken English and raised an eyebrow. Bjelica reached into his briefcase for his new book on Bobby, including previously unpublished speed games, and the Russians ogled it as if it were a girlie magazine.

We were confused about what to do next. Joshua's eyes were smeared with sleep, and he was impatient to leave. "When are we going to the circus? You promised, Daddy." Disgusted, I asked one of the journalists on his way out where people buy tickets to the match. "There are no tickets," the man said, "not unless you know someone in the Politburo."

"Bruce Pandolfini. Bruce Pandolfini." It was Dimitrije Bjelica, a torrent of glamor and good will. "I read your column in *Chess Life*. It is very good," he said, smiling radiantly through his Black Sea tan. "Don't worry, you will get your credentials. Believe me." Bjelica offered to try to help us buy tickets that afternoon at the Hall of Columns. Then he said, "We will play some blitz, yes? I'm a FIDE master* and a very good speed player." He added with a glint in his eye, "I've played hundreds of blitz games against Tal. I played him on the morning of the day he lost the world championship back to Botvinnik."

---

* Fédération Internationale des Echecs, the international governing body for chess, headed by Florencio Campomanes of the Philippines. A FIDE master has gained his master's rating in FIDE tournaments and is, generally speaking, somewhat stronger than a U.S.C.F. national master.

Moscow seemed to be teeming with chess challenges for Bruce, who looked miserable about it. Apparently Eastern European chess masters were curious to see how the master from *Chess Life* played the game about which he had written hundreds of columns. But Pandolfini hadn't played a tournament game in more than twelve years and rarely had time for casual games. He no longer considered himself a player, but it was a difficult point for him to explain.

At twenty-six, he had been among the fifty best chess players in the United States but recognized that he lacked the talent to become one of the fifty best in the world. A world-class player must have immense talent. It is like being an opera star: regardless of how hard you work, you must have the voice; there is no way around it. Pandolfini knew he would never be as good as the grandmasters whom he had admired as a boy, and he didn't want to be a fringe player—a utility infielder, as it were, in the world of chess—so he stopped playing and devoted himself to teaching and writing. He is noncombative by nature, and a lover of the art of chess, and he had made a reasonable though often rocky life choice. But in fielding challenges within this dusty temple of chess, half a world away from the Manhattan Chess Club, the telephone, his students, his cramped little studio, his deadlines, his incomplete manuscripts, his beseeching and frustrated agent and editors, he was feeling counterfeit and trapped, like an aging gunfighter who has lost the speed of his draw.

From the Central Chess Club, we took a taxi to the House of Trade Unions, an eighteenth-century palace in which the championship would be determined. A huge banner advertising the match billowed across Marx Prospect, but for all of Moscow's chess fever, the games were played in a hall that was at least one-third empty. Like the Bolshoi Ballet or the Obraztsov Puppet Theater, the match was nearly impossible for a citizen to get into unless he was a party official or a friend of someone important. A phalanx of police stood behind steel barricades on the far side of the avenue near Red Square and ordered thousands of chess fans to keep moving. Many stoically circled the block as if awaiting a sudden biblical cloudburst of tickets. People craned their necks toward the squat dull-green building, which was badly in need of a paint job, and clumps of fans stopped and peered at posters featuring Karpov and Kasparov until the police prodded them on.

The splendor and excitement of the games seemed to catalyze the frustration and despair of many Russians. A Jewish chess master ahead of us in line talked about his problems. "I am a despised enemy in my own land," he said. "I am not allowed to work. I'm not allowed to play in most chess tournaments, and for the others I don't have the rubles to enter. I'm not allowed to leave for Israel. How am I to survive?" Bitterly he explained that Russians with a politically dissident point of view received a fast *nyet* at the Central Chess Club, where people stood on line each day pleading for tickets.

Inside the House of Trade Unions, just beyond the line of police, Karpov and Kasparov were making their first moves. Pandolfini, Josh and I walked around the block with the crowd. Men plotted to pay ten times the price of a ticket to the first seller, but there were no sellers. The scene was reminiscent of Madison Square Garden before the first Ali-Frazier fight, when people were desperately waving fistfuls of hundred-dollar bills for tickets. But this group was quieter, more resigned; they'd been through it all before.

Occasionally when we swung past the front of the building a long, shiny Mercedes limousine would pull up and a Russian dignitary would walk into the House of Trade Unions. Everyone seemed to lean toward the big black car as if it were filled with largesse.

Bruce and I felt ridiculous; apparently we had traveled to the Soviet Union for nothing. We considered asking someone going in with a ticket to tell Bjelica that we were waiting outside. But it was an unrealistic plan. How would someone find Bjelica among the thousands inside, and in any case what could he do?

Then Pandolfini spotted a man wearing several cameras around his neck who had walked out of the faded building and was crossing the street. He ran off and spoke with the man, a photographer for a Russian magazine. When he returned a few minutes later, he had a ticket. Men standing nearby sighed and kept walking.

I offered to go in and try to buy two more tickets. I felt bad about leaving Josh and Bruce walking around the block. But if I never got in again, at least I'd be able to describe the hall with Karpov and Kasparov sitting across from one another. I walked up to one of the police manning the barricades, half expecting to be furiously waved down the block, but at the sight of the ticket he shrugged and motioned me inside.

KARPOV AND KASPAROV played in the Hall of Columns, a majestic room with snow-white Corinthian columns, walls hung with silky crepe and newly waxed parquet floors reflecting sparkling crystal chandeliers. A century earlier it had been a ballroom for Moscow's rich and famous, including Tolstoy, Pushkin and Turgenev. These days it is used for important trade union conferences, concerts and special political speeches, as well as important chess matches. Kremlin watchers in the United States gauge the importance of a Soviet political event by whether it is held in a site such as the Hall of Columns or at a less prestigious location.

Immediately on entering the hall, I was aware of the noise. People were greeting old friends, chatting, coughing, walking in and out. Television cameras were mounted in the center aisle. Technicians adjusted their cables and walked about with their tools clanging. Fifty or sixty photographers were close to the stage, jockeying for angles and snapping away. Although pocket chess sets were officially forbidden inside, hundreds of people were holding them in their laps, analyzing the present position. Friends argued about the game and lustily cheered moves. It sounded like a dinner at the old Lüchow's on 14th Street in New York City.

Despite the beauty of the setting, Bobby Fischer would never have agreed to play under such conditions; the noise would have driven him crazy. Nor would he have accepted the simple straight-backed chairs provided for the two players, which were similar to the ones occupied by their fans. In Iceland Fischer had bickered over the proximity of the audience and the placement of television cameras: at first he wanted them out of his field of view; then he didn't want them at all. A close friend of Fischer's had said that if Bobby had had his way, he would have played his matches in a sealed room located in the middle of a desert, miles from the tiniest distraction. But Karpov and Kasparov didn't seem to mind the commotion.

Before a critical move, the large room was quiet except for a rustle of anticipation. People were on the edge of their seats, waiting to cheer the home run, the game breaker. Would their man push the c-pawn or the f-pawn?

In the final minutes of a close game, when the players had to move quickly because of the pressure of the clock—each man had to make his first forty moves in two and a half hours—the crowd roared like boxing fans at Madison Square Garden. An indignant referee waved his arms and white lights signaled silence, but no one paid any attention. A young man with the job of moving the pieces on the large display board ran feverishly back and forth from the players to the board. Sometimes in his anxiety he posted a move incorrectly, and then the crowd would scream at him and the lights would flash again. The cacophony and the amateur staging gave tremendous urgency and dramatic appeal to the near-perfect chess being played.

MANY PEOPLE IN the audience were able to speak a little English. I asked several whom they wanted to win. They seemed equally divided; both men were great heroes. Then I asked where I might buy two tickets, and although there were many empty seats, everyone answered that no tickets were available.

I was approached by a delicate-looking man with thick-rimmed glasses who introduced himself as Volodja Pimonov. He spoke English well but with a little hesitation and a hint of a foreign accent. He was dressed in loafers, a western-cut gabardine jacket and a quiet but stylish sports shirt. From his dress and cultured use of language one might have guessed that he was a university professor. Later that afternoon I learned that he was a writer for the prestigious Soviet chess magazine 64, and a Shakespeare scholar. He was immediately sympathetic to my predicament and offered to lend me his ticket. It was my plan that Bruce bring Joshua into the hall, put him in a seat, then return for me.

By the time I got outside the House of Trade Unions, two hours had passed, and Bruce and Josh looked a little desperate. For most of the time, they had been walking around the block. Josh was sleepy and hungry and had complained incessantly. Not knowing what else to do, Bruce had stopped and tried to play a game with him on his pocket set. When a policeman forced them to move they crouched behind a phone booth and resumed the game. With irritation, the same policeman again asked them to move on.

I gave Bruce the two tickets, mine and Volodja's, and sent him inside with Josh while I waited around the corner. I was uneasy about leaving Josh alone inside, but all went well.

On the first floor of the House of Trade Unions was an elegant dining hall with delicious, inexpensive snacks: wineglasses of soda, silver trays piled with pastries, dishes of caviar alongside smoked salmon and sturgeon sandwiches. Tall walls of mirrors extended the palatial dining room into an infinity of appetizing selections. Josh ate piece after piece of French bread smeared with sour cream and caviar, until he spotted another little boy about his size munching chocolate pastries. Soon they were rolling toy cars across the shiny floor—Anton's Zhiguli beeping at Josh's Corvette—and talking at one another in Russian and English, which was more a challenge than an impediment. My son offered Anton a wad of bubble gum, and they began blowing bubbles.

After a while, Josh asked for my pocket chess set. While they had been playing with their toys I had learned that Anton was the nine-year-old son of a Moscow chess master, Grigori Borganovic, and an enthusiastic student of the game. Beside studying with his father four times a week, he attended chess classes at the Pioneer Palace after school. Clearly he would be a formidable opponent, and I was reluctant to give Josh the set. "C'mon, Freddy," Josh said with a swagger. "We're just gonna play a little chess. What's the big deal?" The big deal was that this would be Joshua's first game in Russia, the citadel of chess, and he hadn't been playing well all summer.

In the first game, Anton played a Wilkes-Barre variation which my son had never seen before. "My God," I thought, "even *little* Russians know everything about chess." Josh played in the lackadaisical style he had developed the previous summer, looking longingly at pastries and smiling at passersby. Soviet fans holding cups of espresso paused to watch the two little boys play. Like players and kibitzers in Washington Square, the Russians were curious about little players; maybe one of them would be a world champion someday. Josh hardly glanced at the board, and when he took with his knight instead of checking with his bishop, he had a lost game. I smiled grimly at Anton's father, patted his boy on the head and fought the urge to pull Josh from the room, shake him and exhort him to play harder. It seemed inappropriate for him to be taking the game so lightly. The boys giggled and set up their pieces again. They were playing with them much as children play with jacks in a playground.

Later Volodja came into the dining hall and I thanked him for lending us his ticket. "It is nothing," he said. He watched the children play for a few minutes. By now Josh was looking at the board and had got the hang of Anton's Wilkes-Barre attack; he realized that if he checked with the bishop and retreated it, he was up a pawn with a good position. The two kids were playing in the shadow of Karpov and Kasparov, and from time to time tumultuous cheers filtered from the hall to this children's game. Perhaps the boys fantasized that the cheering was for them.

While we watched the children play, Volodja began to describe his life with disarming candor and passion. The fact that I was an American seemed to represent an opportunity for him. "When I married a Danish girl last year, I fell out of favor," he began. "They feared, I suppose, that I would leave the country. It happens to all people who marry a foreigner. For months my boss at the magazine, Karpov's friend Aleksandr Roshal, has been contriving reasons to fire me. He looks for any excuse. In one of my articles I misspelled the name of a player, and he used this as evidence of my incompetence. He wants me to leave the magazine because if I did emigrate he would be disgraced and perhaps lose his job. It is a common situation here. For example, a Jew is much less likely to be accepted into a medical school because he might try to em- igrate, and this would hurt the teachers who had accepted him. If I lost my job it would be a disaster. I would lose my apartment and would have no money to send my wife. It is unlikely that I would be able to find another job."

Ironically, Volodja didn't want to emigrate; he believed in com- munism. "I have applied to visit my wife in Denmark, but they won't let me go," he said with exasperation. "They are afraid I won't come back. Can you imagine such a situation? I don't want to give up my citizenship; I just want to be with my wife. It is an outrage that I can't visit her. She is very poor and needs my help. The irony of it," he said with disgust, "is that they have turned her from a communist into a right-wing person."

During our weeks in Moscow, we spent a great deal of time with Volodja Pimonov, and always when he spoke of his problems there was great intensity but little hope. He seemed reconciled to spending his life banging on closed doors, writing letters, filling out forms, begging bureaucrats to help, telling his story over and over to foreigners in Moscow. The telling itself had become an urgent ritual; he had become trapped in his story. "Thank you, but there's nothing you can do"; he said this to me dozens of times with his charming smile and sad brown eyes.

I asked Pimonov if he knew where I might be able to find Soviet champion Boris Gulko, and he shook his head sadly. "I don't know what has happened to him. People say different things. I've heard that he is in jail, but I'm not sure. He is one of the greatest players in the world. If they had left him alone, he might have become world champion. But of course they don't want a Jew to be world champion, particularly an outspoken Jew like Gulko."

When I mentioned the Russian grandmaster whom the defector in New York had urged me to bribe with pornographic magazines in order to meet Gulko, Volodja said that the man was playing in a tournament in Odessa and wouldn't be able to help.

Pimonov is a chess player of international master strength. Like devoted players everywhere, he seemed to consider chess as important as love and death. While he talked about his wife, I occasionally stole a glance at Joshua's game. Volodja responded with a sympathetic smile or a fast glance at the position. My divided attention, an embarrassment to me, did not surprise or offend him. Often during our stay in Moscow he would hold forth on the tragedy of Jews in the Soviet Union, the evils of capitalism, nuclear arms or his own insoluble dilemma, his face showing pain, concern or moral outrage, but when the conversation turned to an intriguing issue of chess, his expression would immediately brighten. Before playing, he would become an enthusiastic young man, a bigger version of Josh, excited and concerned only about the coming game.

I introduced Volodja to Pandolfini, who was also watching Joshua's game with more than passing interest. "Pandolfini, I've read your column in *Chess Life* for years," Volodja began. "You are a national master, yes? I can't wait until we have a chance to play some chess. I'm a good speed player." Then he added shyly, "One year I nearly won the Moscow speed championship ahead of Tal. In the deciding game I was killing him. I had mate in three, but then my flag fell."

"Oh, great," Bruce said to me under his breath. "Plays blitz as well as Tal and he wants Pandolfini."

By now Josh was winning game after game from Anton. He was in a rhythm, moving quickly, but concentrating for the first time in months. He was setting up attacks with diversionary feints. His pieces flowed to the right squares, and everyplace Anton moved there seemed to be a trap. Everything was working for Josh. He was like a basketball player who couldn't hit anything but net. But the kids were still giggling, and Pimonov and Pandolfini and even Anton's father were enjoying the games.

When Joshua is playing poorly, I watch every move like a hawk and feel pricked by each mistake; later I can re-create the critical parts of the game—not that he wants to rehash it. But when he's playing like this, I don't follow the moves. I ride on top of the game, relishing the emphatic way he snaps a pawn ahead, the flash of his eyes, the assurance on his young face, the bright neatness of his plan. I realized that while we had been "training" for Moscow, I had become so consumed with motivating him to play well that I had forgotten how much he loves the game.

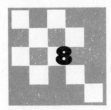

MARK
DVORETSKY

A couple of days later, Volodja pointed out Mark Dvoretsky when he entered the dining hall of the House of Trade Unions. Dvoretsky is the most distinguished chess trainer in the Soviet Union if not the world, with two of his students, Artur Yusupov and Sergei Dolmatov, currently ranked among the strongest international grandmasters. While he stood on line waiting patiently for a cup of coffee, a man shyly approached him with his teenage son and the three shook hands. For the boy, meeting the famous trainer was clearly a special moment. Other men recognized him too, and some made their way across the large room to ask his opinion about the position in the ongoing Karpov-Kasparov game. Clearly this portly thirty-seven-year-old chess teacher was something of a celebrity.

Dvoretsky spoke little English, so I asked Volodja to introduce us and translate our conversation. Dvoretsky was congenial and particularly pleased to meet Pandolfini, whom he knew of from reading *Chess Life*. Indeed, most Russian chess teachers and players knew the American chess magazine and were delighted whenever we gave them a copy. Published by the U.S. Chess Federation, *Chess Life* is filled with profiles of grandmasters, pages of ratings in near-microscopic print, puzzles and the dense analysis of grandmaster games. The magazine is a treasured illicit commodity to Russian players, particularly to Jews who can't get visas to travel and who crave knowledge of the Western chess world; dog-eared copies are secretly shuttled from player to player. Soviet

officials consider *Chess Life* anti-Soviet political propaganda because included in the dense thicket of annotated games are the
victories and defeats of such Russian defectors as Victor Korchnoi,
Lev Alburt and Igor Ivanov—traitors and nonpersons from the
point of view of the Soviet establishment. Even when these players
compete against Russians in international competitions, their results are usually not included in accounts published in Soviet newspapers and magazines, as if the native grandmasters had played
ghosts.

Bruce and I had hoped to meet Dvoretsky to learn about the
Russian system of chess education, which develops so many strong
young players. We wanted to ask him to teach my son for a few
sessions while we observed; since Josh was one of the strongest for
his age in the United States, we assumed that Dvoretsky would
be at least mildly curious.

We were surprised and disappointed when he turned us down.
"No, it would be a waste of time," Dvoretsky said firmly. "I do
not begin working with a student until he is, say, 2100 or preferably
2200 according to your rating system, a weak master. All my techniques are designed for master level and beyond."

This was unexpected. In the United States, once players approach master-level strength there is no systematic education available. Some funding is provided for grandmasters to work with
talented young masters,* but there is no one like Dvoretsky with
a comprehensive system for teaching at the highest level. Instead,
there is an attitude among players that once you achieve the rating
of chess master you can develop further only on your own. Joel
Benjamin, for example, one of our top young players, stopped
studying regularly with a teacher when he was a teenager, at an
age and playing strength that would have made him a desirable
prospect for Mark Dvoretsky. Benjamin explained, "Who could be
my teacher? What could he know that I don't already know? It's
useless studying with someone you can beat."

* The American Chess Foundation, a nonprofit organization, funds master-level chess tour-
naments, school chess programs across the country and private lessons for exceptional young
American chess players who demonstrate potential in tournament play. A.C.F. has funded
Joshua's lessons with Bruce Pandolfini since my son was seven.

Mark Dvoretsky's best students are stronger chess players than he is, but they still develop rapidly under his tutelage. Joel Benjamin's rational point of view is symptomatic of the basic differences between the ways our two societies perceive chess. In the United States players consider it a game with rules to be learned, openings to be memorized, techniques and tactics to be mastered. They are preoccupied with ratings, which reflect their playing strength relative to others. If a player's rating goes up a couple of dozen points, he glows as if he had won the lottery.

American players generally don't speak of chess as art, and metaphysical questions about the game make them uneasy. There are few examples of the kind of creative criticism that is common in the fields of literature, art and music in the West. Most chess writing is dry technical analysis relevant only to serious students of the game.

Perhaps this is an aspect of a defensive mentality. Examining the aesthetics of chess would somehow be peculiar and inappropriate in an environment where with a few exceptions its best practitioners live tragic, deprived lives. American society tends to regard serious players as an eccentric group whose intelligence is useless. They are treated as if they are naughty curiosities, children who never grew up, outrageously self-involved people who spend their days hedonistically playing a game instead of learning a useful trade, building a career, getting on with life. Unlike poets or painters, American chess players can't defend themselves with the claim that they are pursuing an art; our culture simply doesn't consider chess art. "The only people who care about chess and chess players here are other players," said Russian defector Igor Ivanov, the leading money winner in North America in 1984. (He cleared less than ten thousand dollars after expenses for his year of labor.)

Professional players in the United States are bitter about their poverty and lack of recognition, but they don't do much to improve their image. Failure seems to beget more failure. Even at the best tournaments the players are a ragtag group, sweaty, gloomy, badly dressed, gulping down fast food, defeated in some fundamental way. Many of them tell you that they ought to be doing something different with their lives, which is reasonable, considering that even the most brilliant are impoverished. Others explain that they are playing chess full time for the money, which is unconvincing since they could make more doing almost anything else. Generally speaking, professional players are reluctant to own up to their passion for the game, almost as if it were akin to admitting a preference for deviant sex. But despite social and economic pressures, these most rational of men keep at it year after year, forswearing more profitable and reasonable life choices.

In the Soviet Union, the devotion of professional players to chess is economically feasible; chess players of international strength are supported by the state, and an instructor's income from teaching is greater than that of a Soviet doctor or engineer. Enthusiasm for the game is also a reflection of social values. Thousands of Russians play in parks throughout the city, and even nonplayers follow chess in the papers. The top players are national heroes and are as revered as, say, Michael Jackson, Don Mattingly and Clint Eastwood in our country.

Writing on Soviet chess in 1949, Mikhail Botvinnik, then the world champion, explained the success and the psychological advantages of the Soviet player: "What is there in the Soviet school which distinguishes it fundamentally from the foreign school? Most important of all [is] the social position of chess. . . . We Soviet masters . . . know that this is a socially useful cultural activity and that we are bringing benefit to the Soviet state."* In short, chess is a barometer of Russian cultural supremacy. When Fischer defeated Spassky in 1972, wresting away the world championship that Soviets had come to believe was their permanent treasure, there was a national fear that something was rotten in the land.

Chess is part of the Soviet national consciousness, like baseball or football in the United States. Because of its metaphorical resonance and the logical and mathematical purity of the game, it represents vastly different things to different people. Over the years there has been spirited debate in the U.S.S.R. over whether chess is an art, a sport or a science. Players such as Boris Spassky and David Bronstein often describe chess lyrically in terms of in-

---

* M. M. Botvinnik, *Izbrannye partii* (Leningrad, 1949), pp. 11–12.

tuition, fantasy and romanticism. In Bronstein's book *Chess in the Eighties*,* the game becomes a metaphor for life, an occasion for social criticism in the manner of Christopher Lasch or Susan Sontag. Russians write short stories and poetry about chess. At the same time, the Soviet school of chess has been distinguished from other styles of play by its rigorous use of scientific methods of experimentation and systematic analysis. For Mikhail Botvinnik, now retired, and for others interested in developing artificial intelligence, chess provides the raw material for serious scientific investigation into the nature of human intelligence.

Since the twenties, chess has also been regarded as a training ground for Soviet political life. In his book *Soviet Chess*, D. J. Richards writes: ". . . the qualities of the ideal chess-player coincided with those of the ideal Communist: both needed to be resourceful and inventive, to have a feeling for both strategy and tactics and to possess an iron determination to overcome all obstacles on the path to ultimate victory."†

Soviet politicians attempt to make political hay with chess. They barter for the favor of top Soviet players, and in turn the players milk the politicians for political and material advantages. As mentioned earlier, Karpov and Kasparov both have enormous political power, and it is well known that Karpov is a millionaire.

While it is common for Russian players to be ordered to lose games for the good of the state, many citizens consider chess a part of man's moral education, a training ground for the principles of honor and truth and for the harmonious development of personality. Dvoretsky, whose pupils have had a success unparalleled by the students of any teacher in the West, sounds more like a psychoanalyst or an Eastern mystic than a chess teacher. "When I take on a student I work on his personality as a whole, not just chess knowledge," he said. "I'm not interested in teaching people how to memorize. Rather, I develop the psychological capacity for making decisions in different situations. For me, analyzing the drawbacks of a chess player is much the same as analyzing the

* D. Bronstein and G. Smolyan, *Chess in the Eighties*, trans. Kenneth P. Neat (Oxford: Pergamon Press, 1965).
† D. J. Richards, *Soviet Chess* (Oxford: Clarendon Press, 1965), p. 39.

drawbacks of his personality. I suppose my process is analogous to your psychoanalysis, and correcting weaknesses in the personality will ultimately correct fundamental weaknesses in play.

"I will give you an example. One of my students liked to draw his games. This was an aspect of his indecisiveness as a person. He was too dependent on me in chess, and on other people for other aspects of his life. Drawing his chess games was only the symptom of a larger timidity. So at one point in our work I refused to allow him to draw; he could only win or lose. To be free of his draws was a tremendous revelation for him, and he began to play with great creativity and fighting spirit. The next step was for me to withdraw from him; I would give him no advice at all. It was upsetting to him, but in this way I was still teaching him. Soon he began to win major tournaments and became a strong grandmaster.

"I collect examples from different tournaments in order to develop skills. These exercises are very complicated and are designed to help a pupil not just in chess, but to solve central psychological problems and to teach thinking. Yusupov profited greatly from working with my problems. For a time he was failing in the most important tournaments, and when we analyzed his games I realized that he was very keen on his own conceptions but was not being attentive enough to the possibilities of his opponent's position. I wanted Yusupov to enter into his opponent's mind. When you have a successful attack going you may not notice a surprising defense. It is natural not to see what a resourceful player in a losing position may do. Therefore I gave Yusupov exercises to develop his sense of intuition.

"I take talented expert-level players and bring them to grandmaster strength in two years," Dvoretsky went on matter-of-factly. If so, this is extraordinary, for in the United States, young players frequently linger at the expert level for several years before gradually becoming weak masters. The difference in skill between a chess expert and a grandmaster is enormous—say, the difference between a lower-minor-league baseball player and a major-league all-star.

Dvoretsky began to demonstrate a complicated rook-pawn endgame problem whose unexpected solution became clear only after one of several possible variations was traced ten moves deep. "Even in obvious situations, things aren't really obvious," he began while quickly moving the pieces. "It is easy to find moves when you are attacking, but at the same time there are subtleties you are not likely to notice that in the end will cost you the game. My exercises are filled with latent threats."

"His problems were extremely sophisticated," Pandolfini recalled later. "I had to work very hard to follow his ideas, though he assumed that I was getting them without any effort. I've analyzed with Fischer, and it was the same kind of experience. Bobby would move the pieces in a blur, assuming that I understood but not really caring if I did or didn't. If I'd walked out of the room, Dvoretsky wouldn't have noticed; he was in a world of his own."

While Dvoretsky explained his puzzles, there were many distractions. Josh and Anton were again playing chess nearby, sitting on the floor of the dining room, their mouths bulging with huge gobs of bubble gum. Occasionally there were bursts of applause and we would glance at a bank of television monitors to check the progress of Karpov and Kasparov's game.

A burly, box-jawed man stood beside me listening to every word Dvoretsky said, his stony face only inches from my little tape recorder. I assumed this newcomer was a chess fan straining to follow Dvoretsky's complicated analysis, so I smiled at him and said hello. The man didn't answer, and his expression never changed. Soon half a dozen other men were standing around us rigidly eavesdropping as if we were filming an E. F. Hutton commercial. Dvoretsky continued his lecture, but Volodja, beside himself with rage, lost the thread of his translation. "He's a KGB agent," he said in a voice loud enough to be heard fifty feet away. "Why do they do this to us? We're talking about chess, not war!"

AFTER THREE FRUSTRATING days of arguing and pleading at the Central Chess Club and a call to the American embassy we were given press credentials, but time and again Soviet officials nervously explained that it would be impossible for us to visit chess schools. By an unfortunate coincidence, they were all closed for repairs. It was as if we were asking to see missile factories. And whenever I brought up Boris Gulko, my conversations with Russian grandmasters and chess officials alike came to an icy end. Gulko, I discovered, was one of the most famous political dissidents in the Soviet Union, and it seemed unlikely that I would ever find him.

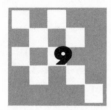

VOLODJA

Most mornings in Moscow we went with Volodja Pimonov to museums and churches or took Josh to play chess in one of the many parks or chess clubs. Usually we drove in Volodja's rattling Zaporoszhets, which he had recently hand-painted muddy blue. Each time we set off he said the same thing: "I hope the car won't fall apart before we get there." To buy it, he had earned extra money teaching Russian to foreigners a few years earlier, but such good fortune was unlikely to come his way again, he felt, and this would probably be the only car he would ever own. He was proud of the car, but also embarrassed, and fretted constantly about it: "Sounds like something is wrong with my transmission." Or "Why is it stalling? It must be my carburetor." Or "There is something wrong with the lock on the driver's side. Do you think you could help me fix it? Finding parts is impossible." For him the car was a connection to the Western world of drive-in banks and movies, superhighways and garages with automatic doors, which he read about in magazines or heard described by his wife during their phone conversations—a world he was likely never to see. Whenever the car rattled or coughed, he looked stricken.

Volodja's curiosity about the West was like an unwelcome lust. He was filled with questions, but the answers agitated or silenced him. During one discussion about journalism I told him that after finishing an article I never showed it to the person I had written about for approval. He was baffled by this. "To write an article about Karpov and not show it to him first would be slanderous here. A writer would lose his job."

"But if you showed it to him and he demanded a change, it might compromise the honesty of the article," I said. It was a new idea to Volodja, and he didn't know what to make of it.

I had the uneasy feeling that Volodja was making large decisions based upon what he learned from us. Often he looked at my face for signs of hidden motivations, and sometimes when he smiled sadly I knew that I had failed some test. "The problem with you people," he said (meaning Americans), "is that you want to be number one in everything. You will be the end of us with this competition. Better houses and better cars, more missiles, more ships." But though he was often critical of the West for its politics or materialism, he craved its hidden possibilities. It outraged him that he was not allowed to look and judge for himself. "You say that you write on a personal computer?" he asked, and in the rearview mirror I could see that he was wide-eyed. "I've never seen one."

"The way is broken," Volodja said one morning as Josh and I sat in the back seat jammed against the jack and spare tire, our feet in two inches of muddy water. He meant that this stretch of road on the way to Sokolniki Park was potholed, and that we should brace ourselves. He was checking the rearview mirror frequently to see if we were being followed. It was illegal for him to be driving foreigners, and on this dreary morning the nameless consequences of being caught made us all feel uneasy.

In Sokolniki Park a chess club nestled within a little forest of birch trees. It was raining steadily, yet two old men in tattered coats sat beneath the trees at a rickety wooden chess table staring at a position. Inside a damp, narrow room we found seventy or eighty Russians playing chess at long tables, while more men lined up behind the players waiting for a turn. They were laborers, dressed in heavy overcoats and caps, with ruddy, fleshy faces and thick, weathered hands. They moved the worn wooden pieces as if they were laying bricks and mortar.

Josh waited behind a heavyset, bald-headed man. When his opponent lost, Josh took his seat. The bald-headed man looked irritated but motioned for him to begin. At first Josh moved the pieces quickly, and Bruce worried that he would blunder. As Volodja scrutinized my son's moves, I wondered whether he was thinking of his own early days at the game, when he had been considered one of the most promising schoolboy players in Moscow. The heavyset man played slowly, with a disapproving expression; this was not a place where children came to play. But many other players were curious, and as the game went on perhaps a dozen men gathered to watch. Josh began badly against an opening he had never seen before, but once down a pawn he began to play thoughtfully and managed to win it back in the middle game. He concentrated like an adult; on one critical move he thought for twenty minutes, his hands cupping his ears. Sometimes Josh falls deeply into a chess position. Time passes and he doesn't notice. His face becomes serene and he doesn't look like a seven-year-old. His mother says that at such times he plays as if there were an old chess player inside him who wakes up for his games.

After an hour and a half the Russian offered a draw. When Josh agreed, the man's face spread into an enormous toothless grin, and he got up from his seat and enveloped Josh in a bear hug. "New Fischer," he said in English to his friends, who were surprised and delighted that a little boy could play so well. They all patted Josh on the shoulder and slapped me on the back for being his father. The love of chess hung in the air like the smell of good food.

One of the men who had watched Joshua's game was Valentin Arbakov, who, like Vinnie in Washington Square, managed to eke out an existence giving laborers time odds for kopecks. Volodja said that as a speed player Arbakov was roughly equivalent to Tal, among the best in the world, but that he lacked the discipline for the slower game. Many grandmasters came to Sokolniki Park to test themselves against Arbakov, and though he was rarely sober, he almost never lost. Yet there is no career for a speed player in Russia or anyplace else.

Volodja, who had never really focused on Joshua's play before, was excited and announced with urgency that his talent would come to nothing if he didn't develop quickly. He spoke half in Russian, half in English as the men stood around listening. "Josh must develop a willingness to work at the game. He must trust Bruce completely. But speed chess isn't good for him. It ruined me. I never became a grandmaster," he said plaintively. It was a great sadness in his life. Arbakov shuffled his feet on the muddy floor and agreed; yes, Josh must study very hard and avoid speed games. His breath reeked of vodka.

THE COSMOS HOTEL was strictly off-limits for most Russians, perhaps because of its grandeur or the likelihood of meeting wealthy Westerners there. Before our visit, Volodja had never been inside. All guests at Intourist hotels are given identification cards that they must show to a guard at the door. When a writer I knew was leaving Moscow he gave his card to Volodja, who clutched it as if it were a ticket to paradise. Now he would be able to get into the Beryozka shop in the lobby to buy Western tobacco and scores of other commodities not available to Russians. If he could manage to borrow several hundred rubles he could buy a Western camera or stereo, sell it in a secondhand shop for five times what he'd paid for it and be able to send some money to his wife in Denmark.

Volodja and other Russian intellectuals we met chafed at the frivolous curbs imposed on their personal freedom—sanctions against driving in a car with foreigners, traveling out of the country or entering certain stores. Despite the risk, they seemed almost eager to break the rules, explaining that they could not bear to live stunted lives.

Walking through the front door of the Cosmos with Volodja was a nervous moment. I clutched my room key, also an acceptable form of identification to show at the door, and found myself leaning away from him; if he was stopped by the police, maybe my complicity would go unnoticed. It was disgraceful, but each time we walked into the hotel, I felt the impulse to distance myself from him.

The Cosmos is a grand illusion, a rendition of Russia artfully crafted to appeal to the Las Vegas, Atlantic City and Club Med vacation set. It is a glitzy, baldly decadent palace of materialistic and corporal pleasures. The hotel's brown, curving façade seems to have been patterned after the Fontainbleau Hotel on Miami

Beach, but the Cosmos is bigger and better. Its creators selected a futuristic theme; scores of bars, discos and restaurants have a zippy Star Trek atmosphere, new-wave music and intergalactic names. Looking out the window of our room, cut from the same mold used by Holiday Inn and Hilton for their antiseptic look-alike rooms, the eye travels to a sleek rocket ship on top of the AeroSpace Museum, poised to lift off from the gloomy Moscow morning.

The hotel is located on the outskirts of the city, miles from most things a tourist would want to see, but it provides the tourist— particularly a Westerner—with everything imaginable to entice him to stay inside. There are AMF bowling alleys to keep tourists in shape for Sunday league games, masseurs standing by to knead away tensions and a heated Olympic-sized swimming pool. If you want Russian atmosphere, the hotel provides plenty. The acres of lobbies are sprinkled with big-screen television monitors showing nature documentaries about Siberia, adventure movies with beautiful Russian landscapes and quaint Russian cartoons to entertain restless kids. If you are feeling tired or lazy, you simply throw your feet up on a luxurious Finnish leather sofa, sip a Beck beer and watch Russia on the tube. There are endless books and postcards to take home, demonstrating that you have ventured behind the Iron Curtain, and legions of helpful Intourist guides happy to describe Russian culture and history by the hour. A weary American could not feel more pampered or more at home.

Lengthy menus in Cosmos restaurants feature such old-time Russian favorites as hot borscht and chicken Kiev, but the waiters invariably guide diners to beefsteak and French fries. Night after night they explain that it's a shame, but akroshka or pyelmeni is not available this evening. The dining halls are like giant spaceships and serve food of the quality you would expect at a Ramada Inn.

For the traveling businessman there are luxury shops filled with glistening furs for the wife and a large selection of gorgeous English-speaking prostitutes lounging around the lobby. If you are needy but shy, such meetings are discreetly arranged by a dour lady stationed on each floor. It is common knowledge that the girls of the Cosmos have an ongoing association with the KGB.

Leaving the Cosmos may seem unnecessary, but if you do decide to venture out, you are encouraged to make arrangements through your guide. In this way the hotel is your host wherever you travel in Moscow. If you want a tour of Russian war monuments or would like to attend the puppet theater, the circus or the Bolshoi, just pick up the phone. A limousine is standing by to take you and to hurry you back the moment the curtain falls, in time for caviar, champagne and late-night disco at the hotel. If you decide to stay downtown later than expected, the driver waits (at least our driver did) until you are ready to return. It is hard not to wonder if his motivation goes beyond courtesy.

For late-night dining and dancing there is a little Bohemian disco in the basement of the Cosmos, trendy enough to attract crowds of yuppies if it were in New York, with little snacks expensive even by Upper East Side standards. The all-night bars at the Cosmos are captained by heavy-lidded men who speak liquor and money in a dozen languages. Like bartenders around the world, they exchange smiles and tired sympathy for tips. At six in the morning they straggle downstairs to the garage where they park their shiny Mercedes. Word has it that bartenders in the Cosmos are among the wealthiest of Russians, and that the payoffs to get these jobs are tremendous.

From the militarylike security at the front door, one assumes that the authorities have as much invested in keeping Russians out as in seducing Americans to stay inside. It is a stretch for a Marxist idealist to reconcile the reality of daily food lines and scratching out an existence on a hundred and fifty rubles a month with Americans enjoying the jet-set life at the Cosmos for a hundred and fifty rubles a day. How can a Russian like Volodja not be dumbfounded by this epic billion-ruble concoction, Moscow's homage to capitalism?

ONE EVENING VOLODJA ate dinner with us in a glittery restaurant on the first floor. His wife had called him from Denmark two days before to say that during her last visit to Russia she had become pregnant. She was feeling too sick to work and had no money, and he didn't know what to do. She was afraid to join him in the Soviet Union for fear the baby wouldn't be permitted to leave. "Do you realize," he said, "I may never see my child?" Back in New York, Bonnie was also pregnant, and I wanted to talk with my new friend about fatherhood, but it wasn't appropriate; my own happiness seemed unfair.

During other nights out, Volodja had ordered for us, but in the Cosmos he whispered that the waiters must not hear him speak Russian; it could be dangerous. We ordered beefsteak and French fries. Soon a West German band started playing the latest European hits. We were sitting beside the dance floor, which was crowded with men in business suits dancing stiffly with busty women in tight skirts alongside a few gorgeously dressed Russian couples— the children of politicians, we were told—stylishly executing the newest Western dance steps. The darkened room seemed to move with slinky electronic rhythms and blinking lights.

Later, upstairs in our room, Volodja said wearily, "Several years ago I was shipped off to a collective farm. It is not unusual if the workers in the district cannot harvest the crops in time. But it was very strange—doctors and university professors living in a cramped and freezing hut. Our lives and careers were completely disrupted because the people in the village wouldn't work."

I was nervous when Volodja talked about his life in our hotel room. What if the room was bugged? It would take an army to listen to all the conversations in all the rooms of the Cosmos; still, during our stay we kept making resolutions to be discreet. Bruce and I continually cautioned Josh not to mention Volodja by name or to ask questions about the problems of Jewish chess players. He was confused about the need for secrecy and would say, "Who's listening? The KGB? But who are the KGB? Why are they listening?" In any case we would eventually forget discretion and talk about everything.

At 10:30 P.M. we watched a television special about the chess match, which was followed by the news. It was the week of President Reagan's long-awaited meeting with Prime Minister Gromyko, and Moscow television was filled with images of chess and war. Newscasts began with stories about Karpov and Kasparov, followed by clips of Reagan pounding his fist like Mussolini or of U.S. Marines training with bazookas. One didn't have to be a

grandmaster to conclude that while Russians engaged in their sym-
phony of sport, Americans practiced war.

"What about that Korean spy plane?" Volodja asked.

"Terrible," I answered sharply. I felt self-righteous about the
Korean plane.

"You know," Volodja said, "most of the European journalists
here felt that the Korean plane was part of a spy mission. At the
very least it was doing something provocative to see how we would
respond."

"Even if that's so, what's the justification for shooting it down?
Why not force it to land?"

He nodded. "I think it was the second plane which caused the
alarm here."

"What second plane?" I hadn't read about any second plane.

"Our radar showed one plane; then the blip broke into two. At
first the two planes were flying close together; then the second
plane, apparently smaller, flew off."

"The story here is very different from the one in the States. We
heard nothing about a second plane," I said. Political conversations
between us often ran up against such walls, for we made our judgments on the basis of different "facts." Often we felt bewildered;
who was right? "What do you think happened?" I asked. "Why
was the plane shot down?"

"I think the generals were drunk that night."

It seemed like a reasonable theory: generals in some backwater
area, drunk on vodka. "Something like that will be the end of us
all," I said.

For the last several days, Josh had been coaxing Bruce and
Volodja to play chess. Bruce searched for excuses, but this evening
Josh insisted and had his way. In their first games, Bruce was
deferential, attempting to lure Volodja into a kind of pas de deux.
If he won a pawn, he acted as if it were an accident, or even offered
a little apology. Volodja was oblivious and played for every advantage. While Pandolfini used timid, drawish openings, Volodja chose
dynamic attacking lines from the latest issues of *Shakhmatnyi byul-
leten* and *64*. Again and again he wedged apart Pandolfini's pawns
with state-of-the-art opening traps. Bruce struggled and lost the

first six games, four of them on time. It seemed as if he wouldn't be able to win a game. Volodja was a tiger, pouncing on each move. The instant the flag on Bruce's clock fell Volodja immediately set up the pieces for the next game. For him these wins were like accumulating wealth. He was insatiable; perhaps winning helped him forget. Bruce hung on in weak positions, trying not to lose.

Josh was beside himself and couldn't bear to look at the games. He believed his teacher's playing strength was at least equal to Bobby Fischer's and couldn't imagine Bruce taking a beating. As the games continued, he became crazy with tension and bounced like a beach ball from sofa to bed to bathroom. When he knocked over a lamp, no one noticed.

After an hour or so, Bruce managed to draw a few games. This was the happiest part of the night for him. They were intricate positional games, well played, with a handshake at the end and no loser. But the competition turned sharply on one game. It was a rook-pawn ending in which Pandolfini's passed pawn had advanced to the seventh rank, with his rook blocking the pawn's advance. As Volodja pressed the clock he commented that Bruce was playing the ending incorrectly. "Otherwise you would have a won game," he said confidently. But he was wrong; his opponent's win was clear after three more moves.

Now Volodja started losing. Pandolfini played with a melancholic expression and, regardless of the time on the clock, moved his pieces in a calm, unhurried way. But he had become more familiar with his opponent's style and choice of openings, and despite his demeanor his game had become more aggressive. Volodja played in a fury. He seemed to move faster and faster, banging the clock for emphasis but making mistakes. He had wanted to be invincible, and falling short of this, his game began to collapse. In his rush to win he knocked pieces from the board. In one game he hung his queen and barked at Josh to be quiet. Bruce kept trying to guide the marathon to a conclusion, but Volodja wouldn't allow him to stop.

Josh fell asleep at two in the morning beneath a pile of bolster pillows. Each night in the hotel he carefully constructed a fort on top of his sheets, his protection from "the baddies who are listening."

At three I walked downstairs with Volodja. The lobby was empty except for a dozen whores who chatted with the policemen near the front door. Emerging from the excesses of the past hours, Volodja's face was timid and a little embarrassed. "Bruce's knowledge of the endgame is sophisticated," he said thoughtfully.

As he walked to the front door, I wondered what the guards would think: Who is this man leaving the hotel at this hour? Is he Russian? What would happen if they stopped Volodja and asked for his papers? But they didn't.

Back in the room, Bruce was lying in bed looking as if he were about to burst into tears. "What's the matter?" I asked. "You couldn't have played better."

"And I hated every minute of it. Did you see how upset he became?"

It was a strange moment; we had traveled all the way to Moscow to see the world championship and to observe Russian chess life, and my son's teacher was confessing that he couldn't bear to play the game. He might lose, he might win; either way it was a crisis. "I like to draw," Bruce said unhappily, "but that's hard to do unless you play like Petrosian."

DURING OUR SECOND week in Moscow, Volodja became increasingly afraid. He had been observed spending afternoons with us at the match and driving us around Moscow. His boss, Aleksandr Roshal, accused him of subversive activity and threatened to fire him immediately if he continued to see us. Pandolfini and I felt terrible about having added to his difficulties, and we urged him to keep his distance, but Volodja wouldn't hear of it and clung to us as to a lifeline. He asked dozens of questions about the professional opportunities that might be open to him in Europe or the United States, as if the answers would get him a visa. He was speaking to all of his friends, trying to track down Boris Gulko for us, and hoped that if I wrote about the dissident in Western magazines, I could also discuss his own situation in order to pressure the authorities to allow him to visit his wife.

One morning when he picked us up Volodja told us with great agitation that he had been fired. "To take away a man's work, that's fascism," he said. "But if I call a press conference, I will be called a political enemy and sent to prison. It's ironical about Roshal," he went on, talking about his boss, who was Karpov's close friend. "For his whole life he has wanted to defect to the West. He has openly discussed it with his friends. Now he exercises tyranny against Jews and anyone else who wants to leave. Kasparov's mother despises Roshal for his attitudes about Jews and is afraid that he will try dirty tricks during the match. I must call my friends this afternoon, the people I know who have applied for emigration and been turned down."

"Why?"

"In circumstances such as mine, people have disappeared. I live by myself. Telling people about my situation is my only safeguard."

THE
PRESSROOM

In the Hall of Columns, Anatoly Karpov and Gary Kasparov played on a stage flanked by two large display boards. Karpov wore a gray business suit; the challenger dressed more casually in a sports jacket and sweater. Sometimes Kasparov strolled the stage between moves with his hands behind his back, as if he were walking in a park. When he sat at the table, centered on a large oriental rug, he would scratch his tightly curled black hair and glance furtively at Karpov. He was a tense young man trying to appear relaxed. The older and more experienced Karpov rocked in his chair, and his eyes rarely left the board until he was sure of a win; then he would pick at his teeth and look out at the crowd like a king.

In the chess world Karpov is called the Fetus because of his diaphanous complexion and frail physical makeup. But in the early days of the match, while he built his lead, he grew immense. On the stage he seemed to tower above his younger and larger opponent, and when he looked at Kasparov he didn't bother to hide his contempt.

For the first half hour of each game, Pandolfini, Josh and I would watch the two men from the balcony. Josh leaned his elbows on the railing and observed them through the wrong end of his binoculars. I was afraid he would drop the glasses and hit someone below on the head. After the opening moves we watched on television monitors in the pressroom on the third floor, but sometimes, when the players were under time pressure, we returned to the balcony. Then Josh would root exuberantly for Kasparov and throw rapid analysis at Bruce while spectators seated nearby gave us dirty looks. Most of his blitz tactics were pure fantasy. Excited by the crowd and loyal to his man, my son saw sacrifices and mating combinations all over the board.

THE PRESSROOM ON the third floor of the House of Trade Unions was jammed with chess stars of the past, notable Moscow personalities, journalists and television crews seeking interviews. There were banks of phones, telex machines and a score of screens showing closeups of the two brooding sportsmen. At demonstration tables clusters of grandmasters unraveled an infinity of possibilities.

When we were in the pressroom, Josh was on his own. He preferred to sit at the front table with a past United States champion, Grandmaster Arnold Denker, Gary Kasparov's friend Eric Schiller, International Master Jonathan Tisdale and the oldest active grandmaster, Miguel Najdorf, a living legend in chess circles. Television commentators frequently questioned Najdorf, Denker and young Waitzkin about the newest wrinkle in the current game while crews filmed the interviews for millions around the world. Late at night we would watch Josh on the television in our room. During one interview he demonstrated a winning line for Kasparov with bubble gum all over his chin. Each time Yuri Averbakh, past president of the Soviet Chess Federation and a FIDE arbiter for the match, entered the room, he paused to give Josh a hug and smiled like a politician while photographers snapped their cameras.

The level of excitement at the match was equivalent to that at the Rose Bowl or an NCAA basketball championship, but from the point of view of an American who lacked sophisticated chess knowledge it would be difficult to say why. World championship chess is a strange and nearly unrecognizable relative of the game most amateurs play. Day after day passes without a checkmate, without a player's either winning a piece outright or making a recognizable blunder. The two best players in the world calculate and conceive of strategies for long stretches of minutes and then make the quietest moves. In the middle game they often calculate ten or more moves ahead; in the endgame, when most of the pieces are off the board, they may think ahead even further. According to a chess master who is also proficient at other games, Karpov's and Kasparov's deepest calculations, which involve the retention and mental manipulation of numerous possible positions, are roughly equivalent to doing the *New York Times* Sunday crossword puzzle in your head. They do all this in the hope of eventually weakening a square, doubling a pawn, giving a bishop a little more room, seizing an open file, overprotecting a strong point, improving the position of a developed piece or gaining a tempo. These advantages are hardly discernible. Each man tries to figure more deeply, but more often than not their calculations match perfectly, and a well-disguised offensive thrust is anticipated and answered with a compensating defensive move.

Grandmasters of approximately the same strength aren't exactly playing to win but rather seek to maximize the possibilities of winning without taking an unacceptable risk. They are like two men balancing on a tightrope. Sometimes a player will strum the rope a little with a toe, as if idly passing time, in the hope that he will catch his opponent leaning the wrong way. But he knows that if he plucks the rope too hard, it is more likely that he will lose his own balance and tumble, rather than his opponent. While the game is being played in the air, the only ones who truly understand their sleepy feints, counterfeints, wiggles and taps are the two men on the rope. Far more often than not, the contest will end with both men still balanced.

Karpov's and Kasparov's strategies were far beyond most of us in the pressroom. In addition to extraordinary chess genius, world-class grandmasters have a mental file of hundreds of thousands of complex positions and opening variations accumulated from experience and study—an encyclopedia of chess history to help speed their analysis during games. This allows them automatically to play moves that appear esoteric and inexplicable to the amateur. Still, everyone in the pressroom analyzed and tried to beat them to the punch. Movie stars, politicians and journalists scrutinized the boards for a knight fork or a mate in two, tactics far too obvious for grandmaster play. I spent many intense hours trying to relate positions on the monitor to ones I'd experienced with Josh in our living room. When you've traveled six thousand miles to watch chess, you try.

Usually there were about twenty grandmasters in the room, and after virtually every move of a close game, one of them would offer an opinion. "It's an easy victory for Karpov; Kasparov must resign," one would say. Minutes later from across the room another grand-master would slowly rise from his chair and state gravely, as if historians were taking notes, "Kasparov is clearly ahead." Denker had the habit of changing his mind two or three times a game, and each pronouncement was flashed to Europe and South America by telex. Without the time and quiet to study the position system-atically, the blitz analysis of the grandmasters was not much dif-ferent from Joshua's fairy-tale interpretations. The intuitions of these sages were affected by wishful thinking and by jealousy, but mainly by the imperative need to say something into a camera or to appease a pesky journalist who was late filing his story. In the pressroom, Karpov's and Kasparov's advantages depended not so much on the position of the pieces as on whom you asked, and while the clock ticked to the end of a game, each opinion seemed loaded with significance.

Everything in the pressroom was big news. One afternoon Grandmaster Alexandria, dressed in a black slinky dress, moved through the room like Lady Brett Ashley. When I asked her for an interview, she sat on a stool, crossed her legs and glamorously swept her hair back. Before I had finished my second question we were bathed in spotlights. Every time I interviewed people in the room the same thing happened; cameramen assumed that when the American writer asked questions it must be important.

Dimitrije Bjelica was a dynamo, turning out articles in different languages for various papers. Like a track star he raced from phone to phone, belting out stories. "I never write a thing; there's no time," he said. One afternoon while he took a frantic break, I mentioned some piece of gossip about Bobby Fischer. The follow-ing morning the story was printed in two different newspapers.

"Who's winning?" I asked Dimitrije on another occasion. He looked weary this afternoon—weary with chess. He shrugged: who knows, who cares? But a few minutes later he was standing in front of the cameras discussing the game with crackling confidence, as though he had direct access to Karpov's brain.

A Russian journalist was making a fortune exchanging dollars for rubles. "There is absolutely no risk," he said. "Two rubles for every American dollar. You can exchange as much as you want." A Russian photographer whispered to me that I should watch out for the guy; he was with the KGB. The KGB was like Zorro; the name was on everyone's lips. They were bigger than life, but maybe they weren't there at all. How could you know for sure? Maybe the photographer was jealous of the journalist, who carried a wad of rubles as thick as a loaf of bread. Western newsmen were standing on line to exchange their money. At this exchange rate an American would get more than twice as much for his dollar, but the Russian was making a killing; the normal rate on the black market was five rubles for a dollar. "I was with three women last night," he said. "Do you want Russian women? It's no problem. You like big women? Whatever you want." He reminded me of a Puerto Rican fence in New York I'd once known who prided himself on his ability to deliver, on twenty-four hours' notice, any model of any appliance you wanted.

Each day Alexander Kostyev, the senior coach of the chess department of the U.S.S.R. Sports Committee, was at the match, shaking hands with old friends and watching the monitor. I introduced myself and explained that I would like to visit one of the special chess schools. He was prepared for my question. "It is too bad, but all the schools are closed for repairs," he said, repeating what I had already heard.

"Surely there must be someplace in Moscow where children are studying with teachers that isn't closed for repairs," I said. Kostyev acknowledged that this might be true. "The only thing you can do is to ask the permission of Nikolai Krogius," he said, referring to the head of the chess department of the Sports Committee. "Unfortunately," he added, "Krogius is taking his rest in Georgia."

It was the fourth game of the match. After two draws, Kasparov had lost the third game. On the TV monitor he appeared tired, and now he strode around the stage, trying to rouse himself. Eric Schiller, Kasparov's American friend, was edgy and banged the pieces for emphasis while he analyzed in a commanding voice. When he offered an opinion, newsmen jotted it down in their notebooks. "Gary's okay," he said to one. "I spoke to him this afternoon. Had a little cold but he's feeling much better."

"Bruce," Arnold Denker called to Pandolfini in the whiskey voice of an old gin-rummy player from the Catskills, "Bruce, I switched hotels. Now I'm at the Rossiya. But what a mistake. The room is just terrible." Then, turning to someone behind him, "It doesn't work. Did you look at the skewer after rook takes pawn?" Then back to Bruce. "There's no hot water, no room service. The Cosmos was terrific. They had everything. Stay where you are."

Denker, suntanned, fit and smiling in a neatly pressed summer suit, looked young for his seventy-one years. Speaking to Josh, he pointed in the direction of Miguel Najdorf. "That man is a living legend. He beat Alekhine. Botvinnik." Josh looked confused; he glanced around the pressroom, assuming that Alekhine and Botvinnik were at one of the tables. "He beat Bobby Fischer," Denker added.

"You beat Bobby Fischer?" Joshua asked, finally impressed, and Najdorf smiled.

"Did you ever play Bruce Pandolfini?" Josh asked, glancing respectfully at his teacher.

"Miguel, I still remember the game against Botvinnik in forty-six," Denker said. "It was forty years ago and I remember every move."

A journalist asked Denker what he thought of Kasparov. "He's a genius!" he exclaimed. "Half-Jewish, half-Armenian. How could he miss? If only Petrosian had been half-Jewish. Because he had the other half, the Armenian.

"Miguel, have you ever gone back to Warsaw?" Denker went on. The silver-haired Najdorf shook his head without taking his eyes from the position on the board. Born in Poland, Najdorf had sought asylum in Argentina in 1939. Back home, his family had been murdered in a concentration camp.

Grandmaster Iosif Davidovich Dorfman, Kasparov's top aide, came into the pressroom and agreed to answer a few questions. I asked him whether or not Kasparov's Jewish background was a disadvantage in the match. "It seems clear," I said, "that Karpov's team is much stronger. I've been told that most top grandmasters are afraid to associate themselves with Kasparov." Dorfman, himself a Jew, looked uneasy and, before saying anything to me, spoke in Russian to a man standing nearby. Then he replied that if I asked these kinds of questions he wouldn't be able to continue the interview.

KARPOV CONSIDERED HIS position for half an hour, then pushed a black pawn and looked confidently out at the audience. Kasparov appeared to be startled. Reporters raced around the pressroom looking for their favorite players to interview, while grandmasters moved pieces and scratched their heads. "He played my move," Denker said merrily.

After a minute or two, Kasparov pushed a pawn in defense. "That was idiotic," said Eric Schiller and banged down his rook. "Gary, what are you doing? You're gonna blow another one."

"Eric, what's the big deal?" said Denker. "I like black's position, but it doesn't mean he's winning."

Mikhail Tal moved around the pressroom like a cat. In 1960, at the age of twenty-four, he became the youngest man ever to win the world championship and according to Fischer was one of the ten greatest players who ever lived. During an era when grandmasters were fighting for microscopic positional advantages and chess seemed to be evolving into an era of draws spiced by occasional dry technical wins, Tal blasted everyone off the board. In the spirit of the nineteenth-century romantic players, he went for the home run, sacrificing his queens and rooks for mate while many of his defeated opponents claimed lamely that his thrilling sacrifices and combinations were unsound. Now, at forty-eight, wild gray hair flowed from his head, and his eyes bulged with genius, or perhaps madness. He moved from one table to the next and paused for a moment, glaring at the position. While he stared there was complete silence. Eventually he would move a piece or two, and the grandmasters would nod. For several minutes after Tal moved on, they left the position alone, as if it were holy, but eventually their own ideas began to take hold again and they would start moving the pieces and making predictions to reporters.

Now Karpov played pawn takes pawn. "He's made a mistake,"

shouted Denker. "Where's Najdorf? I've gotta make a bet with Najdorf. I'm gonna give him eight to five."

"Gary's okay, Gary's okay," Schiller muttered, trying to reassure himself. Tal, Polugayevsky and Josh Waitzkin saw winning chances for white; Dolmatov and Dvoretsky liked black. The place was going berserk; someone was winning.

In the midst of the bedlam, Kostyev, who was in charge of youth chess in the U.S.S.R., appeared with a short, handsome man dressed in a stylish tight-fitting sports shirt, Levi's and cowboy boots, who was holding the hand of a skinny little boy. "This is Yugenil Gik and his son Sasha," Kostyev said to Josh. "Would you like to play a few games with him? Sasha is a talented seven-year-old player."

Gik was one of Karpov's aides and a collaborator with the champion on many books. He hadn't been in the pressroom long before journalists were throwing questions at him about the match. We walked to a chess table near the telex machines, trailed by reporters and photographers. Gik was congenial but said little; he waved to people with the relaxed assurance of a winner. "Is Joshua a champion for his age in the United States?" he asked. I said that he was among the strongest players for his age.

The children began to play. Josh moved too rapidly and blundered away a pawn on the seventh move. Sasha took more time and Gik smiled. Pandolfini shook his head: C'mon, Josh, concentrate, slow down, play chess. Photographers snapped the kids from all angles.

I asked Gik if the size of Karpov's team was an advantage to him in the match.

"Karpov plays the game, not his team," he answered curtly.

"Is Karpov nervous about the match?" I asked.

"Karpov is never nervous. He doesn't know what it is to be nervous." Now Gik twitched when his son neglected to take a pawn that was a sitting duck. At first Josh had been distracted by the photographers, but soon he began to develop an attack. Sasha, a dreamy little boy, didn't seem to notice.

The Karpov-Kasparov game hung in the balance. Reporters hurried around the room asking questions. Several of them asked Gik about Karpov's position, but Gik waved them aside. Sasha's position had become desperate; he was staring blankly at mate in three. The tendons in Gik's face were bulging; he was furious. It was an emotion I knew well. It was all the father could do not to grab his son and scream, "What are you doing! Look at the board! You're throwing away the game!"

"Do you want your son to become a chess professional?" I asked Gik a few minutes later.

"Why not, if he had talent," he answered in disgust. A dozen moves into the second game Sasha had lost his queen and was struggling to play on. When Gik barked at him to resign, the little boy turned over his king, more upset by his father's anger than by the chess game. Josh began to set up the pieces again, but Gik said, "Enough," and led Sasha out of the pressroom.

A half hour later, Karpov and Kasparov adjourned in a fairly even position. The following morning *Pravda* carried an analysis of their game, and beneath it a photograph and caption describing the match held at the same time between little Sasha Gik and the American boy Josh Waitzkin. The caption didn't mention a winner.

NOT
CLOSED
FOR
REPAIRS

On a damp chilly morning a few days later, Josh, Pandolfini and I stood on a corner watching several hundred Russians standing in line to get into a large supermarket. We were waiting for Anna, a chess teacher at one of Moscow's prestigious sports schools, whom we had met at the Hall of Columns. She had agreed to allow us to visit her class even though she knew that if her superiors found out she might be dismissed.

After a twenty-minute wait, I saw Anna walking stiffly toward us. She was a beautiful, statuesque woman, and for some reason this made her extreme nervousness more unsettling. She understood English quite well but could barely speak a word and became flustered and turned beet red when she tried. As shoppers glanced at our display of pantomine and Pidgin English, we eventually pieced together her plea that we not talk English at the school; if we were spoken to, we should just nod. School administrators would be standing at the front door, and we should walk quickly past them.

We hurried into the school without incident. Anna stationed us in the back of her classroom and gave each of us a thick stack of three-by-five cards of endgame positions with illegible notation. After our cloak-and-dagger introduction, we expected something fantastic; perhaps we would be privy to secret research or a high-tech learning device.

The classroom was designed for hard work, with worn desks and uncomfortable wooden benches anchored to the floor. On the wall were photographs of Karpov and other great Russian grandmasters and a bulletin board celebrating the chess accomplishments of past students of the school. In this "sports school," one of two in Moscow, young chess players took a class each morning with Anna in addition to a normal secondary-school curriculum. Twenty-five nine- and ten-year-old children were in the room, an elite group selected for their ability from many thousands of youngsters in secondary schools throughout Moscow. All except one were boys. We looked at the backs of their heads and wondered which among them would be the Karpov or Botvinnik of the twenty-first century.

In contrast to her nervousness with us, Anna was composed and eloquent before her class. For the entire two hours she lectured and asked questions about a single king-and-pawn endgame position from an Akiba Rubinstein game. As she discussed every conceivable variation, the children took copious notes as if they were college students. After an hour Josh became impatient; he wanted to play. With Bruce he rarely studied a single position for more than fifteen minutes. At seven years old, he regarded chess only as a game and was patronizing about the necessity for deep study. He wanted to get his hands on Anna's students, whom he was certain he could beat.

Bruce was impressed with Anna's class. She was a bright, thorough teacher with a keen sense for the pace at which her students could absorb technical material. We were looking for secrets, but there were no secrets, no techniques that American teachers didn't routinely use. The advantage for children here was simply their constant exposure to the game. Day after day they were drilled in the fundamentals of chess for more hours than fourth and fifth graders in the United States study math.

Most mornings, before we went touring, Bruce spent an hour working with Josh. Usually they set up their chessboard on the second-floor balcony overlooking the cavernous lobby of the hotel. After Anna's class we returned to the Cosmos at eleven-thirty, and Bruce decided to work with Josh before lunch. It was a mistake; my son was saturated with chess instruction.

"Now what else did you consider?" Pandolfini asked while Josh gazed down at the hubbub in the lobby. "You didn't consider e5, did you? You're still not considering it. Sit up. Let's get down to business."

Josh shaded his forehead with his hands so that his teacher couldn't see his eyes and struck the pose of a contemplative player.

"You're not racking them up this month, Tiger," Pandolfini said. "It's not easy to get master-class points when you're gazing off into space."

"I'm not doing so badly. How many points do I have this month?" Josh asked, trying to engineer the conversation away from the lesson.

"Josh, forget the points," said Bruce, caught in his own trap. "White to move and win."

"I was right, wasn't I?" Josh asked combatively. "Rook to d1."

"That's not the point. You didn't study the board. You're moving before even *I* know the answer. I want you to have at least two different plans before you move. Each plan should have at least three or four moves." Josh was shaking his head in agreement but shutting Bruce out. Pandolfini was impatient. Perhaps watching Anna's class had made him edgy; maybe he and Josh had spent too much time studying openings and not enough on the endgame; maybe he had allowed Josh to play too much speed chess; maybe he hadn't been systematic enough in his teaching. The Russians build chess players slowly and methodically, as if they were constructing tall buildings.

Sometimes I'm delighted by Bruce's ambition for Josh; at other times I find it frightening. He has said that Josh has the talent to become a master before his twelfth birthday, a chance to become the youngest American master ever; that's his goal. But perhaps Josh isn't as good as Bruce thinks or won't be willing to work hard enough. Josh is secretive about his dreams. What if he decides to give up chess? Could Bruce sense it and gracefully let go, or would he keep pretending that his pupil's growing distance or distaste for the game was only a stage in the learning process?

Josh and Bruce were working on the same Rubinstein endgame position that Anna had taught in her class. Her students had been attentive, but now my son couldn't bear to look at it.

"So why is black better? Take your time."

"Black has the advantage," Josh said, pushing himself, "because white has more islands. If you have more pawn islands, you have weaknesses."

"That's right," said Bruce, but before the words were out, Josh had cleaned the pieces from the board with a sweep of his hand in order to bring the lesson to a quick conclusion.

"Okay, Josh, set the position up again, and if you get it wrong you lose master-class points."

"Okay, I don't care." Josh shrugged. "It's good for my practice."

"It took players hundreds of years to come up with the theory of positional chess," Bruce said sternly. "Rubinstein was one of the greatest endgame players of all time. Did you know that?"

For the past fifteen minutes, while Bruce had been lecturing him on endgame technique, Josh had been furtively fashioning a glider from a paper napkin beneath the table. "This is the best one I ever made," he announced and lofted it off the balcony.

A middle-aged man who had been sitting beside them watching the lesson had been itching to play and challenged Bruce to a game. Pandolfini graciously declined but suggested he play against Josh, who couldn't have been happier to put Akiba Rubinstein behind him. He was like a racehorse breaking from the gate, and the man was lost after fifteen moves.

A COUPLE OF days later a master with whom we had become friendly invited us to attend his class at the Pioneer Palace. This visit confirmed our suspicions that the Pioneer Palace was not closed for repairs and that the secret to Russian chess training at the elementary level was nothing more than devotion to the game and hard work. Here Josh played games with half a dozen talented nine-year-olds and beat each of them. But would he be able to keep pace with them over the next several years, and would he want to? For my son and other American kids, chess is a question of trade-offs. More chess means less time for homework, basketball and friends, who know or care little about the game. Josh thrives on the excitement of tournaments, but he also loves fishing, base-ball, basketball, soccer, tennis and video games. He was now study-ing two hours each week with Pandolfini, doing half an hour of problem-solving three or four evenings a week and, if there was no tournament, playing once or twice a weekend in the park—a total of six or seven hours of chess a week; there was simply no time in his life for more. But his Russian counterparts were studying ten hours a week in the sports school, another ten hours with a master at the Pioneer Palace in the afternoon, and each night after dinner they were urged by their parents to study positions. At an age when American kids dream of becoming firemen or baseball players, the children in Anna's classroom already were specialists who knew what they were going to do when they grew up. Such specific and rigorous early training goes against the spirit of liberal arts education and of making mature life choices during or after college, but clearly it is the most efficient way to manufacture a new generation of grandmasters.

Joel Benjamin describes what it is like to analyze positions with young Russian grandmasters: "It was obvious that in certain endgame positions the Russians knew it was a win or a draw simply by looking at the position, while I had to figure it out. This gives them advantages in tournament play." These players had spent countless hours studying the grammar of chess while Benjamin had played sports with his friends in Brooklyn.

ONE AFTERNOON WE arranged for a tour of Moscow through an Intourist representative at the hotel. Our guide, Yuri, a pleasant young man with acne on a fleshy face, was a student of languages at Moscow University. Although he spoke with a slight hesitation, he was fluent in English, and his knowledge of some aspects of American culture was astounding. He had a passion for American sports and pop music and peppered us with questions about Meat Loaf, Madonna and other rock stars. He knew the lifetime statistics of Kareem Abdul Jabbar, Doctor J. and Bernard King and earnestly described the moves of basketball players he had never seen. He took us to a score of monuments that celebrated the Russian Revolution, delivering a mechanical little speech at each of them. When I asked him if there was much premarital sex in Moscow he became so embarrassed that he couldn't answer.

Two days later we were eating lunch in the cafeteria at the

Cosmos when I realized that I had left my wallet in the room. I took the elevator up, turned into the corridor to our room and bumped into a busboy—Yuri dressed in a white jacket. I greeted him enthusiastically, but he rushed off down the hall. I followed him and called his name. From the second-floor balcony I watched him race down the long staircase and out the front door of the hotel.

Pandolfini was upset when I told him what had happened and went up to the room to see if anything was missing. Our travel vouchers and money were all in place, but Joshua's journal was open. "I left it open. Were any of my books missing?" Josh asked with alarm, referring to his collection of Snoopy books.

Soon it became clear that we were being watched constantly. One morning in a museum I sat down on a bench to take a few notes in my journal, and a man immediately sat down beside me and peered at my notebook. All morning he followed me from gallery to gallery. When Josh gave his little friend Anton some toy cars in exchange for several Russian chess books at the Hall of Columns the next day, the books were sternly observed, as if the children were passing state secrets.

BORIS
GULKO

More than ever I wanted to meet Boris Gulko. Still, I was apprehensive when I received a call on our room phone in the hotel saying that a meeting with "our friend" had been arranged. What if the meeting was a setup? If we ended up in jail, what would happen to Josh? By now we'd been away for three weeks and he had become homesick for his mother. He wanted to call her and tell her that he missed her and that the KGB was following us. This was all Bonnie would have to hear.

On a damp gray morning Josh, Pandolfini and I stood outside a boarded-up café wondering if we were being observed. We had been told that Gulko would take the metro to a stop near our hotel, that Volodja would pick him up, and if they weren't being followed they would stop for us.

In a few minutes Volodja's small car pulled up, and he gestured for us to crowd into the back seat. Next to him in the front sat Gulko. I suggested it might be safer if we talked in the car, but he wanted us to come to his flat to meet his wife and son.

Volodja nervously checked the rearview mirror. "Boris has just won the semifinals of the Soviet championship," he said. I was surprised, because there had been no report of his participation in newspapers or chess magazines, and most players and chess journalists I had asked said that they didn't know what had become of Gulko. "Oh, I am allowed to play a few games a year," he said, "but they are never reported. If I win a tournament they only write who came in second or third." Gulko said that he had played

Kasparov twice during the past three years and won both games. Almost no one beats Kasparov, and such news would have been on television and on the front page of *Pravda* were Gulko not a refusenik, one of the living dead.

Boris Gulko is a distinguished-looking white-haired man of medium height with a small pursed mouth and a gentle face. He appeared to be fifty-five or sixty. His speech was serene, almost in the manner of an Eastern mystic, except for a sharp laugh that was filled with irony. At times there was an eerie disparity between his subject and his tone of voice. For example, he would describe a period of intense physical and emotional trauma—a hunger strike or a brutal beating—almost in passing, as if he were beyond feeling pain. I was shocked when Gulko told me that he was thirty-seven. He smiled. "If you don't eat for forty-two days you too will look sixty," he said.

I asked if he'd been following the match.

"I would love to go, but Krogius won't sell me a ticket," he said, referring to the head of Soviet chess. "Perhaps I would be an embarrassment. Two years ago I got in touch with Karpov about my problems, but he refused to help."

Even during the early stages of the Karpov-Kasparov match there had been discussion among Russian intellectuals, grandmasters and journalists about whether the event was a legitimate contest. In several of the early games we had attended, Kasparov had advantages and had failed to follow up on them. Later in the match, he aroused the suspicion of grandmasters and chess journalists around the world by offering draws in games in which he seemed to have winning chances. Miguel Najdorf said that Kasparov's play was inexplicable and a disgrace. "I wouldn't offer draws in such positions, and I'm seventy-five years old," he said. In the *Times* of London, chess columnist Harry Golombek wrote: "Perhaps Kasparov has been warned not to play well and has been given to understand that the consequences for him and his family would be disastrous if he did."

I asked Gulko if he was surprised by Kasparov's poor play and whether he thought it was possible that the challenger had been ordered to lose the match because the Central Committee didn't want a Jew to be world champion. "It is impossible to know this for a fact," Gulko answered. "Perhaps Kasparov is just playing poorly. He is an emotional young man. But in Russia chess is political and it is difficult to refuse if you are asked to throw a game. If they don't want a chess player to play, like me or Bronstein, for example, they'll stop you for years.

"A player's creative life is ruled by chess management," Gulko went on in his unsettling calm voice. "In 1953, in the Zurich interzonal, Bronstein was ordered to draw a game against Smyslov. Bronstein had winning chances in the game, and if he had won it, it's likely that he would have won the tournament and played against Botvinnik for the world championship. But in this instance, more important than Bronstein's Judaism was the issue of keeping an American out of the championship, because if Bronstein had won that game it also would have given Sammy Reshevsky a chance to win the tournament. The Soviet action was directed against Reshevsky, an American who is also a Jew.

"In 1977, the year I won the Soviet championship, Viktor Baturinsky was the leader of Soviet chess. Because I was a Jew he tried to make certain I'd lose. In two instances players were asked to lose games so that their opponents might finish ahead of me."

IN THE DISTRICT where Gulko lived there were hundreds of large new apartment buildings, all painted the same blue and white. They could have been lower-middle-income housing in Far Rockaway except that they looked out on farmland dotted by small huts.

We parked behind one of the buildings about half a mile from Gulko's flat, where he said it was unlikely that anyone would be watching for him, then walked through alleys, beneath clotheslines and across sandy playgrounds. After seeing Soviet grandmasters shuttled to the Hall of Columns in limousines and fans bothering them for autographs, I found it strange to be sneaking through backyards in the company of a Soviet champion. We kept glancing behind us to see if we were being followed.

The Gulkos lived in a little flat in one of the large blue-and-white buildings. There was a small bedroom for the boy, David, and in the living room, where Boris and Anna slept, were a comfortable sofa and shelves filled with books about art and chess.

Anna Akhsharumova is a pale, thin young woman, with an odd suppleness like a Modigliani woman. Whereas Boris looked old for his years, Anna, who was twenty-seven, could have passed for a teenager. She was dressed in a simple sweater and blue corduroy pants, but what immediately caught my eye was the gold six-pointed star she wore on a chain around her neck. I had not seen one before in the Soviet Union. The Gulkos are not very religious and the star worn by this shy, introverted woman seemed to be a political statement.

Like her husband, Anna has been a Soviet champion; she won the women's title in 1976. Without a doubt the Gulkos are the most talented and titled chess couple of all time. In fact, there is no sports marriage as accomplished as this one; perhaps if Chris Evert and Jimmy Connors had married it would have been roughly equivalent. Since they applied for emigration to Israel in 1978, the Gulkos have been barred from most tournaments. On the rare occasions when they have been permitted to play, their results have been either omitted from the public record or outrageously manipulated. Last year Anna was allowed to enter the women's championship. The deciding game was against Nana Ioseliani, who, like Karpov, is popular with the Soviet establishment. Anna was declared the winner when Ioseliani ran out of time. Three days later a group of bureaucrats announced that Ioseliani would be given more time to complete the game. It was an extraordinary violation of the rules, and when Anna refused to continue, Ioseliani was awarded the win. "They did not want me to win the championship again because we are Jews and refuseniks," Anna explained simply.

"My difficulties began in 1974," Boris said. "I won seven tournaments in a row, which is very rare in Soviet chess. In spite of my success, or perhaps because of it, I began to have troubles. I was not allowed to travel abroad to tournaments. In the 1975 Soviet championship, I was in first place, ahead of the former world champion Tigran Petrosian, when a story was circulated on television and in the newspapers that my friends were losing to me on purpose. Petrosian said in *Izvestia* that it was impossible for a grandmaster to win so many games in a row without help from friends. These stories were so unpleasant for me that they interfered with my concentration. I began to play badly and finished second to Petrosian.

"In the 1976 interzonals, the elimination matches to determine the challenger for the world championship, I was the only Soviet player without a trainer. In 1977, after I won the championship of the country, I thought my fame would help me, but I was mistaken. Most of my difficulties, I suppose, relate to being a Jew. All Jewish chess players have had problems. At times, even Tal, the great Russian world champion, has not been allowed to travel abroad for tournaments. The same was true for Bronstein, even when he was one of the two best players in the world. Kasparov's mother changed his name from Weinstein, hoping to avoid the problem. Did you know that there are many Jewish chess players in the Soviet Union strong enough to be grandmasters, but they don't have the money to enter tournaments? No one ever hears of them."

While we talked, Anna served tea, sandwiches and a delicious homemade apple pie. It was important to our hosts that we eat a lot and look at their treasured books and photographs.

Listening to the Gulkos and to other Soviet Jews during the trip, I got the impression that as long as they didn't make waves, Jews were not so much actively harassed or persecuted as actively ignored. Jewish complaints fell on deaf ears and their accomplishments disappeared. It was as if they were asked to live invisibly.

"In 1978 Anna and I applied for emigration to Israel. I wanted to live without chess management, but chess management didn't want to live without me." Gulko laughed quietly. "Until then we both were paid for being chess players, but after we applied for emigration all income stopped. They didn't invite me to any tournaments, even those in this country. For two years I was not allowed to play a single game. For two years I waited. It was destroying me. Anna was in the same situation. We went on a hunger strike in 1980, and after that I was allowed to play in the Moscow Open. I suppose they didn't consider me a threat to win, because it was a very strong tournament and I was out of practice."

To the dismay of the authorities, Gulko did win, and during the awards ceremony at the Central Chess Club, he asked to speak. A hush fell over the gathering as he addressed the Soviet Chess

Federation and asked that Victor Korchnoi's wife and son be allowed to leave the Soviet Union to join him in exile. After the speech players and guests paused to shake Gulko's hand.

Volodja Pimonov witnessed Gulko's courageous speech at the Central Chess Club. "Afterwards, I drove the judge of the tournament home," he said. "The man was trembling, because authorities were already saying that it was his fault since he was the judge. After such a debacle they must find a scapegoat."

In 1982 the Gulkos tried to publicize their situation by demonstrating outside the interzonal tournament. "Anna and I waved posters saying, 'Let us go to Israel.' We were arrested and thrown in jail for the night. A few days later I returned to the tournament, which had been moved to the Sport Hotel for increased security. This time I did not intend to demonstrate; I simply wanted to watch the chess. There was a large crowd outside the hall hoping for tickets. A large man with the face of a dog came over and kicked me and smashed me in the face. Then a policeman appeared, the dog man said that I had beaten him, and I was arrested again. The crowd got to see a more interesting show than inside the hall—a former champion of the Soviet Union being kicked on the street.

"A month later we went on another hunger strike. After twenty-two days the doctors told Anna that she must eat or she would die. I had nothing but water for forty-two days. We did it to gain the attention of chess players around the world. But they couldn't help us.

"My savings are gone now. For a while we received parcels of clothes from Jewish organizations in the West, but they no longer come. I think they are impounded by customs. The clothes were useful because I could sell them in a secondhand shop for money to buy food. Our financial situation is critical, but the biggest pain is not being able to play. When we applied for emigration we were among the strongest players in the world. These years have been a creative death. My life now is mostly waiting. I've lost many years. I don't know how many more I have left."

Later Boris played a game against Josh, and then demonstrated several of his recent unpublished games. The calmness of his voice gave way to passionate chess talk and even peals of laughter. "You have to be a grandmaster to understand," said Boris, moving the pieces; at this moment all of us could feel the sublime importance of chess in this deprived little home. "I conceive of chess as an art form," he said, showing us an original combination with two knights while Anna watched him as if he were reciting poetry. "I will only play in a way that interests me," Boris said. "For me chess is finding ideas, beautiful, paradoxical ideas."

Ten minutes after we waved good-bye to Gulko in the parking lot, we were stopped by the police. Volodja whispered that we must not speak English. He was questioned at length about a supposed illegal turn before we were allowed to go on. Volodja said he was certain they knew we had been at the Gulkos'. "You won't be allowed to leave the country with your tapes and film," he warned. "If they are confiscated, it will be very bad for me. Maybe you can make some arrangement?"

"What kind of arrangement?" I asked nervously.

GAINING ACCESS TO the American embassy on Tchaikovskovo Street was like trying to enter a fortress before an attack. Guarding the outside perimeter, Soviet soldiers demanded passports in order to intercept Russians seeking asylum, as well as to record the names of everyone who went inside. Word had it that all visitors to the embassy were secretly photographed. Within the gates a Marine in a metal-and-plastic cage skeptically asked our business. When I explained that I was a writer and needed to see the ambassador he became flustered and politely pointed out that it wasn't easy to see the ambassador.

Inside the embassy there were gaily colored rooms in various states of disorganization and disrepair. Bulletin boards displayed cheerful, homey notices about baby-sitting, Russian lessons, cake sales and square dances. The place had the rambling, upbeat look of a progressive lower school in New York City.

Bruce, Josh and I were led to the third floor, and after a few minutes the acting ambassador hurried into the room to say that he had no time for us today. I said we'd wait. Eventually his assistant appeared and asked what I wanted. Before I'd finished two sentences he said in a booming voice, "I'm sorry, but there is nothing I can do to help you." Then he scribbled on a large notepad:

"This room is bugged. All the rooms at the embassy are bugged, even the ambassador's office. Write what you want on this pad."

"I'm sorry, but there's nothing to be done," he said aloud again, pointing to the ceiling like a character in a Woody Allen movie. I described our situation on the notepad and asked for help getting my notes, tapes and film out of the country. In reply the assistant scribbled that he would discuss our problem with the acting ambassador, and that we could wait in the coffee shop downstairs.

The three of us sat at a table sipping tea. Noticing the banners of NFL teams on the wall, Bruce and Josh began to discuss the Jets. Sitting beside us were two young American diplomats dressed in Brooks Brothers suits. One was briefing the other, who had just arrived in Moscow. Both of them were tense and their rapid-fire whispering was quite audible.

"So what about the ICBMs?"

"Well, they're using three different types."

"Are they aimed at Alaska?"

"Yeah."

"What about the borders?"

"They have the defenses, but the technology is primitive."

Having just learned that the ambassador's office was bugged, I thought it was bizarre to be listening to this conversation in the middle of the lunchroom.

Soon the ambassador's assistant was back. "Do you want to give me your notes?" he wrote on a pad.

"No. I want you to make copies," I wrote, and then handed him a package containing my tape cassettes and film.

"That's going to be hard. The copy machines aren't secure." What madness, I thought. My chess notes were hardly espionage material.

Next to us the two young diplomats were shaking hands. "So when are we going to get together for a game of table tennis?" one of them asked.

The ambassador's assistant shook his head. "You can't imagine what it's been like living here for two years," he said aloud.

A FEW DAYS later, Bruce, Josh and I took the midnight express to Leningrad. We were looking forward to seeing the Hermitage and the circus, and to being away from Russian chess politics. When we left the Moscow station, the passengers in our sleeping car were crowded in the corridor, chatting and looking out the windows; then, one by one, they drifted into tiny sleeping compartments.

We were shocked when a large hulking man threw his suitcase on one of our two bottom bunks. Intourist at the hotel had confirmed that our room on the train was to be a private one. I found a woman conductor and tried to explain that the man didn't belong here; besides, other compartments were half-empty. But when the man said a few words to her, she walked away. He was middle-aged, emotionless, silent. We'd been followed by other men with the same stony countenance.

The KGB man walked back into the nearly empty corridor and stared out the window. After a few minutes we noticed him exchanging remarks with another large man who occupied an adjacent room. Volodja had warned us that after visiting the American embassy we would be regarded as spies. I recalled the fear in his voice on another occasion when he'd said, "In circumstances such as mine, people have disappeared." Pandolfini and I quickly decided to spend the night in the corridor with the door to the room open. Josh could go to sleep in the top bunk, where we could watch him. If we needed to call for help, maybe someone from one of the other compartments would hear us.

Josh lay on the top bunk reading while Pandolfini, our uninvited guest and I stood in an uneasy vigil in the corridor. We looked at a chess position from the sixth game of the match while the man stared out at the darkness. Long after everyone else was asleep and the doors between cars were locked, the man moved into the compartment, got into his bunk and turned off the light. I went in and turned it back on.

Sometime later Josh signaled to me through the half-open door. He whispered in my ear that the man, thinking he was asleep, had opened our luggage compartment. When Josh sat up, the man returned to his bunk. I told Josh that he should try to sleep. For the next five hours, Bruce and I stared at the same chess position.

Exhausted but safe in Leningrad, we called Volodja in Moscow, who told us that on the day after our interview Gulko had been picked up by the police for questioning. He didn't know whether or not Boris was still being held.

TWO DAYS LATER at the Moscow airport about two hundred people waited on line to clear customs. In front of us a Russian hockey team leaving for a match abroad was in festive spirits. The line moved quickly until we reached the agent. Pandolfini was taken away to a room and strip-searched; his notebooks, mostly analyses of the chess match, were taken away and photocopied. Three agents pored over each page of my notes, and for an hour several others listened to my little tape recorder. All my tapes of interviews in Russia, as well as the important pages from my notebook and my film, were already en route to New York. The cassettes I was carrying now had been recorded years before while I was doing a story in the Bahamas. The Russians were so intent on hearing fishing captains talk about the techniques of catching blue marlin that I didn't think they'd let us leave.

For the first time during the trip, Josh looked scared. Where was Bruce? Could he go to the bathroom? They wouldn't let me take him. At last, seconds before the gate closed, we were allowed to board our Finnair flight to Helsinki.

When the plane took off, Josh yawned and said, "The end." Minutes later he was asleep in my lap, looking, for the first time since he'd waved good-bye to his mommy, like a very little boy.

I felt enormous relief, and then the heady sensation of having gotten away with something. We were all okay, I had my notes, and soon I'd be sharing stories and Russian caviar with my wife and friends.

But then I thought about Gulko and Volodja and others I'd met. I wouldn't be able to call or write Volodja; it would be dangerous for him. I recalled a conversation with a famous Soviet grandmaster during our first week in Moscow. I had asked if he considered Gary Kasparov's Jewish background a disadvantage in the match. The man became oddly foreboding. "Write nothing negative," he'd said, waving his finger back and forth. "Nothing negative. The chess world is small, and your little son is part of that world."

13

THE
CHESS
SHOP

The proliferation of subcultures and eccentricities in New York City tends to obscure the madness of a life devoted to solving complicated puzzles. The plight of brilliant jobless and even homeless chess players in Washington Square fits seamlessly into a landscape of unpublished poets hawking photocopies of poems in front of bookstores, painters showing their canvases on sidewalks and musicians playing outside concert halls, waiting to be discovered. Struggling artists live here amidst an illusory swirl of impending success.

Except for a handful, chess players don't have such illusions. The game has a severe analytic quality that makes self-deception difficult. Unlike the undiscovered poet who, despite the harsh criticism of his peers, lives on his fantasies for the day that he will be recognized as the next Dylan Thomas, even a young chess player can usually gauge his talent. When Josh was six, he played several games against a pudgy thirteen-year-old who was the top player on his high school team. He beat Josh every time, but a couple of the games were close, and afterwards the boy seemed gloomy about his performance. He explained that if he didn't make significant improvement during the next year, he would wind up as just another wood-pusher. Despite his celebrity in school, he seemed to know that he didn't have it.

While thousands of basketball kids on the city's playgrounds are convinced of their golden future in the NBA, chess children, except for the very youngest, respond with remarkable frankness and accuracy when asked about their playing strength and potential in comparison to their peers. A twenty-year-old who has been playing and studying chess for seven or eight years and has gained a rating of, say, 2100, which places him in the top 3 or 4 percent of all the tournament players in the country, will have few illusions about becoming world champion, or even about playing a single game that will compare with the masterpieces of Alekhine or Bronstein. Despite his desire, he knows as well as he knows the spelling of his own name that he is simply not in the same league as other twenty-year-olds rated four hundred points higher. Still, more likely than not he will continue to devote a tremendous amount of time to chess, either because he loves the game more than anything else in his life, or because there is nothing else he can do as well, or in some cases because he simply can't bear to give it up.

In New York City alone, there are hundreds of excellent but not exceptional chess players who spend most of their waking lives in coffee shops, parks, clubs and at tournaments, playing five-minute or five-hour games, studying books on openings and endgames and feeling confused about whether they are artists or reprobates. But in Greenwich Village, even such futility has a certain cachet. In the grim light of a New York winter, the regulars in the clubs, with their dog-eared books, creased clothing and singularity of purpose, seem to share an irreproachable nobility with the down-and-out heroes of Knut Hamsun novels or with Isaac Bashevis Singer's hopelessly impoverished Warsaw writers. Somehow they are winners for clinging so fiercely to their ways.

Since becoming a chess parent, I tend increasingly to think of New York in terms of chess. Besides Madison Square Garden and a few favorite restaurants, the places I am most drawn to are the chess corner of Washington Square, the Village Chess and Coffee Shop on Thompson Street, Fred Wilson's chess bookstore on East Eleventh Street, Bryant Park and the corner of Forty-first Street and Seventh Avenue, where in the shadow of towering office buildings and X-rated movies, chess masters and even an occasional grandmaster sit on folding chairs and create gorgeous combinations against passersby for nickels and dimes despite the exhaust fumes and the cold. For me, Carnegie Hall has little to do with music;

rather, it is where the Manhattan Chess Club is located, and where Josh plays on Friday nights in the blitz tournaments.

At the end of a jog around Washington Square, I often stop by the chess shop on Thompson Street. Through the window, which is checkered with chess sets of exotic design for sale, I recognize nearly every player. Most of them are here every day that the weather keeps them from playing outdoors in Washington Square. A few play in the shop year round, regardless of the weather, as if this cramped little room, where players must pay seventy-five cents an hour, invests their avocation with more status than does the park. They play with unflinching seriousness, as if life depended upon the flick of a piece or the snap of the clock—and it does. Some of these men have lost jobs and wives playing night after night, usually against the same opponent. The ones who have one or two steady partners have become as tight-knit as a family and think the idea of playing someone new is ridiculous. After years of games against the same opponents, the moves have become more like old habits than chess, and taking on someone new would be risky.

One would think that when players sat with their faces only a few feet apart, their feet occasionally brushing beneath the table day after day, month after month, there would be some intimacy. But this doesn't seem to be the case; the players know little about the private lives of their partners and aren't curious to learn more. The game is everything. Partners are usually well matched, so a day's success is generally based on who concentrates better and is more able to shut out distractions. "You can't play well if you're worrying about your wife or your job," one man explained. But from time to time one of them will whisper conspiratorially to me that he will soon be giving up the game.

One man—I'll call him Jim—made a small fortune in the stock market earlier in his life. For the past seven years, since his wife left him, Jim has played in the chess shop or, weather permitting, in Washington Square. During these years of thousands of games, Jim's chess ability has neither improved nor declined, and his happiness in life relates to his daily success against one or two opponents. In 1986 Jim spoke to me about chess with distaste.

"There's no point to it," he said. "It's a hostile game. Everyone here hates one another." His eyes glowing with intensity, he announced that soon he would give it up. Several months later he came over to me again and repeated his intention. It was as if the chess shop were a penal colony with walls and bars. A year ago, one of Jim's regular partners suddenly disappeared. I knew him to be a gentle, literate man who was greatly distressed by his addiction and who often spoke of quitting; nevertheless, I was afraid something might have happened to him. But when I asked Jim, he disgustedly waved my question aside. The man was no longer around; that was all that mattered.

At times the Village Chess and Coffee Shop feels comfortable, like a familiar gallery in a museum. At the end of my evening jog, it is a pleasure to say hello to the players and to watch a few games—sometimes more than a few. It is remarkable how quickly the hours pass there. During the last couple of years, I've learned the mannerisms and styles of the players. Although I no longer play, I have acquired an appetite for chess literature and for watching games. In truth, I've become a persistent kibitzer, hooked on observing games in the same way that some are addicted to baseball or bridge or spy novels. In the evening, when I leave the coffee shop, I sometimes look back through the glass window at the faces riveted on the chess pieces. Night after night, the same men sit across from one another in the same chairs. They seem to have no sense of the passing of time.

JOSH
AND
BRUCE

With its dense architecture and crafty manipulations, its subtle attacks, intensity and unexpected explosiveness, chess is like the city. Lives in small, thin-walled New York apartments are racked by differing sensibilities jangling at the edge of private space. Competing for territory, we attack one another in indirect ways. For example, in my building there is a man who tyrannizes his neighbors with his off-key attempts to be a jazz-and-blues singer. While he belts out his favorite standards, I cannot write. Whenever I mention my irritation to him in the hall or write him a note, he sings louder, as if trying to convince me that he really is an undiscovered talent. In a state of helpless rage, I contemplate clobbering him with a two-by-four as he races up the stairs after work, eager to begin crooning "Moonlight in Vermont."

When it is time for Joshua's chess lesson, I pray that my neighbor won't sing the blues and that the super's kids won't jump on the trampoline upstairs. It is a special time: we take the baby to the sitter so she won't pull the pieces off the board; Bonnie can't run the dishwasher or washing machine; she tries to prepare dinner quietly because a dropped pot might cause Josh to lose his train of thought.

Week after week Bruce urges Josh to look deeper into the positions they study. While they commune over the pieces I sit in the kitchen wondering how the lesson is going. I'm tempted to watch, although I know that Joshua is distracted by my presence.

When I can't bear to stay away any longer, I watch the two of them for a few minutes from across the living room. Typically, Bruce leans back in his chair and sips coffee. Josh sits at the board, his head cupped between his hands. I can see his eyes flashing from piece to piece, his face taut and serious. He can't find the answer. He glances up at Bruce for help and then back at the board. His lips move, "Take, take, take, take, take, take," while he nods his head to the beat of his mumbling. He is in trouble. Bruce won't help and leans back in his chair with a supercilious expression that both spurs our son ahead and angers him. His brow furrows in frustration. The mate is eight moves from the position in front of him, and he isn't allowed to move the pieces until he figures it out in his head. He almost has it, but not quite. At the point in his analysis where the lines have been cleared of pieces and the mate should be crystal clear, the king standing like a lone figure on an empty avenue, he gets lost. He doesn't see the critical check, and after a few seconds the imagined position of the pieces grows fuzzy in his head and he must reconstruct it again. "Take, take, take, take, take, take . . . knight to f8," he says without resolution.

"That's a nice try, Josh. I considered it myself, but you can see why it doesn't work, can't you?"

"Because the queen protects along the diagonal," Josh says glumly. He begins to chew on the neckline of his polo shirt while his teacher sips his coffee.

At the age of six, Josh resisted instruction, and Bruce taught him indirectly by playing speed games and offering delectable bribes for rare moments of seriousness, but by the time he was eight, their lessons often resembled meditations. When Josh looked up from a difficult position for a hint, Bruce would say inscrutably, "I am only here to help you look. You have to find the answer yourself."

After years of study there is a tendency for young players to depend too much on their teachers, making moves mechanically in tournament games because it was suggested in a lesson that they were correct. Bruce has to be careful not to overteach. If Joshua's imagination for combinations is constrained by too much information or by the fear of displeasing his teacher, then Bruce will have done more damage than good. When Josh's games become dry and repetitious, Pandolfini is angry with himself; it means that he has concentrated for too long on one aspect of the game and that his pupil has fallen into a rut. It is all too easy for a teacher to make such a mistake.

Joshua's relationship with Bruce is delicate and always changing. At times there is great trust and warmth, as if Pandolfini were a third parent. Sometimes Josh feels that he will not be able to play without his teacher standing in the wings. When he is fresh and attentive, he inspires Bruce to teach long, ingenious lessons. By the end of a two-hour session, Josh has a bright pink spot on each cheek, and Bruce is pale, a little out of breath and completely drained. Nevertheless he will telephone a couple of hours later to mention a new idea to overcome a bad habit or to propose an extra lesson. During two- and three-day tournaments, he will call each night to go over the day's games in search of an idea that might help on the following morning.

When Joshua is playing well, the two of them seem to complete each other. The pupil brings his imagination and competitive spirit to bear upon the ideas that the teacher writes about in his articles and books. Hours of memorizing openings, of wrestling with problems and of endgame exercises translate into wins and a gradually maturing chess style. Soon after turning eight, Josh won twenty-six out of twenty-seven tournament games and placed first in tournament after tournament, including the New York City Primary Championship. Playing among his peers, he seemed unable to lose. In all likelihood he would be the number-one seed in the National Primary Championship in the spring.

Through Josh, Pandolfini was playing the game he had given up thirteen years before, but without the burden of having to endure either losses or wins tainted for him by the pain inflicted on the loser. For the most part Josh thrived on tournament play. He would wake up on Saturday mornings and ask excitedly, "Is my tournament today?" Unlike his teacher, he felt terrific when he won. When Josh did well, Bruce, like the teachers of other talented children, was undoubtedly spurred on by the hope that he was teaching a future champion.

* * *

ALTHOUGH PANDOLFINI WORKED at presenting a pleasant, even exterior, his interest in Josh's chess study rose and fell in relation to many factors, including the chaos or happiness in his life, his publishing commitments and how much sleep he was getting. Josh always noticed when Bruce had other things on his mind, and he rated his lessons in much the same way as his teacher judged him by awarding "master class" points, decorative stickers and colored stars. At the end of their lesson, while pasting dinosaur stickers in Joshua's lesson book, Bruce might say, "You did some good work today, Tiger, but you were a wise guy. I'm only gonna give you twenty-one points." After Pandolfini left, Josh might say, "Bruce seemed distracted today," or "Bruce was very sharp."

When Josh was feeling bored with chess, or too tired after school to concentrate, he was apt to feel irritated with Bruce. Then he would sit as far away as possible from his teacher, his hands covering his ears as if trying to shut out the street noise, but in fact trying his hardest to tune out his teacher. There were periods when he simply couldn't bear the rigor of his lessons. Playing chess was one thing, but analyzing with Pandolfini was work. During weeks of trying to wake up his distracted student, Bruce's softness and good humor would give way to prodding lectures that Joshua either didn't understand or didn't care to heed. Pandolfini's attempts at politeness took on the sound of irritation, and Joshua's little jokes, which during good times were grace notes to serious study, became examples of his lack of concentration. As though he himself were the reason for his pupil's poor play, Pandolfini would complain at the start of a lesson that he had been working too hard and was tired. It must have occurred to him that all these hours of study might come to nothing, that this clever little boy might not really be a chess player after all. When Josh was playing poorly, Bruce looked frayed and was harder to reach on the phone. During these periods Josh would point out that his lessons weren't as long as they used to be, that Bruce looked distracted and complained a lot, and that his teacher didn't really like him anymore. Bonnie and I would assure him that this wasn't so, but in fact there were periods, as in all marriages, when they weren't fond of each other.

Pandolfini had become my friend as well as my son's teacher, but I saw that when we got together frequently or spoke regularly on the phone, Josh tended to withdraw from Bruce and to be less interested in his lessons. At such times, without ever talking about it, Bruce and I called each other less often and rarely socialized. Joshua's chess was more important to both of us than beer and good conversation.

FOR PANDOLFINI, AS well as for other teachers, like Sunil Weeramantry, Svetozar Jovanovic and Bobby Fischer's former teacher, John Collins, there is little or no irony about the endeavor of imparting large doses of arcane chess information to young children. Once, during Joshua's first year of study with Bruce, I asked Collins, the dean of American chess teachers, how often a talented youngster ought to study with a chess master. He answered immediately, "Every day," but then added sadly, "Of course it's not possible."

One afternoon at the Manhattan Chess Club before his weekly lesson with Pandolfini, Josh, who was then six, paused to watch seventeen-year-old Maxim Dlugy, the strongest player for his age in the country, take his lesson with a Russian emigré, Vitaly Zaltzman, who is one of our few master-level trainers. With his customary baby brashness my son offered a few suggestions to Dlugy and Zaltzman. They spoke in Russian and for the most part analyzed without paying any attention to him, but later Zaltzman came over to me and asked, "What is his rating?" When I explained that Josh, who at that time was sitting on a telephone book to see the pieces, had never played in a tournament, Zaltzman looked at me quizzically. Why not?

IN THE PRIMARY grades of the Dalton School on the Upper East Side of Manhattan, children learn reading, writing and arithmetic within a carefree environment of playacting, backyard archaeological expeditions, musical productions and museum and farm visits, all administered by good-natured and tolerant teachers. But in the chess class, Svetozar Jovanovic, a Yugoslavian emigré, lectures to his six-to-nine-year-olds with the ceremony and dry sobriety of a no-nonsense college professor. Dalton's chess program, designed and run by Jovanovic, is the most ambitious and successful primary and secondary school chess program in the United States. Following the Soviet and Eastern European example, all children at Dalton are introduced to the game, and those with talent are encouraged to pursue advanced studies in an after-school program. The results are extraordinary. For the past several years, out of the top fifty chess players eight and under in the United States, nearly 30 percent went to Dalton, a medium-sized private school.*

Like no one else I have ever met, Svetozar Jovanovic has the ability to communicate the sublime importance of chess. At the start of a class, he looks at his giggly group of children poking and kicking one another, their mouths smeared with after-school snacks from the newsstand on Lexington Avenue. Sternly he takes off his glasses and pinches the bridge of his nose with his thumb and forefinger as if to say, Why am I wasting my time on you guys? Soon the children become quiet and attentive. Jovanovic places a basket of beat-up pieces in front of each player, the kind of basket used to serve hamburgers and greasy fries at diners. His manner and conviction invest these chipped little armies with enormous power and tradition, as if the class were about to participate in an ancient rite. He begins by describing a game played a hundred years ago, his English heavily accented and laden with Russian chess jargon, and his eyes sparkle while he speaks about traps and combinations.

Many of his students, the children of millionaires, professionals, politicians, actors and rock musicians, wear designer labels. Jovanovic's suits are disheveled, and he bemoans the privations of the chess teacher in America, but against all worldly logic he has these little kids believing that nothing is more important than this game— neither violin or tennis lessons nor weekends in the country. Chess is the real thing; it is sport, art and philosophy rolled into one. In his Yugoslavian accent, the names Alekhine and Botvinnik take on the religious significance of Moses or Jesus.

Jovanovic tells parents that it is important for the children to be

---

* In 1987 the Dalton School won the national championship in both the primary and elementary divisions. In 1988 the school won both divisions a second time and in addition won the national junior high school championship, competing with a team consisting primarily of fourth-, fifth- and sixth-grade players.

well-rounded and that schoolwork comes before chess, but during the one hour he spends with their kids each week, the game is larger than anything else, and he tolerates little fooling around. Again and again he sternly reminds the kids that if they don't concentrate here, they won't be able to attend to business during tournaments. He teaches them Russian so that they will be able to study Russian chess material. He drills them in problems and frequently explains that talent is no substitute for hard work. With pomp and circumstance he rates his players against the great Yugoslavian youth teams of the fifties. Jovanovic knows by heart thousands of games that talented children have played over the past thirty years, and when one of his students blunders into a trap, he can recall a similar disaster that happened seventeen years ago to an eleven-year-old in Yugoslavia.

Once, after Joshua had been accepted at Dalton, he lost a game in a local tournament to a ten-year-old. Jovanovic called later in the evening to inquire if our son was in bed yet; he wanted to talk about the game. While riding the subway back from the tournament to his apartment in Washington Heights, he had been analyzing Josh's game in his head and had found a forced win for him on the seventeenth move. They played through the moves and quickly agreed on the pity of it: a forced win if only Josh had seen it. Perhaps someday Jovanovic will be lecturing a seven-year-old about moving too quickly and will bring up the example of Josh Waitzkin's horrible oversight in 1986 against Vaughn Sandman.

"THIS IS DRIVING me nuts," Josh said to Pandolfini during his lesson. He had been staring at the same position for nearly an hour, and wanted to turn on the Bill Cosby show, or to run outside and play football—anything to get away from this maze of chessmen, which he had rearranged in his head a hundred times. But after nearly three years of studying, there was another part of Josh that couldn't bear to let it go like this. If Bruce were to say, "Okay, let's forget about it, Tiger," the position would nag at him for the rest of the evening. While Pandolfini rocked back in his chair and waited, it occurred to me that I had never studied anything this intensely before I was a college senior studying for comprehensive

exams. As a student, I was rebellious and looked for shortcuts;
nevertheless, I have little patience for Joshua's laziness and his
lapses of concentration. It has become one of my greatest joys to
watch my son work through difficult chess ideas, solving problems
I couldn't begin to comprehend.

Bruce knew his pupil very well. If he'd told him to look back at
the board and try again, Josh would have argued or changed the
subject. Pandolfini waited. In a few seconds Josh had worked
through his resistance and was biting his shirt and mumbling,
"Take, take, take, take, take, take." Then, suddenly, "Oh! It's so
simple," and he banged his head with his hand. Both of them were
smiling. Pointing at squares and pieces and talking excitedly in a
garble of algebraic notation, Josh demonstrated his lengthy plan
while Bruce looked a little bored.

During these sessions the two of them were working on process
more than on problems. Josh was learning to look further into a
position, to restrain his first impulse in order to consider it from
different perspectives. During their first year, Bruce had asked
him always to consider at least two plans. Then he began asking
for three or four plans. When Josh complained that he couldn't
look deeply enough without moving the pieces, or couldn't hold
the position in his head long enough to find the answer, Bruce
urged him on like a physical therapist of the mind. At times when
my son was thinking, I could see the strain of it on his face, as if
he were stretching his brain like a muscle. Finally he would say
something like "I forgot that pawn was there. It's so simple. What
an idiot I am."

At the end of a tense lesson, the two of them sometimes played
a few speed games, with Bruce giving Josh five-to-two time odds.
Occasionally Josh won one of these games. Bruce would giggle and
look embarrassed at the winning move, but whenever this happened Josh was never sure if Bruce had played his hardest or had
merely allowed him to capitalize on a preconceived weakness to
emphasize the lesson of the week.

For a young student, the teacher has mythic powers; he is the
inventor of chess and the final word. At the age of eight, Josh
furiously defended Pandolfini's ideas against amused grandmasters;

he considered the notion of being able to defeat Pandolfini in a serious game impossible. Yet within several years he would probably become as strong a player as his teacher, Bruce remarked matter-of-factly, and then he would need to study with someone else, in all likelihood a grandmaster. Generally speaking, young chess talents develop quickly if they work at it.

OCCASIONALLY PANDOLFINI AND I met for dinner, and inevitably our conversations turned to what he and Josh had been doing in their lessons. One night he explained that for the last few months they had been working on positional ideas. After a pause he added, "There has been great progress, but now we have to return to chess tactics. Then we'll do more positional work, then more tactics." I nodded; apparently it was like tacking a sailboat, and it made perfect sense. After a couple of beers Bruce spoke of Steinitz's pawn formations and his theory of building a crushing attack by gaining advantages so small that they were almost impossible to perceive. My understanding of grandmaster-level chess is impressionistic. I will never be able to strangle my opponent positionally, but I love the idea. When Pandolfini is in top form, I feel as if I'm playing the game myself. He drank more beer and described Alekhine's great battle with Capablanca in 1938, and what it was like to analyze games with Fischer in the sixties. During these dinners it seemed as if Josh and I had embarked on a thrilling adventure; we were tracking the greatest players who ever lived.

At other times Joshua's chess work struck me as ludicrous. Perhaps he had been playing poorly or apathetically, or I was in a bad mood and all serious endeavor seemed pointless. In this frame of mind, my son's chess education mortified me. I recalled the description of Victor Frias, an international master, of the life of the American chess master as "a vale of tears," and felt chagrined with myself for encouraging this dead-end preoccupation. At that time Frias, one of the best players in the country, was driving a cab all night to eke out a living. Once, years before Josh became a player, I rode from the airport in a taxi with a driver who told me that he was a grandmaster. He described the places he had been and the people he'd beaten. I decided that he was a liar, but perhaps I was wrong. Probably some of Frias's fares have decided that he was lying when he mentioned his games against Korchnoi, Yusupov, Belyavsky and Larsen.

What are we doing? I would ask myself. Why is Joshua's chess so important to me? It is a question that nags all chess parents. Unlike the tennis prodigy, the great young chess player has no pot of gold on the horizon. At tournaments parents clasp their trembling hands, root as if it were life or death for their kid and dream the lusty dream of their child's immutable, unmatchable genius. Breathless and flushed from rooting and worrying, they say to one another, "This world is much too narrow," or "There's too much emphasis on winning," or "I don't like how much time we're putting into this." Everyone nods, and listening to all this doubting one would think that the parents were about to wrench their kids out of the children's chess circuit. But at the next tournament there they are again, commiserating with one another about the craziness of so much misspent passion.

PLAYING
FOR
THE
TITLE

Unlike chess in parks, in coffee shops or in many clubs and adult tournaments across the United States, the National Elementary Chess Championship (consisting of a primary division, grades K–3, and an elementary division, grades 4–6) is a well-organized and attractively staged event. Enthusiasts in cities like Syracuse, Charlotte, Pulaski and Terre Haute bid against other interested groups for the right to hold the tournament. Directors plan for a year ahead to ensure a smooth operation, with playing conditions far better than in most master-level tournaments. At considerable expense, more than six hundred children and their parents travel to the event from all across the country, and they are treated with decorum and respect.

At the nationals, players compete against one another for seven rounds over the course of two grueling days. To become a national champion you must win all seven games, or at the very least score six wins and a draw. The competition is fierce, and no matter how good you are, it takes luck to win. One sleepy game, a brief lapse of concentration, the careless touch of a wrong piece, and it's wait till next year—unless you're too old to compete in the tournament next year.

In recent years, organizers of the championship have taken pains to protect against mishaps and protests. In the primary division, parents are not allowed in the playing room, which reduces the possibility of cheating or emotional scenes. The top games are televised into lobbies and waiting rooms, where the parents can

watch their kids, assisted by the expert commentary of chess masters—often the teachers of the players on the screen—who study
the moves with the seriousness of NASA scientists scanning their
monitors at the moment of lift-off. Often teachers of other players
watch the televised games to scout the competition for their own
students. Newspaper reporters and television crews do interviews
between rounds. Invariably, the proud teachers and parents of the
winning children are asked, "Is your kid the next Bobby Fischer?"

The pomp and circumstance of the nationals greatly heightens
the importance of games between children, and naturally it makes
both them and their parents nervous. Parents are both excited and
burdened by winning and losing, results which seem to portend
the future. Such intensity plays havoc with one's perspective—
immortality itself may seem like the prize—and even the weakest
players and their parents dream of winning.

IN THE 1985 National Primary Championship, held in Charlotte,
North Carolina, Josh was the number-one seeded player. It is both
exhilarating and frightening for a child to be considered the one
to beat, to know that the coaches of other top players are concocting
deep traps to beat you; that until you lose and get knocked off the
first board, all your games are televised and scrutinized by coaches,
parents and other players. For these reasons, Josh was nervous in
Charlotte; in addition he was disappointed because two hours before our flight Bruce had called to say that a publishing deadline
made it impossible for him to be there.

Nevertheless, Josh played well. In the first six rounds, he scored
five wins and a draw, and going into the last round he was tied for
first place with three other children. If he won his final game he
would at the very least tie for the championship. In the deciding
round he played against David Arnett, a gifted player from Dalton
who would later become his best friend.

While they played I sat on the lawn outside the junior college
where the tournament was being held. The game was televised in
the lobby of the building, and about a hundred people were watching the screen, but I didn't want to see it. I leaned against a tree
near some other parents whose children weren't competing for top

places. They were in a gay mood, laughing easily and exchanging plans for the summer. I envied them for being able to appreciate this pleasant, breezy afternoon and wished I could be more casual, less single-minded. But one more win and Josh would be national champion. I felt misshapen by tension and by my desire for my son to win. I tried to respond pleasantly to passersby, but I could feel my heart racing in my chest as though I had just run a mile. The consequences of losing were vague and unspecific but seemed immense, like impending doom or grief. Yet at the same time I was certain that this couldn't happen, and I tried not to allow myself to fantasize about our victory, our ecstatic joy and high fives, the long-distance calls I would make to my New York friends with the incredible news; such thoughts were bad luck. Before the game I had walked around the same blocks, past the same trees that I had walked before Josh's wins in the earlier rounds. I reminded myself not to drink water until after the game, another ritual of support. While he played, I played against my superstitions.

The game lasted only twenty minutes. I would have guessed that they were still in the opening when David came out of the building with a toothy smile. I asked if he had won. He nodded yes and said something about Josh's having fallen for a trap. Then Josh appeared, his face looking washed-out. He was attempting to be casual and trying not to cry, but he looked defeated, as if some of his life had been taken away. I put my arm around him, gave him a kiss and said that it didn't matter. Later I realized that I repeated this a few times as if it were a question, until he nodded yes, it didn't matter.

But it wasn't true and we both knew it. We were both wondering how he could have lost. He had been so sure of himself. He didn't believe that any child his own age could beat him when he was trying his hardest. What could have gone wrong? The great players are supposed to win the big ones; he had heard this on television dozens of times during basketball and baseball games. Did it mean that he wasn't a great one? "Maybe I just don't have it," he mumbled. "Sure you do," I said. "It was only one game." He had fallen for a trap that he had studied several times with Pandolfini. Why? Did he have a lousy memory? Josh had always worried about his memory. He didn't seem to be able to learn the openings as quickly as some of the other top players. An eight-year-old doesn't feel like a child at such a moment; he feels like a loser. You're not supposed to be careless when you're playing for the national championship, he reminded himself. During his lessons, Bruce had told him many times, "Tiger, one careless move could cost you the nationals. Take your time and think." Josh kept shaking his head. He should have taken a few more minutes and found the right move. Now he wouldn't be able to get the game out of his mind for a long time.

IN THE SUMMER, after we get out of town for a few weeks into clear air and sunlight and away from the pace of lessons and tournaments, the justification for being a chess parent tends to desert me altogether, even though the motivation persists against all logic. While we swim and fish, I wince when I recall the pandemonium of our New York lives. I worry that my ambition for Josh will outstrip his desire to play. I worry about the tyranny of his heady national ranking. Wouldn't it be wonderful if he could just play chess the way he plays football and basketball, without being concerned about his rating, or about what little kid in California is catching up with him, or about not being national champion? I wonder about the payoff or penalty down the road for a little boy who feels like a failure when he is less than number one. When was I ever number one in the country at *anything*? I've never even *known* anyone who was number one at anything besides my son— and yet this is the standard by which he judges himself.

ONE DAY AT the beginning of that summer, Josh said, "Everyone tries to beat me. I'm expected to win, and when I lose it's a big deal." He'd been feeling down-in-the-dumps since losing at the nationals.

For the most part, my son doesn't talk about his feelings, but on this day he wanted to. "Sometimes I wish I could give it up for a while," he said.

"For how long?" I asked.

"Maybe for two weeks."

"You can," I answered, although it sounded as if he meant two years or forever. "Don't pick up a chess set. Forget about it." It was good that summer was here. Maybe we could both forget about the game for a while.

There was a moment of silence between us, and then I took a deep breath and asked the question whose answer I dreaded: did he sometimes think about giving up the game entirely?

Joshua's eyes became misty. "How could I do that?" he said in a trembling voice. "Chess is my life."

THE
CHAMPIONSHIP
OF
BIMINI

All my life I have had enormous passion for games and sports, so much so that all else has often seemed banal. The sport that I am best at is fishing. I have good eyes and, for some reason, an animal sense for where to drop my baits. I've never been particularly handy at picking up the newest knots or had motivation to stay abreast of fashionable techniques of the sport, but usually if there are fish around, I can catch them.

My father introduced me to fishing when I was six or seven years old. We fished together for flounder and eel off docks and out of runabouts on Long Island Sound; then when I was thirteen he began taking the family on winter fishing trips to Bimini, a tiny sun-scorched island fifty miles east of Miami. By coincidence, it was the same year that I read Hemingway's *Old Man and the Sea* in *Life*, and I came to the Gulf Stream armed with notions about the heroism of killing large fish that you think of as your brothers. In those days the fish off Bimini were plentiful, and hooking blue marlin, sailfish, dolphin, wahoo, barracuda and tuna became more important than anything else in my life—more important even than practicing my one-hand push shot and my throw from short to first.

I was thirteen when I landed my first marlin. I will never forget the sight of that enormous blue beast bursting out of the ocean toward the clouds, nor will I forget the smile on my father's face as I posed for a photograph beside the two-hundred-pound fish at the Big Game Club's weigh-in station. His pride was immeasurable. He caught the eye of admiring tourists and Bahamian dockhands, and his expression seemed to be saying, What a future my boy has.

Spurred on by my father and by Hemingway, during my teenage years I was out on the water at every opportunity, more often than not trolling the oil-slicked waters of Manhasset Bay after school for baby bass, or bottom fishing with sandworms for sea robins and eels. It didn't matter that the catch was modest; even murky Long Island Sound seemed filled with adventure and mystery, with makos and marlin finning out behind the next wave. I voraciously read books on the pioneers of angling and envisioned my place among them: the Waitzkin kid alongside Zane Grey, Lou Marron, Kip Farrington, Mike Lerner, George Lyon and other rich, gray-haired men who had trolled away large portions of their lives on oceans with exotic names. I knew the weights, lengths and girths of record gamefish caught on various line strengths more accurately than I knew the batting averages of Yankee players. I looked forward to the day I would open *Sports Illustrated* to the section that celebrates teenage sporting achievements and view myself holding a heavy bent-butt fishing rod next to an angry-looking broad-shouldered blue marlin hanging from a scale.

As an adult, I bought a small fishing boat, and Bonnie and I have lived frugally through the winters to fish in the summers in the Bahamas. Between marlin strikes there is time for daydreaming, and as I gripped the steering wheel and watched my handsewn mullet and horse ballyhoo baits skip and slide across the wake, I often would recall my father's excitement and happiness fishing these same waters thirty years before. He rarely fished himself, preferring instead that my brother and I handle the rods. While we pulled in our fish, he stood behind us and rooted like any Little League father, as if we were accomplishing life's great deeds. Sometimes I felt as if I were reeling in his love.

IN RECENT YEARS I have fished the waters off Bimini with my son. Josh seems to have inherited my love for the water and for fishing. Most mornings before we go out in the boat to troll for sailfish and marlin, he walks to his favorite fishing spots along the shore or off a crumbling dock. He carries a bucket with his bait and a knife inside, his little fishing rod slung over his shoulder, and if I do not intervene, he casts his bait all day without noticing the sweltering sun and the mosquitoes.

In the seventies and eighties the island has become distinguished more for its burgeoning marijuana and cocaine trade than for its marlin fishing, which has gradually declined until catching one is now a rare event. While we pull baits across the glassy calm waters in front of Bimini Harbor, Josh reads *The Hardy Boys* and pesters me to take him into shallow water where jacks and barracuda are abundant, and instead of daydreaming about the coming NFL season or marlin fishing with my father, I find myself thinking about chess games Josh has played. I wince at close losses and feel thrilled all over again at wins against surprised adults in Washington Square. I love to talk about the game with him, particularly about what he thinks of different opponents—who's improving, who's overrated, psychological tactics, the kids he hates to play.

But in the summer of 1985, after the nationals, Josh wanted to take a break and I tried not to mention chess. For the past two summers, fretting about cutting my son off cold turkey from the chess world has made it more difficult for me to concentrate on fishing. Before we went to Russia, there was a month on Bimini when he didn't play at all, followed by a month playing exclusively against me—which, in retrospect, was far worse than not playing—and it hurt his game. This summer I was feeling concerned about whether losing in the seventh round of the nationals would dampen his enthusiasm. In July some of the other New York kids were going to Sunil Weeramantry's chess camp; others were playing in a city-funded program in Central Park with U.S. Champion Lev Alburt and other grandmasters and were practicing at local tournaments as well as at the Friday-night blitz tournaments at the Manhattan Chess Club. They were all getting better while we trolled for marlin.

I was determined that Josh live a well-rounded life, go to a good school, play sports, fish and go to movies and shows with his grandmother; at the same time I knew that the best chess kids in the world study and play all the time. Svetozar Jovanovic, the coach at Dalton, where Josh was enrolled for the following fall, says firmly to his little students, "A young chess player must study and play at least an hour every day. It is the same as being a musician. It doesn't matter how large the gift is; he must practice." When speaking to other children and their parents, Jovanovic often referred to Joshua's success as an example of what talent nurtured by hard work can do. This bothered me, because I doubted that Josh would work at all if I weren't there to urge him on, and I wondered when the motivation would pass from me to him—or whether it would ever happen. When I told Jovanovic that we were going to take the summer off from chess, he took off his glasses and said firmly with narrowed eyes, "Two weeks, no more. Even the most talented cannot afford more than that."

I know that Jovanovic is right. Susan Polgar, the great teenage Hungarian international master, and her two little sisters play forty to fifty hours a week. Instead of going to school, they only play chess. In the morning they study with a grandmaster who specializes in openings; in the afternoon a grandmaster comes to their home to work on tactics; in the evening they are visited by a third grandmaster, a scholar of the endgame. In casual games, the Polgar girls move the pieces with hardly a glance; they know the board the way great pianists know the keys, and their casual manner conceals deadly combinations and perfect technique. While they play, fans swoon over their prodigious gift for the game and call them "born" chess players, "naturals." How can you hope to compete with such "naturals" if you play only six or seven hours a week and take the summer off? As I trolled, I found myself imagining the great strides Josh would make if he worked around-the-clock with three grandmasters.

IN THE SOVIET Union nine months earlier, I had told Pandolfini that I wanted to remove myself from Joshua's chess life. Each morning for the last two weeks they had been working on the game and my head was filled with jargon that I didn't understand. I was angry with my son for not concentrating during his lessons, and even while we were being tailed by the KGB I worried more about his chess. "Why can't you remember to move your knight to f6?" I snapped at him, echoing Pandolfini without having the slightest idea why he ought to move the knight to f6. For the rest of the afternoon I remained irritated with him because he had forgotten about knight f6.

Being a chess father was too painful and took too much of my time, I told Bruce. Joshua's career seemed to be swallowing me, and I wanted Pandolfini to do more. I suppose that I wanted *him* to be the chess father. Bruce looked at me with his sympathetic brown eyes and nodded; whatever the problem was, he'd take care of it. For the moment, I felt better, but we both knew that it had been idle conversation. Who but a father or mother can accompany a child to all-day tournaments to make sure that he has his lunch and doesn't eat too much candy or exhaust himself playing football between rounds? Over the years Pandolfini has heard my complaints from scores of other parents. Recently one ambitious parent offered him a significant amount of money to board his talented seven-year-old son at Bruce's home for a year to study chess seven days a week. This father was convinced that at the end of this period of nonstop work his son would be recognized as the new Bobby Fischer. I can imagine Pandolfini seeming to nod agreement to this obsessed parent's proposal while trying to figure out the right tactic by which to duck out graciously.

All of the top young players have at least one parent behind them, encouraging, assisting, worrying. In a sense, the child is only one part of a team. Regardless of his gift for the game, he can't compete at the highest level without a good teacher and a supportive parent. During the last two years, it has become clear that I am the coach and Bruce is the teacher. He drills Josh on the openings, hones his tactics and trains him in endgame technique. I decide which tournaments we'll play in and how much practice he should have the week before. I log his weaknesses and strengths during games and point them out to Pandolfini. I remind Bruce to give him homework, and I pester Josh to do it. I make sure he is asleep early on Tuesday night so that he won't be tired for his Wednesday lesson.

Bonnie often chides me for thinking more about the chess player than the boy, and I nod sheepishly; I am guilty of this crime. It is hard for me to remember Josh before he was a chess player. It's terrible, but when he wins or plays brilliantly my affection for him gushes. After he plays badly, I notice that I don't walk as close to him on the street, and I have to force myself to give him a hug. Luckily Bonnie is exactly the opposite. When he loses, her motherly instincts are aroused and she pampers him. Then Josh allows himself to be taken care of like a little boy who needs his mommy. I think that Bonnie is somewhat removed from Joshua's chess only because I am so involved. She sees her role in our adventure as the voice of moderation. She frequently reminds me that my relationship with Josh is much more important than his chess, and reminds our son that if he never played another game, his father would still love him. But when Josh and I go off to weekend tournaments without her, she grieves. I have a hunch that if I weren't around, Bonnie would be nearly as profligate in her chess parenting as I am.

One afternoon while we trolled in the Gulf Stream Josh asked if I would find him a football league to play in. "It's bad for chess," I said without thinking. "Too many hits on the head."

"C'mon, Freddy," he said impatiently, "I wanna play football." For the next half hour this aging all-star football fan argued with his eight-year-old about why football was out of the question.

When I think about Joshua's chess life on the boat, I drift away from marlin fishing, forgetting to check the baits for seaweed and to look at the sky for circling birds. But I am only mildly disturbed that I've lost my edge as a fisherman; it has become clear by now that it is Joshua's chess, rather than marlin, that gets my blood hot.

ONE MORNING ABOUT five weeks after we arrived on the island, Josh and I took our skiff across the lagoon from South Bimini, where we were staying, to North Bimini. He steered, and we trolled a couple of small jigs for barracuda and jacks, but nothing hit. I couldn't wait to get out of the blistering late-morning sun, but Josh wanted to cut up a little fish he'd caught earlier and cast for mangrove snappers off the Game Club dock. When I was a boy I had landed a ten-foot black-tip shark off the same dock one night, and ever since he heard the story, Josh had taken to carrying a

hand line, and after catching a small snapper he would hook it in
the back and swim it out with the tide as a live bait for shark.

But this day we hadn't come to the Game Club to fish for sharks
or mangrove snappers. Earlier that week I had read in the *Miami
Herald* that an open tournament was about to begin sixty miles
away in the Diplomat Hotel in Hollywood, Florida. The article
included brief profiles of some of the most talented scholastic players who were flying in from across the country for the large tournament, including several New York players whom Josh competed
against regularly. Reading the piece, accompanied by pictures of
young chess players, filled me with misgivings and indecision. How
could it be good for Joshua's chess to stop playing for two months?
No one else had taken the summer off. Why had I made this
quixotic decision? For fishing? My immediate impulse was to fly
to Hollywood and register my son, but then I realized it would be
a mistake. He hadn't played a game in six weeks; he'd be crushed
and we would both feel miserable.

The article also mentioned that former world champion Boris
Spassky would be playing in the tournament. Probably he would
give a simultaneous exhibition or a series of lectures. Eight months
earlier, Spassky had played in such an exhibition in New York
against forty players, including Josh, and afterwards we'd had dinner together. Spending time with Spassky had been stimulating,
and also unsettling. During the exhibition he had been an elegant,
articulate and witty ambassador for the game. In his lecture he had
imitated the nasal speaking voice of Karpov, the raw, youthful
energy of Kasparov, the paranoia of Korchnoi. In the simultaneous
exhibition he had rocked back on his heels in mock horror when
Josh took one of his pawns, and with regal courtesy he had offered
draws to mediocre players. He was a wonderful showman, but
there was something sad about a former world champion's having
to perform regularly in chess sideshows in order to make a living.

During our dinner Spassky spoke about Bobby Fischer with
affection and respect, and about the Russian chess establishment
with bitterness. Though he was not yet fifty, the greatest moments
of his life seemed already behind him. "Bobby never offended
me," he said, referring to their time in Iceland. "He was always a

gentleman. To tell the truth, I was a beaten man before I ever came to Reykjavik. There were so many lies being told about me in the Soviet Union that I was exhausted when I arrived for the match. And Bobby was a good opponent for me. For some reason, even though he was the stronger player, I could usually guess his moves. But back in Moscow after the match I was lambasted by the Soviet Sports Committee as if I had tried to lose."

"Was Botvinnik among those who attacked you?"

"No, but Botvinnik was glad I lost. I think he felt that my becoming champion tarnished his reputation. He hated being forgotten."

Now in two days Spassky would be sixty miles away, answering the same questions about Karpov, Kasparov and Bobby Fischer, telling his stock jokes and anecdotes and then flying off to perform somewhere else. I recalled his telling me that he loved the game but hated the way of life of the professional player: "Don't allow your son be a chess player," he had said. I had nodded; of course Josh should do something else with his life. But at the same moment I was imagining him competing against the top grandmasters in the world. This is a contradiction in my life that I don't understand: not wanting my son to suffer the unhappiness of a poor, itinerant player does little to snuff out my reckless enthusiasm for his early chess career.

It would be a mistake for Josh to play in the Miami tournament, but the idea had titillated me, and I wanted to see if he was still sharp after his layoff, and whether the nationals had dulled his enjoyment of the game.

THERE IS ONE chess player on Bimini—I'll call him Cornelius— and a couple of days later I arranged a match with him. Joshua's interest was pricked by the idea of playing for the championship of Bimini. At ten in the morning, the appointed time, we walked into the Big Game Club bar, where the temperature plummeted forty degrees, but Cornelius wasn't there. Through tinted windows we looked outside at postcard images of the Bahamas. "Jeez, it's cold," Josh said, pulling his arms inside his T-shirt. "Let me go outside and cast a few times while you look for him." He couldn't get his mind off fishing.

We were the only ones in the bar besides Cooper, the bartender, tall and a little gray around the temples, who had been working here for more than thirty years. He asked me about Bonnie and the new baby. Cooper and I have known each other for a long time.

"Have you seen Cornelius?" I asked.

"No," he answered; from his tone, it was clear that Cooper didn't approve of Cornelius, who is a heavy drinker.

"Josh was supposed to play him this morning, but I guess he forgot."

"Play him what, man?"

"Chess. Don't you know that Cornelius is the champion of Bimini?" Cooper shook his head as if I were nuts. Cornelius is no champion of anything except booze, he was thinking.

Bimini is a tiny community of about twelve hundred people. Over the past dozen years, island gossip has switched from illicit sex and big-fish stories to tales of hometown smuggling, piracy at sea and drug-related murders. When I first came here, men made their living fishing for conch or crawfish or working on gamefish boats. Today, most industry is drug-related. At night planes from Colombia drop hundreds of bales of marijuana into the ocean near Bimini, where they are picked up by high-powered speedboats for the sixty-mile run to Miami. Each morning young men and some of the old-timers who used to be fishermen run their small boats to atolls south of the island, where they search for waterlogged bales of marijuana that were overlooked by the speedboats the previous night. A whole generation of Bimini men have become wealthy on the waterlogged refuse of the big-time drug trade. Other Bimini men (it is rumored that Cornelius is among them) off-load drug planes that occasionally land at night at the South Bimini airport.

Cornelius was indeed the chess champion of Bimini, but no one knew or cared. With the burgeoning drug traffic, it seems that both chess and fishing have become dying arts on the island. Cornelius won the title years ago when a dozen fishermen played the game in the evenings at one or another of the tiny bars along the main road. "There were some good players then," Cornelius recalled, "but now it's only me." The other players had either moved away or were dead.

After leaving Cooper, Josh and I strolled down the dusty main road with our rolled official-sized tournament chessboard and brown bag filled with Staunton pieces, searching for Cornelius. The midday sun was so bright it was hard to see even with sunglasses. We stopped at every bar along the way, but no one knew where he was. We asked the Conch Island Woman, who sat on a crumbling wall next to her rusty little table, which was set up on the street. Her hot jars of conch and green pepper were marinating in the sun, the delicious smells carrying down the Queen's Highway. She fanned mosquitoes off her legs and shook her head; she hadn't seen him. Josh was whimpering about the burning street and stopped to dip his feet in every puddle. I was getting angry. I wanted my son to play chess today and couldn't let go of the idea. I kept thinking about Susan Polgar and her two little sisters in Hungary getting better and better, and about the chess tournament in Florida. How could Cornelius have forgotten about the match? By now Josh was hoping we wouldn't find him. The tide was beginning to come in and the afternoon fishing off Brown's dock figured to be terrific. I asked a couple of drunks if there were other chess players on Bimini, and they directed us to a man who worked in the tiny insurance office. "He's better than Cornelius," said the guys, who were sharing a bottle. But when we found the man sweltering over his application forms, he explained that his game was checkers.

Sometime after lunch we finally found Cornelius sipping a beer at Ozzie Brown's bar. I was so pleased to see him that our three-hour search was forgotten. I had no idea how good a player the Bahamian was, but he had weight lifter's arms and an inscrutable, dangerous face, and it made me nervous to think of Josh playing him. I had arranged the match with conviction, but now I asked myself why I was pitting my little kid against this dope-smuggling thug. In the moment of excitement and dread I always feel just before Josh plays, Cornelius assumed his place in the pantheon of champions beside Smyslov, Tal, Botvinnik and Karpov. The Bahamian even yawned in the world-weary manner of an old champion patronizing a beginner.

* * *

THE CHAMPIONSHIP OF Bimini was played in a breezy room paneled in dark, varnished wood with large open windows looking out onto the picturesque harbor. This place was filled with ghosts. On the walls there were scores of yellowing photographs I had first admired with my father—photos of tremendous marlin that had been caught in these waters in the thirties and forties by Ernest Hemingway and other all-star anglers I had read about in fishing books.

"Are you ready?" Cornelius asked Josh. He was as dusty as the road and smelled of twenty years of beer. He wore a thick gold chain with a shark tooth on his neck, the mark of coolies in the Bahamian drug trade, who more often than not carry their entire worldly wealth on their hands and neck.

Josh asked me, "If I do good, will you buy me a vanilla shake at Bob Smith's?" Then he pushed his center pawn two squares, and Cornelius did the same, picking up his pawn between fingers burdened with heavy gold rings. Josh anchored the center with pawns and a bishop, and Cornelius pushed his pawn on the bishop file and developed his knight. On the fourth move, Cornelius prematurely brought out his queen. Perhaps it was a variation popular among Bimini bone fishermen of the sixties or a try for a fast win against a kid, but it was a mistake. If Josh played properly, Cornelius would be behind in the development of his pieces, and the queen might be vulnerable to an attack. All my son had to do was bring out his knights and bishops to their natural squares, but he looked indecisive and fidgety. Maybe Cornelius was a master and there was a deep threat hidden in this early queen move. But Josh had played games against dozens of masters and half a dozen grandmasters; usually the development of their pieces was slow, and their attacks built gradually and were unstoppable. Park players made crazy, unpredictable moves which often lost but sometimes could beat you quickly. What was behind this queen move? He was trying to size up Cornelius and at the same time trying to get used to analyzing a position after six weeks away from the game. After thinking for several minutes he brought his queen out to the third rank. "Oh, wow," Cornelius said beneath his breath, as if he had never expected such a dangerous move from a little guy. Now the position looked balanced and neat, with the queens on opposite sides of the board. Josh had matched the Bahamian's unsound threat with an unsound one of his own.

Cornelius pushed a pawn two squares. His center looked very powerful, protected now on the diagonal by the queen, and I could tell that Josh wasn't sure what to do. Hesitantly he took a pawn. The Bahamian smirked. He was quietly taunting and lulling his opponent and Josh had fallen for the bait. Now Cornelius pushed a pawn to the fifth rank, forking Josh's queen and bishop. My son's cheeks flushed; he was playing like a beginner. After the inevitable exchange Josh had traded his bishop for three pawns, with his queen sitting in the center of the board and his pieces undeveloped.

I could barely contain myself; this was the result of his long layoff. Josh had forgotten to develop his pieces and had fallen into a beginner's trap. Instead of analyzing he was thinking about barracudas and ice cream. How many times had I told him, "You can't play without trying your hardest. You've got to concentrate."

On the street a native passed and hailed Cornelius. "How you doin' against the little fella?"

"All right, all right."

Now Josh moved a knight to the edge of the board. How could he do this? When he was six Pandolfini had taught him that "a knight on the rim is very dim." Placed there, the knight can attack fewer squares than in the center of the board and is more easily trapped. Josh's position was a mess.

Cornelius pushed a pawn and Josh developed his other knight. Cornelius pushed another pawn. He was making quiet moves and seemed to be waiting for another blunder, but his passive play was allowing my son counterplay. Josh moved the first knight toward the center of the board. All of a sudden his position didn't look so bad; there had been a point to the knight on the rim after all. Now he had two strong knights in the center flanking an attacking queen.

The Bahamian scowled and considered the position. Finally he brought his knight back next to his king, which freed the queen to defend along the diagonal. On the next move he was planning to shift the knight to the other side of the board, where it would be more useful. But the move was a disaster. Josh immediately checked Cornelius with his queenside knight, forcing him to bring his king out to the second rank. Falling behind had somehow focused Josh and he was finding the moves easily. Now he checked with the other knight, and when the Bahamian pushed the king again, Josh moved the first knight for a discovered check from the queen. Cornelius was out on his feet, no longer bothering even to find the best escape squares. On the next move, with a big smile Josh forked the king and the queen with his queenside knight, and it was all over.

They played two more games, which Josh won easily. He was into the flow of playing again, attacking weak squares, developing his pieces, playing smartly and opportunistically, the way he had learned from Pandolfini. As they played on, Cornelius grew increasingly restless and sullen. By now it had dawned on him that Josh was not winning by luck. The Bahamian wanted to put this match behind him and be the champion of Bimini again.

I should have been delighted that my son was winning, but I wasn't satisfied. When Cornelius was thinking, Josh looked out the window instead of studying the board. I thought of Alekhine, who had once said that a chess player's world must be only the chess position in front of him. Even here on Bimini, beside the deep blue water of the Gulf Stream, with the sexy rhythms of a reggae band drifting in from the bar, Alekhine would have bent over the pieces for hours without letting his eye wander, a timeless, contemplative chess machine. Josh was winning, yet I focused more on his missed opportunities. He might have won more quickly and elegantly; his game lacked the crystal clarity of Capablanca's; his combinations were predictable. It annoyed me that he tapped his leg to the music and that his eyes drifted from the position to the photographs of gamefish on the wall. Josh crushed Cornelius, but it didn't mean anything; the Bahamian was a patzer who hung pieces.

LOSING
IT

In the fall of 1985, Josh trans-
ferred from the Little Red School House to the Dalton School. But
in the first few weeks of the fall term he was homesick for his old
school and friends, and his unhappiness was so large and persistent
that we thought we had made the wrong choice. As if to prove his
point, he lacked all enthusiasm for chess, and his play was poor
after the summer's layoff in Bimini. When his chess friends came
over to visit and challenged him to a game, he looked pained and
suggested Monopoly or something else—anything else. It was dis-
tressing when Joshua's friend Ben Rosen asked me, "Why doesn't
Josh like chess anymore?"

The first lesson with Pandolfini in the beginning of September
was disastrous. They had arranged to meet on a Sunday morning
at the Manhattan Chess Club, but when Josh arrived, Bruce was
still working with another student.

While we waited, a spindly little boy came over and asked Josh
to play blitz. "I'm gonna crush you," he said. Josh shrugged, and
they began to play. The kid was seven and moved his pieces instantly, as my son had been inclined to do at that age, seemingly
without thinking. Josh was rusty and unsure of himself and moved
slower and slower as the game became more complicated. When
he ran out of time, the other boy had used up barely two minutes
on his clock. They played two more games and Josh lost each of
them. He couldn't move as fast as the other boy, and when he
tried to, he blundered.

It was the first time that my son had ever felt soundly defeated by a child younger than himself. Among his peers, he had always been the best player. When he lost, he viewed it as an accident, a momentary lapse, and usually his opponent would savor a win against him as an unexpected stroke of fortune.

At eight, Joshua's chess career had gone topsy-turvy. In the nationals he had lost the most important game of his life to David Arnett, and now a little boy, shorter and younger, had beaten him almost without effort. My son wasn't feeling like such a great player anymore. During the lesson that followed, he had trouble listening to Bruce. The chess problems were too hard, and he couldn't figure them out. It was Sunday and he wanted to be at home on the sofa with his little sister, watching cartoons on television. "Look at the board, Josh," Bruce snapped. "Why are you looking out the window?"

Jeff Sarwer, the boy who had beaten Josh that morning, was considered a genius by the regulars at the Manhattan Chess Club. Some of the old-timers who had watched Bobby play as a child referred to Jeff as a young Fischer. They had said the same thing about Josh two years before, when at six he had first played his witty, tactical games at the club, but by now this was old news. Joel Benjamin, himself once a brilliant prodigy, said that Jeff Sarwer was the strongest player for his age that he had ever seen, and Vitaly Zaltzman, his teacher at the time, touted him as the best for his age in the world.

Jeff and his nine-year-old sister, Julia, didn't go to school. They were tutored by their father, a Canadian citizen, and spent most of their day at the Manhattan Chess Club playing and studying with various masters. Sometimes little Jeff would be snapping off five-minute games against club regulars at midnight and then would be there the next morning eagerly challenging members as they sleepily wandered in. He considered himself different from other chess kids. Chess was his life; the others were dabblers. "None of them can beat me," he said with a disconcerting, hard-edged condescension. "I play like a master and they don't know what they're doing." He didn't spend time with other chess children, preferring the company of strong adult players. As if to further distance himself from his peers, many of whom dressed with preppy casualness and were taxied to the club by maids, he wore scuffed sandals and the same grimy running suit day after day and had the hair shaved off his head. For adults and children alike, playing against this pencil-thin child was a disconcerting experience. As he formulated ingenious attacks, one could not help wondering about the extraordinary mechanism computing away beneath his shiny bald scalp.

During the following year Jeff Sarwer was the subject of much discussion in the New York children's chess world. The parents of some of the top players argued that their kids would show just as much promise if they too studied the game forty or fifty hours a week, but that regardless of talent, it was wrong to keep a child out of school. Some parents felt that since Jeff didn't attend school, he shouldn't be allowed to participate in scholastic tournaments. But many regulars at the Manhattan Chess Club sympathized with Mike Sarwer's ambition for his son. Some of them were openly bitter that their parents had not gotten behind them as young players, and they championed Jeff's eccentric life-style as a kind of homage to the game. He was seen as the ultimate chess experiment: a child with exceptional aptitude who would have unlimited time and the best teachers in order to grow to his full potential.

IN SEPTEMBER, PANDOLFINI was late delivering two instructional books he was writing, including one on Bobby Fischer's games that later became a best seller among chess books. His editor was calling him every day, and Bruce was having trouble completing the manuscripts. Like many writers, he was anxious about the quality of his work. In addition, in his capacity as executive director of the Manhattan Chess Club he had to deal with pressing financial and organizational problems. He was expected to start fall chess programs at four secondary schools, and the parents of his students, back from summer vacations, were eagerly calling to schedule lessons. Each morning his answering machine was flashing with fifteen or twenty urgent demands. Desperate to finish his books, Pandolfini stopped returning phone calls, including Joshua's and mine. He wasn't sleeping, he had stomachaches and he couldn't eat. He had no time for chess lessons. During a two-week period he canceled three sessions in a row, and my son decided that his teacher didn't like him anymore.

For Josh the evidence was mounting that chess was filled with disappointment and pain. After two years of success and winning, the game was making him feel like a loser, and he tried to shut it out. One afternoon Pandolfini rushed over from his studio for half an hour, feeling that a short lesson was better than none. He barely said hello and taught as quickly as possible, trying to cram two weeks' worth into thirty minutes, and left feeling frustrated that Josh wasn't concentrating. Twice more he came over for quick sessions, talking more in algebraic notation than in English. He was so harried that he didn't notice that my son rarely looked at him. After these whirlwind meetings Josh wondered what had gone wrong between them. Bruce no longer kidded around or talked about the Jets and Knicks. He had stopped pasting stars and dinosaur stickers in Joshua's little black book and no longer awarded him master-class points at the end of their lesson. Bruce must have decided that he was no longer worth the effort. It was hard for Josh to talk about it. Chess made him agitated and unhappy, which in turn made his father unhappy. But when I confronted him, he assured me with a pained expression on his face that he still loved the game.

Bruce and Josh struggled through a number of sessions. I was hoping that Bruce would be able to pull my son out of this slump, but toward the middle of October, Josh excused himself from a lesson, found Bonnie in the kitchen, and cried softly so that Bruce wouldn't hear. "I can't do it," he told her. "It's too hard."

"It went badly—very badly," Bonnie told me later. She had been watching the lesson from the kitchen door. Instead of looking at the board, Josh had stared at the clock and had sometimes covered his ears with his hands. He didn't want to hear about the Samisch variation of the Nimzo-Indian. He couldn't have cared less about mating with a knight and a bishop against a king.

"He doesn't enjoy the game anymore," Bonnie said firmly. "It's stopped being fun. He can't bear his lessons with Bruce." She was saying things that I had been trying to ignore; it's easy to tune out a little kid when you have fame and glory squarely in your sights.

"Haven't you noticed? They're not the same together. They used to be such friends, but now Bruce hardly cracks a smile. He acts toward Josh like a frustrated boss on the verge of firing a lazy worker. Both of you have forgotten that he's a little boy."

Bonnie went on to point out that for months I had been oblivious to Joshua's feelings about chess; I was so intoxicated by his potential that I couldn't see what was happening. While she talked, I was thinking that if only my son and I could have a serious conversation, everything would be okay. It was just that he was out of practice and in a bad mood. The tournaments would begin soon, and despite his loss to David Arnett in the nationals, he was still the highest-rated primary player in the United States.

"You must be blind," Bonnie said angrily in response to my silences and equivocations. "Don't you understand? He doesn't like playing anymore."

OUR LITTLE CHESS team was in a state of chaos and dejection. Josh didn't want to play, and whenever I managed to get through to Bruce on the phone, he sounded frazzled and exhausted. I was facing the possibility that there would be no more tournaments, no second chance to win the national championship, no more splendid contests in Washington Square. When I thought of Joshua's life without chess, the alternatives—good grades, Little League games and clarinet lessons—seemed mediocre and boring.

Finally I arranged a dinner with Bruce to discuss our crisis. He looked thin and drawn. While he described his harried eighteen-hour day, he kept glancing at his watch. He knew that he had to be somewhere else, but he couldn't remember where. He said he was falling behind on all his deadlines. He couldn't write well when he was so tired, but there was no time to rest. I was apprehensive that he was about to say he no longer had time for Josh, and that we would have to find another teacher.

Instead, Pandolfini began to describe an idea. His mood changed completely, and he began to laugh and relax. After thirteen years he was considering playing in chess tournaments again, but the other players wouldn't recognize him. He would dress in elaborate disguises; perhaps he'd wear a long beard and a flowing black cape and speak in one of several accents he had been practicing. He would do very well in the tournaments, perhaps even win a couple, he predicted. For one thing, he would have no rating and the best players would take him lightly, which would be an enormous edge. Also, he knew much more about the game than when he had last played in tournaments. Most important, in his disguises he could play without pressure because it would be impossible for Bruce Pandolfini to lose. Each time he began to establish a small reputation, he'd change identities and begin anew. The fantasy of playing again seemed to free Bruce from the clutter and anxieties of his life. He was intrigued by his quixotic idea, experiencing aspirations he'd first felt as a teenager while playing through the chess masterpieces of Alekhine at the Marshall Chess Club, imagining himself building impregnable positions and humbling the best players in the world. Somehow, he assured me, he'd make room in his hectic schedule for this secret life.

While Bruce talked on, I realized that years of writing articles for *Chess Life*, lecturing at universities and producing popular instructional books had made playing the game he loved too threatening. If he did poorly, wouldn't it tarnish his reputation as a writer and teacher? But wasn't it also possible that his reluctance to play might quietly infect a student of his? At eight, Josh was also trapped by a reputation—reluctant to play, afraid to lose. "You know why I didn't want to play Ben," he had said to me a few days earlier. "Let's just say that by accident I lost a game. He'd tell everyone in school."

At seven, Josh had often been referred to as a genius, and for Bruce it had been wonderful to have such a highly regarded student. For both of them it had been like living in a Peter Pan fantasy. Josh could fly and couldn't fall. When he lost a game playing against adults, he came out a winner nonetheless; invariably he was praised for his talent and potential. Perhaps without realizing it, Bruce and I had fueled this illusion of invincibility. To each of us it was unacceptable for him to lose to other children. Before he was old enough to write, Josh had learned that winning was the most direct way to his father's heart. I was insatiable for his wins, and we didn't talk about losing; that was an unacceptable reality that he had to wrestle with on his own. Even when he lost a game to someone who was several years older and had a higher rating, Bruce was quick to point out Josh's carelessness and how easily he might have won; rarely did he praise the other child's ingenuity.

AN EXCEPTIONAL STUDENT is likely to be a losing financial proposition for a teacher. While his wife or girlfriend is urging him to find wealthier pupils, the teacher finds himself scheduling extra sessions with his star, lessons that are sometimes not paid for. There is never enough time to cover the material, and one-hour lessons frequently stretch into a third hour. In addition, the teacher spends time planning tournament strategies, photocopying problems, scanning foreign periodicals for the newest opening lines, searching bookstores for out-of-print material, worrying about results. He does all this because he is infatuated with his student's potential, riding hopes that are unlikely to come to fruition and that he would be embarrassed even to admit. Perhaps his student will become a national champion someday, maybe even world champion. For the teacher, this would be like becoming a champion himself.

In the back of his mind, Pandolfini had a goal. Given Joshua's rapid progress as a seven- and eight-year-old, he had a chance to become the youngest American master ever. Almost without realizing it, Bruce had picked up the pace. In the past Josh had solved problems faster than any child he'd ever worked with, and the more difficult they were, the better he liked it. Gradually Pandolfini had begun to talk to my son as an equal, often verbalizing complex chess variations without demonstrating them on the board. This saved time, but for a while he didn't realize that Josh would sometimes nod without understanding; it simply wasn't in his nature to admit to a weakness. Also, on some days, or even for entire months, Josh seemed to be able to grasp master-level concepts. At such times his chess ability was years more advanced than during those periods when he couldn't bear to face the stern demands of his lessons. During the first years of my son's play, Bruce had often reminded me that such inconsistencies were normal for a child, but lately he and I had both expected a more even performance. Pandolfini was impatient for his pupil to begin playing advanced contemporary openings, which would raise the level of his game, but Josh had trouble memorizing the moves. He also had difficulty recording his moves accurately in notation during tournaments, and would expend more energy scribbling and erasing on the scoresheet than in playing; as a consequence, until he learned to write with more dexterity, his offhand games were more creative and sophisticated than his tournament ones. Sometimes Bruce accused Josh of not trying—younger kids could write the moves accurately—and my son would complain bitterly that he *was* trying. He was so good at some things that it was easy to forget that his aptitudes for different tasks were uneven, just like those of other seven- and eight-year-olds.

The realization that he might be losing Josh was a terrible blow for Pandolfini, who had begun to feel like part of our family. Twice a week after the lesson he had sat at our small kitchen table eating dinner, discussing Joshua's homework, or what school he ought to go to, or expressing pained concern about a second-grade infatuation that had turned out badly. On his own, he had spent many hours worrying about his pupil's future and systematically plotting its course. Now he had to face the fact that their lessons simply weren't working. When he tried to introduce new material, Josh sat at the table with a sullen expression, fooling with a ball or a toy car, waiting for Bruce to leave.

He'd been pushing Josh much too hard, Pandolfini realized. In preparing for the nationals the previous spring, he had treated his student like a robot, cramming variations into him that my son found inaccessible or unattractive. He had tried to ignore Joshua's willfulness and age, and had grown increasingly impatient with his resistance to various time-honored ideas. But perhaps this stubbornness was a vital component of Josh's fighting spirit and chess intuition. By nature Bruce tended to be pacifistic and compliant, whereas his pupil was competitive and pugnaciously opinionated. Perhaps the well-intentioned but constant drilling of chess principles was taking the guts out of our little player, ultimately even contributing to a fear of playing. Bruce wondered whether he had wanted Josh to win too much. Perhaps he should have allowed his student to discover more for himself, even if it meant losing games and rating points. Maybe early success had been a trap for both of them.

Pandolfini and I decided that he and Josh had to get away from serious chess, to forget the imperatives of winning and the endless memorizing of opening variations that had taken all the fun and game out of the game. Bruce threw all of his plans and programs out the window. Chess would have to become fun again or Josh would quit. In fact, he might quit anyway; he had to have the room to make that choice. To play with enthusiasm and creativity he would have to be allowed to discover why and for whom he was studying. It wouldn't work if he was doing it all for his father and his teacher. Bruce would have to start listening to his pupil, and at this moment Josh was thinking more about his new school than about chess. He hated taking the bus in the morning; he felt sick from the driver's cigar and the plastic smell of the van's upholstery; he couldn't stand what they served for lunch. He and Bruce began to talk about such matters during their lessons. Josh was excited about the math program at Dalton and showed Bruce a tricky conceptual problem that he had figured out in less than ten minutes. Then he timed his teacher while he solved it.

Like a married couple who have been going through bad times, the two of them had to learn to laugh together and to begin to worry about each other. One afternoon my son asked Bruce why he looked so gloomy, and Pandolfini talked about his bad day. Then Josh talked about a pretty girl in his class, clasped his hands and hoped fervently that she liked him. He asked Bruce whether he should risk asking her over and then worried about what would happen if she said yes. What do you do on an afternoon play-date with a girl who doesn't like football?

Pandolfini allowed chess to become incidental to other matters. When he brought the game up he did so gently and without urgency. He set up chess problems for Josh to solve, simple ones of the sort he'd introduced two years earlier. He timed his student on the clock, and they both laughed while Josh tried to find the mate before Bruce had all the pieces in place on the board. After fifteen or twenty minutes of this Pandolfini would stand up, yawn and say, "C'mon, Tiger, let's go outside and toss the football."

Twenty minutes of beginner problems and an hour of shagging long passes became a chess lesson. After a couple of weeks of this they started playing speed games as well, but they chatted about football at the same time, and when Josh blundered Bruce turned it into a joke.

Almost overnight, Pandolfini could see that everything was coming back together, but he didn't want it to happen too fast. One afternoon Josh beat him in a seven-minute game without odds of any sort. Afterward, Bruce told me that he had never seen Josh play such an elegant, original combination. The two of them continued to joke and to talk about sports, keeping chess on the back burner. Bruce gave his student a new little black book, and every lesson he crammed it full of superstar and Day-Glo dinosaur stickers. Sometimes they spent a third of the lesson fooling with the book and the stickers.

By now my son was looking forward to seeing Bruce again. His coach at Dalton, Svetozar Jovanovic, had also been concerned about his unhappiness and had arranged events to integrate Josh into the school. He called to invite Josh to play a simultaneous exhibition against the primary team, assuring him that afterward the children would know who he was and it would be easier for him to make new friends.

One chilly afternoon late in October Josh asked me if I would take him to Washington Square to play some speed chess. I told him to grab the football and his sweatshirt so that we could have a catch afterward. In the five months since the nationals, this was the first time that, without prodding from friends, his father or his teacher, Josh himself had suggested playing. Walking toward the park, he talked nervously but also with excitement about playing fourteen games at the same time in the next day's simultaneous exhibition. Later that afternoon, he jumped for a pass and fell back to the asphalt on his head. He blacked out for a few minutes and then couldn't focus his eyes. At the hospital the doctor said that he had a slight concussion. The following morning he had a headache, but he pleaded with me not to call Jovanovic to cancel the event. I gave him an aspirin and agreed.

Jovanovic had set up a circle of desks for the exhibition in a spacious Dalton classroom. When Josh arrived, looking shy and insecure, Jovanovic hugged him to his ample belly and presented him to the group of parents and children with all the pomp and circumstance of Yuri Averbakh introducing Anatoly Karpov in the House of Trade Unions. Josh rolled his eyes as Jovanovic listed his accomplishments in chess, and the fourteen kids he was about to play trembled with the importance of this moment.

For the next two and a half hours my son circled the room with the presence and composure of a little man. It was disconcerting to watch. His concentration was unwavering, his expression peaceful, and he seemed years older than the little boy who had cried during his lesson six weeks before. After making his move at each board, he announced it in descriptive notation for his opponent to record on the score sheet. When the position was complicated, he paused in front of the game for what seemed like a long time, though it was probably no more than half a minute. Everyone in the room became nervous during these pauses. Why doesn't he move on? Is he in trouble? Is it possible that Josh Waitzkin is losing? Finally he would advance a piece and move on to the next game, but a little reluctantly, glancing over his shoulder at the position he had just left as if with regret. At some tables which were half a foot lower than the others, he dropped to his knees so that he could better absorb the position. At one such table a little red-haired girl concentrated on her game. Her eyes never left the board, and she was giving Josh a tough time. Now he made a mistake, and immediately she took his rook. "Oh, no," he said and rolled his eyes. He paused at the table a long time before taking back her bishop with his king. When he returned to the board again he analyzed for an eternity, then moved his knight to where she could take it with a pawn. A few moves later he had her in a mating net.

Josh won thirteen out of the fourteen games he played. Later he helped Jovanovic collect the pieces and pack them away as they talked about one of the games. Josh had played a tricky combination to win a rook from a little boy, who afterwards had looked confused and sad. With his arm around Joshua's shoulder, Jovanovic said, "You know, Josh, that was the same trap that Naomi Spiro used against Elliot Lum two years ago in Syracuse." The little chess traps of children ring in Svetozar Jovanovic's head for years.

LATE IN NOVEMBER we were passing the Manhattan Chess Club and on the spur of the moment decided to go up and say hello to Bruce. He wasn't there, but in a far corner Jeff Sarwer, the boy who had beaten Josh in September, was playing a speed game against Michael Rohde, a strong international master. Several other masters were standing around watching the game and chatting. Jeff looked up for a moment, nodded to Josh and then focused on the board again.

After the game was over, Josh challenged Jeff to play a few. I felt sick to my stomach. Bruce had made a point of explaining to Josh that he ought not to compare himself with Jeff, who was a full-time player, in effect a seven-year-old professional. If there had been any plausible excuse to pull my son away, I would have grasped at it. Nothing good could come of this match.

The two of them sat down, and one of the masters jocularly called out for others to come watch "the battle of the titans." The dozen or so men who gathered at their table joked about the size of the players, but everyone was curious. I felt only dread. The adult players watching, most of whom probably hadn't even known how to move the pieces at that age, had no idea that a match between these two was as loaded emotionally as a contest between Karpov and Kasparov.

When they started to play Josh looked composed and eager, and in that moment I knew that even if I had been born with chess talent, I still could never have been a player. I would have wanted to run from this kind of confrontation. The nakedness of the moment was appalling. One of these little boys would lose, and at least for a time a carefully constructed edifice of fantasies and expectations would crumble. The stakes were also bloody for the fathers, but I noticed that Mike Sarwer had stationed himself at a far corner of the room where he couldn't see.

Josh moved quickly and confidently, and Jeff seemed to sense a message, because his thin little fingers began to tremble against his will, indecisively pausing over the pieces as his clock ticked.

Josh won the first game on time with the position fairly equal. He didn't make any mistakes, and in the next two games he checkmated Jeff. The boys stood up and shook hands with the decorum of grandmasters, but there was no meeting of the eyes. When we left the club, Jeff was sitting in a corner crying by himself. He cried for the next hour and a half, I was told later.

Outside I asked Josh what he thought about the games—whether he was stronger or whether Jeff had played poorly—the kinds of crummy questions that chess parents lay on their kids. My son shrugged. "Maybe I'm stronger, but maybe he is. It was just a few games. Next time we play he'll probably get me."

Perhaps at least one of us was beginning to learn something.

A
CHESS
FAN'S
NOTES

Being a chess fan in the United States is a difficult and lonely hobby. Many of the best tournaments are continents away, and even the top ones here get little attention from the media. If I am interested in keeping abreast of José Cucci's New York Open, one of the largest and richest tournaments in the world, and if I don't have the time to hang out at the Penta Hotel on Seventh Avenue, I must buy the Argentinean newspaper *Clarin* and ask my friend Jon Lehman to translate Miguel Quintero's article. If I want the latest Karpov-Kasparov gossip I must read the London *Times* or wheedle information from one of our Russian emigré players, who have their own sources.

While in our country it is acceptable and even respected in many social circles to memorize mountains of arcane sports statistics and to spend time away from work and the family to root for the Yankees or the Mets, there is little empathy for the chess fan. People become uneasy when they realize that you are absorbed in distant board games. To the nonplayer, being a chess fan seems an eccentric, perhaps even seedy, preoccupation.

Unfortunately this view is shared tacitly even by the tournament directors and players, who complain year after year about the lack of money and interest in the game. At most tournaments, the fan is at best an afterthought. The playing area is roped off for the contestants, and for other players who are taking a break or have already finished and are interested in watching games still in progress. Often, in his eagerness to see the action, a fan will creep beneath the rope to glimpse a position over the shoulders of half a dozen grandmasters. But tournament directors are like hawks, and they can always pick out a fan. Again and again, directors shepherd us away from games and threaten to throw us out of the hall if we don't stand behind the rope, where we can't see.

Players in the United States aren't accustomed to having fans around and have not bothered to cultivate graciousness. Rising from hours of sweaty analysis, grandmasters are put off by applause or by unsophisticated questions. Often they are surly, as if the presence of the faithful is a painful distraction.

International Master Victor Frias explains it this way: "Many GMs and IMs consider weak players more or less worthless as people. They have developed this defensive attitude because their own social status is so low. Many fans are highly paid professionals, doctors and lawyers, and despite their interest in the game, basically they consider the professional chess player a bum. Of course the players counterattack. Disparaging the chess fan is a way of putting down the big shot who's always putting you down.

"With a certain justification, American players feel they don't owe the fan anything. Players give a show without compensation. Unlike in Europe, chess professionals in the United States must pay their own entry fee and transportation to tournaments, so if after a game a guy asks me a stupid question, without thinking I give him a dirty look. But if he had to buy a ticket to get into the tournament, and if this covered my entry fee and food for the week, maybe I would grit my teeth and tell him why I lost."

Occasionally I ask a player what happened last week at a tournament in Ohio or in Atlanta, and I can see suspicion cloud his face: Why does he want to know? He's not even a player.

It is different abroad, where chess is frequently in the newspapers and the top players sign autographs, and where games are sometimes televised into auditoriums, which allows fans the release of cheering the good moves of their favorites without distracting the players. Like a spectator at a football or basketball game, the chess fan needs to cheer in order to feel that he has participated in the victory, so that he can feel like a winner himself.

I know that my friends aren't interested in the latest chess news, but occasionally I can't restrain myself, and over a beer, I enthuse about an upset in Barcelona or an up-and-coming thirteen-year-old in Great Britain who has played a brilliant opening variation. But I never seem to learn; it doesn't make for good conversation. In the fall of 1985, in addition to the Karpov-Kasparov rematch, I was looking forward to the candidates tournament in Montpellier, France, one of a series of round-robin events to determine the next challenger for the world championship. Mikhail Tal was playing. What a thrill it would be to have him play for the world championship again! One evening, after reading in the foreign press that the great forty-nine-year-old grandmaster had surged into the lead over some of the best young players in the world, I tried to express my exhilaration to Bonnie, but she wasn't interested. When Tal drew in the last round and had to enter an exhausting playoff with the younger Jan Timman of the Netherlands to determine which of them would proceed to the next round, I knew in my heart that my hero would lose. I was depressed for two days, but I didn't mention it to Bonnie, who probably thought my moodiness had to do with my writing. For the most part I keep my chess life to myself.

Before falling asleep, instead of prognosticating, as in the old days, about which offensive lineman the Jets are likely to choose in the draft, or whether or not Mike Tyson has the potential of a Marciano or a Frazier, I think about the great young Russian chess players: Vaganyan, Yusupov, Sokolov and Dolmatov. Which of them will emerge from the pack to challenge for the championship? Is Grandmaster Shamkovich right in believing that Yusupov's style is better suited for Karpov than for Kasparov? Is Kasparov really the best attacking player since Alekhine? Is Karpov the greatest defender in the history of the game?

During our trip to the Soviet Union Grandmaster Eduard Gufeld insisted that both Karpov and Kasparov were much stronger players than Bobby Fischer. Months later, in bed beside my sleeping wife, I was still upset by his assertion. Fischer was like Shakespeare, Muhammad Ali and Babe Ruth, a figure larger than the game, dwarfing all other players and at the same time raising their possibilities to unheard-of heights. Could the two Russians, who seem destined to play each other again and again, have surpassed Fischer's genius, or was Gufeld's view merely jingoistic posturing?

Like most chess fans, I was infuriated when Florencio Campomanes, the president of FIDE since 1982, stopped the first Karpov-Kasparov match at exactly the moment when Kasparov seemed to have broken his opponent and was moving in for the kill. Newspaper articles and editorials all over the world suggested that the outcome of the match had been rigged by the Soviet government, which was uneasy about the prospect of an outspoken half-Jewish chess champion. In several unusually candid interviews at the conclusion of the match, Kasparov claimed that the Soviet Chess Federation, dominated by Karpov's cronies, had asked Campomanes to stop the match when it became clear that their man could no longer win. Kasparov believed that in addition to the Soviet Chess Federation, FIDE, Campomanes and even the referees had conspired against him. He remarked with dark humor that in a future match he might be able to beat Karpov, but not Karpomanes.

It was a difficult time for a chess fan. How could one root for these great players if their results were predetermined by the machinations of a few overly zealous chess fans who are members of the Politburo? If Karpov cheated or even countenanced cheating on the part of others, what about Vaganyan, Yusupov or even Kasparov and Tal?

Fortunately, basketball, boxing and chess fans alike have encountered such situations before and have developed deep resources. Moral outrage passes, and when it was time for the Karpov-Kasparov rematch in the fall of 1985, I was excited all over again and no longer dwelled on Russian chess politics. The match played itself out like a movie script. Kasparov forged ahead; Karpov fought back. Three times the lead changed hands, and some analysts were saying that both grandmasters were at the top of their contrasting but marvelous games. Karpov jockeyed for safe positions from which he could engage in quiet, devious maneuvering. Kasparov attacked directly and theatrically with combinations and sacrifices. After the nineteenth game, he held a two-point lead, and most experts thought that the match was all over. But then Karpov won the twenty-second game and drew the twenty-third.

If he could manage to win the twenty-fourth game with the black pieces, he would be even in the match and retain his championship. After the first match, dominated by Karpov's back-room political tactics with Soviet politicians and Campomanes, the world champion had been characterized in the media as Satan after the fall. But now, in the final hour of the return match, Satan was up off his back making a Rocky-like comeback. As much as I was rooting for Kasparov to win or draw the twenty-fourth game, I was also rooting a little for Karpov.

ON THE MORNING of the final game between Karpov and Kasparov I was furious that I couldn't watch it live. Seventy-one games between these two men had come down to this last one, and each would be giving it everything he had. For the sports fan, teams and players are often imbued with moral qualities. In the West, besides being known for exciting, attacking chess, Kasparov represented fair-mindedness and hope. Perhaps as champion of the world he would use his influence to help Boris Gulko, Volodja Pimonov and others who wanted to emigrate or who were not allowed to play in tournaments because they were Jewish or had bucked the Soviet chess establishment. Karpov, on the other hand, seemed to stand in the way of better times; the world would be crueler, more gloomy, the morning after he won.

To me the event was as momentous as the first Ali-Frazier fight; yet I knew that no television or radio station would cover the game, and that I couldn't even learn the result until the next day when I read it in the *New York Times*. I'd spend most of my day fretting about what was going on in Tchaikovsky Hall in Moscow. Then I came up with an idea. I called information for the telephone number of Tass in New York and dialed nervously. The phone was picked up by a sleepy-sounding man, who said that his name was Olof. I explained that I was writing about the match for one of the largest dailies in the United States, and that I needed the moves of today's game the instant they came over the wire. (This was only partially a lie since I *had* written about the chess world for national magazines.) Olof perked up. Naturally he assumed that I was on a tight deadline and that his attentiveness to the wire would be a service to millions of readers. Perhaps it even occurred to him that this transmission of sporting news might be a useful cultural exchange between our two antagonistic countries, a small step toward understanding and peace. In fact the only peace in question was the peace of mind of me and my friend Steve Salinger, a strong C player, standing by at the chess set.

During the next several hours Olof and I exchanged phone calls, and with a trembling hand I duplicated the moves played only a minute or two before by the two opponents in Moscow. After each call Steve and I discussed the wisdom of the moves and whose position looked more promising. Perhaps I was feeling guilty about lying to Olof or maybe I was beginning to believe the lie, because as the game progressed I felt more and more burdened by the increasingly complicated position. It was as if the Western world were counting on my analysis, a terrible responsibility which compromised my limited chess intelligence. By the fifteenth move I couldn't make head or tail of the position. Every capture was filled with ambiguity, the pieces seemed to swim in all directions and I even began to be confused about who was playing white and who black.

"Why do you think he put the knight there?" I asked Steve.

"Well, he had to; otherwise it would be captured by the pawn. Where else could he put it?"

By move twenty, the position had become delicate, and even the unflappable Salinger was unsure who was better off. In a second burst of inspiration, I called Grandmaster Lev Alburt, gave him the position and asked for his analysis. Alburt had no idea where I was getting the moves, and to my relief he never asked. Every fifteen or twenty minutes I gave him an update and asked for his opinion. At one point, after venturing that Karpov looked a little better and suggesting some future moves for black, he graciously asked for my opinion. I mentioned an idea that had been suggested a few minutes before by Steve and then added hastily, "But we are very weak." Alburt probably took this to mean that we were weak masters. Why would two patzers be waiting breathlessly all day for telexed moves which they couldn't understand?

On the twenty-eighth move, two terrible things happened in

quick succession. First, Kasparov apparently lost a pawn; secondly, the telex line from Moscow broke down. "You've got to get it fixed," I shouted at Olof. I had made the same demand to the Manhattan Cable Company when they lost the picture during the fourth quarter of a tense Knick game. While we waited, Alburt speculated that Kasparov was worse off, but that he still might have drawing chances. By now I was no longer rooting even a little for Karpov. What would happen to Kasparov if he lost? He had gone way out on a limb making derogatory remarks about Karpov, Roshal, Sevastianov and others in the Soviet chess power structure.

For half an hour the only news Olof had was that the line was out. Finally, when I called him for the twelfth or fifteenth time since the telex had broken down, he said, "I have no more moves, but the last message says that black has resigned." In disbelief I asked him to read it again. Kasparov had won. It seemed impossible. Down a pawn (two pawns, actually, but I didn't know this at the time), Good had triumphed over Evil. Salinger and I danced around my little kitchen as if our families had just been saved from a terrible catastrophe.

IN THE SUMMER of 1985 Grandmaster Lev Alburt won the United States championship for the second year in a row. His chess prowess, his years as a top grandmaster functioning within the Soviet chess establishment and his long-standing relationship with Karpov and Kasparov make him uniquely qualified to comment on their games.

"The quality of chess in their first match was simply miserable," Alburt told me, "the worst in the history of championship play since Zukertort and Steinitz. Both players made many mistakes, much of the play was boring and there were few brilliancies. In the second match the quality was somewhat better and there were fewer mistakes, but the chess was still far from exceptional. This is not surprising; both men had too much on their minds.

"There is a tendency of people in the West to portray Karpov as a kind of villain, and to see Kasparov as a dissident idealist, but that's an oversimplification. Kasparov is also a member of the ruling class, the *nomenklatura*, as well as Karpov. They are both members of the Central Committee of the Communist Party. What makes these matches unique is that for the first time in the history of Russian chess two members of the ruling class are playing for the championship. The real drama here is the struggle between two powerful cliques."

"How does this affect their play?" I asked.

Alburt elaborated with a mixture of fact and surmise. Several weeks before the start of the first match, Karpov was making many phone calls to reach a friend who was close to a general in the army, instead of studying openings. He had come up with an idea that would be more irksome to Kasparov than any opening preparation. He wanted to ask his friend to bribe the general into drafting one of Kasparov's top aides just before the beginning of the match. It would take dozens of phone calls before Karpov accomplished this dirty trick, and meanwhile he wasn't thinking about chess. Of course Kasparov soon caught wind of the plot and was quickly on the phone himself, calling friends to block Karpov's plan.

"Did this actually happen?" I asked incredulously.

"Of course," Alburt answered, as if he thought everyone knew. "Grandmaster Gennady Timoshenko was in his late thirties, old for the army, and had been working with Kasparov for many years. His loss was a severe psychological blow. But it wasn't only that Kasparov lost a top assistant; he also lost a political battle. More likely than not this dirty trick contributed to his poor start in the match.

"There were many intrigues during the course of the match, which was emotionally draining for the players. There were at least ten illegal delays, each of them the result of a power play. After Kasparov won the third game he requested a rest day. With Karpov so depleted, it made no sense, and many people in the West wondered why he had done it. Obviously Kasparov was forced into it; Karpov had been able to put pressure on him through a political connection. For both of them, the war being played in back rooms and on the phone determined the outcome of the match more than preparation, and it didn't make for good chess."

"From reading the papers, I got the impression that the second match was largely free of dirty tricks," I said.

"For the most part that's true," said Alburt, "but in the middle of the match, Kasparov did lodge an official protest with the jury about Karpov's use of drugs."

"I thought it was normal for Soviet players to take drugs."

"There are no rules against taking stimulants, but in each game of the match, Karpov received from his aides a glass of a certain drink, and in his protest Kasparov insisted that the drink should be prepared and delivered to Karpov *before* the game. His objection was that during the game the grandmasters who worked for Karpov could convey a message with this drink. For example, the message might be 'You faced a novelty in the opening and are already in trouble. Try for a draw.' The drink could be distinctive by the container in which it was delivered, or by its smell, taste or color. By these signals it's easy to convey several simple messages. His analysts might signal Karpov that they'd found a winning line and that he should try to adjourn the game. For a player to know that a team of trusted grandmasters considers his position better or worse is an extremely important advantage.

"But there was another factor in Kasparov's protest that was even more important. Different positions require different approaches. In one it could be clear that combinations and tactics are needed. In this situation Karpov would need a drug that would stimulate his abilities for a short period of time to provide an explosion of concentration. Then he could relax. So if his analysts saw that a tricky series of moves was coming up, they might give him a strong stimulant, which would convey the message that he should watch out for a combination and at the same time would provide him with energy. Or imagine a different position: the players have bishops of different colors and Karpov is a pawn down, so a long, careful defense is called for. In this case a strong stimulant, even coffee, would probably not be right because it would give him an up followed by a down. Another drug would be called for which would give him a steady flow of energy. What Kasparov was saying by his protest was 'Let Karpov take one type of drug before the game which will help him—I can't prevent that—but don't allow him to vary the drug from position to position.' "

"Where did you learn about this?" I asked.

"I read about the protest in the newspapers, but the details were related to me recently by some Soviet grandmaster friends in a tournament in Reykjavik. The grandmasters said that Kasparov was complaining openly about the matter."

Alburt had endless inside stories about Karpov and Kasparov, the Mafialike tactics of the Soviet chess establishment and the Machiavellian wheelings and dealings of Florencio Campomanes. He listed recent examples of payoffs and political blackmail in the world of international chess and described in minute detail how a grandmaster sleuth goes about identifying a fixed game between two other grandmasters.

Alburt is the Bob Woodward of the chess world, but for a fan like me who dreams about the resurgence of Tal and about Kasparov's flamboyant sacrifices, maybe it's better not to know too much. The inside dope is depressing, and being a chess fan is difficult enough without it.

CHESS
PARENTS

In the fall of 1985, before the start of an elementary school chess tournament, I found myself standing next to the father of one of the highest-rated sixth-grade players in the country. I complimented him on his son's recent results and he said some nice things about Josh. We were working at being casual, but we were also measuring each other and doing the kind of chess calculation that most chess parents are proficient at. According to a recently published rating list, Joshua's playing strength had taken a big jump and was now nearly identical to that of the man's son, a fact that was reflected in the body English and strained banalities of our conversation.

"It's a nice day," I said cheerfully. Since he was playing against older children, there wasn't much pressure on eight-year-old Josh to win today, and therefore not much pressure on me.

"Too nice to be inside all day playing chess," said the other father, his voice catching a little in his throat.

There were sixty elementary-age children playing in this tournament, and the man's son was considered the one to beat. For a time, it had been heady for him to be the father of the top player, but now it was largely a burden. If his son finished in any position other than first place, they would leave the gymnasium feeling depressed, hardly able to look at each other. Walking past rows of cafeteria tables holding the second- or third-place trophy for his son, he would avoid the eye contact and salutations of other parents, particularly the father and mother of the winner, who would be looking around for praise from parents and coaches, ready to offer assurance to the sixth grader's father that his boy would win next time. Whenever his kid lost he could feel the other parents climbing all over his back. It was like drowning. Parents of weaker players were silently indicting him for having focused so much energy on chess for the past four or five years, for not having been more relaxed and worldly about the game, like themselves. Parents of strong young players like Josh were licking their chops, moving in for the kill. On the way home, he and his son would argue bitterly about what went wrong in the critical game.

The father of the sixth grader glanced at the rating sheet that was taped on the wall and shook his head. "I've never seen the competition so tough in a local tournament," he said, trying to find a way to justify a loss. "You're not kidding," I said, feeling relaxed because of the other father's uneasiness. In a small corner of my mind I began to calculate: Josh is two and a half years younger than the other boy; think how strong he'll be when he's a sixth grader. If things go perfectly he could be a master at twelve, and no one will be able to touch him. And if he's a master by the sixth grade, think of how much better he'll be six years after that. At this moment, while the other father tried to force a smile, Joshua's horizon seemed limitless; he was way ahead of the pack, and I had conveniently forgotten about younger players like Jeff Sarwer, Morgan Pehme and John Valoria, who could already play competitively with my son. They didn't fit neatly into my blue-sky projections.

IT'S PAINFUL FOR the parent of an eleven- or twelve-year-old to deal with the challenge of a younger player. It's as if his child were being personally attacked, or as if the parent himself were being displaced. Despite the steady improvement of a talented child, there is always someone catching up, someone a little smarter, a little better. The parents of the strongest players live nervously with a sense of the irremediable ticking of the clock. When people refer to a six-year-old as a prodigy, it seems to imply that he or she is the only one in the world with this gift. That there may be other little kids with even greater aptitude is a fact that parents tend to resist. But by the time a player is twelve and has been studying for four or five years, he is no longer evaluated by what he might be but by his results and his rating. Unless the child is truly a genius, it is difficult for him and his parents to continue to believe that he will be the next Fischer or Kasparov, both of whom were playing at master strength in early adolescence. Almost overnight, the magic and charm, the admiration and compliments, the seemingly open-ended potential are replaced by limitations and fast-receding possibilities. The little genius is suddenly referred to as a solid player but without the creative imagination or exceptional memory needed to reach the top echelon of the adult chess world. It is always hard to say exactly why his game didn't evolve. Perhaps his early success was more the result of an excellent chess education than of exceptional talent—to a certain extent, a parent can manufacture a top young player by sending him to good teachers and forcing him to study—or perhaps the child simply lost his drive.

"HOW'S YOUR WORK?" I asked the parent of the older boy, trying to steer the conversation away from chess.

"It's a bad time for me," he answered with a frankness that surprised me. "Things are frantic. I've been working on a project for the last two years. It was on the back burner, but all of a sudden there's been a flurry of interest and money has become available to do it."

"That sounds great."

The way he nodded indicated that it ought to be but wasn't. "My boy's in the sixth grade," he said. "This is his last year to win the nationals. I can't walk away from him now. What choice do I have? The deal is gonna have to wait."

For both of us the winter and early spring would be shadowed by the approach of this event so filled with portent. To chess parents, winning the nationals is the gold at the end of the rainbow, the payoff for all the hard work. It is glory, pictures in newspapers, the adulation of children and parents, tangible evidence to nonchess friends that you may not be completely crazy; even more, to yourself it is concrete proof that your child's ability is something significantly more than your own wild hopes and projected dreams.

But for the parent of the sixth grader, the nationals also represented an enormous relief, a finish line. After coaching and suffering through six years of scholastic tournaments, he intended to back away from chess after the nationals. He was emotionally exhausted and worried that weekend after weekend of tension might be ruining his health. After years of allowing his young son's chess life to intrude on his own priorities, it was time to put his house in order, he said. But maybe he also welcomed the end of the tournament grind because in his heart of hearts he knew that his son would never be another Bobby Fischer. Or perhaps he was simply kidding himself; the drug would prove to be too potent, and after the nerve-racking event in Charlotte, North Carolina, he'd tousle his kid's short black hair and start planning for the next tournament.

WHEN A PARENT first learns that his child has chess talent he revels in it. The earliest games are more a form of children's art than a contest with a winner and a loser. While the child is discovering the game, the parents delight in his precocious concentration, in his rapture over complexities, in his naïve ingenuities. His first attacks are like little poems. "Look what he's done," they say to each other; "Look what *we've* done" is what they may be feeling. One father of a seven-year-old told me that the first time his son played eight or nine moves blindfolded he began to cry; it was like beholding a miracle.

Over the years, the parents of all gifted players witness little miracles. One evening when Josh was nine we walked through Washington Square Park on our way home, licking ice-cream cones. It was a cool spring evening and every chess table was occupied except for one, where an out-of-town master sat with his pieces set up, waiting for an opponent. Josh wanted to play, but the chess master was clearly put off by the challenge of a young boy and said disdainfully that he never played for less than two dollars a game. I am against Josh's playing for money, but this time I agreed. Perhaps because of the fragrant spring air or the supercilious expression with which the man moved his pieces, Josh had an unusual composure and power that evening. He was able to focus all his knowledge and will into a force that was almost palpable. He was playing the game the way he would play it someday, and the dozen chess players watching nodded quietly, seeming to know from the start that he would win. Josh knew it also and was smiling broadly over his decisive combination long before the master knocked over his king and disgustedly tossed two crumpled bills out of his pocket.

One would think that an eight- or nine-year-old could no more defeat a master than beat an NBA player in a game of one-on-one. But it is an unexplained and wondrous phenomenon that in chess, as well as in music and mathematics, a gifted child is capable of the creativity and genius of an exceptional adult. The parent of one gifted little boy said that when her son played brilliantly she felt as though she were the mother of Jesus.

THE PARENTS' JOY in their child's precocious play is compromised by nervousness over competition with other kids and by fear of failure. In a children's tournament one can always tell the winners from the losers. Those who have been defeated come out of the playing room with pasty faces; they have trouble speaking, and some of them cry uncontrollably. Winners smile broadly and walk with bounce. At their first tournaments fathers and mothers find themselves emotionally skewered. It doesn't seem appropriate to be rooting for the heartrending sadness of another little kid, but there is really little choice; a parent doesn't want his own child to feel bereft. Hearts harden, and soon the parent of a good player revels in his child's wins against other children.

Other parents, after watching their son's or daughter's painful defeats, remove their child from tournament chess, deciding it isn't worth it. One talented and enthusiastic seven-year-old cried bitterly for twenty minutes whenever he lost a tournament game. His mother, a psychologist, patiently explained to her son that these games weren't important enough to get upset about. "Chess isn't about living and dying," she said, and she urged him to put his life in perspective. Soon the child stopped crying, but he began to lose more regularly; then he stopped playing altogether. Apparently, if one is to be a good chess player one's body and soul must resist any notion of defeat; a player must despise losing in order to struggle for the win. Great players feel traumatized when they lose, and perhaps as a consequence rarely do so.

When chess parents talk about their kids, they try to be offhand about it. As if Jimmy's gift were a delicate flower to enjoy, they try to recapture the spirit of those first moments when defeat and their own emotional investment had yet to become factors and little Jimmy was Magellan first navigating the sixty-four squares. With their friends they may talk about the aesthetics of the game or about the advantages of learning logical thinking as justification for the amount of effort they expend, but for the parents of the top players, all too often winning becomes the dominant motivation. If the child wins he is happy; if he loses he feels miserable or even inadequate as a human being. If he is a highly rated player he worries about his reputation, and his parents may worry about it even more. Troubling though it may be, in time they discover that it has become *their* reputation as well. If he wins a lot they are credited both inside and outside the chess world as being parents of "that brilliant child"; if he begins to do poorly they may feel loss, anger or even shame.

Losing often takes the form of denial. A parent will rarely attribute his son's loss to a brilliant combination played by his opponent. Rather, his kid made a simple oversight or was confronted by an opening he had never seen before, or the tournament director gave him unfair pairings, or he was tired or sick. He wasn't really beaten; he merely slipped up or had bad breaks. This allows the parent to continue to plot his child's future relatively unencumbered by limitations.

CHESS PLAYERS OF all ages are interested in comparing themselves with other players. First- and second-grade children compare their numbers—900 or 1000 or 1050—against one another, and also against Kasparov's and Fischer's numbers: 2740 and 2780. The difference doesn't seem so great. When you're six or seven, becoming a grandmaster doesn't appear to be hard; it's only a matter of playing a little better and getting a higher number. No matter how good or bad they are, the littlest kids are convinced they'll win the next game, and even after they have lost several and have no chance to win a trophy, they play on as if first place were in reach. They all believe that someday they'll be great players. At scholastic tournaments their naïveté and optimism are infectious and lighten the dreary stairwells and hallways where they wait with their parents for the next round. But when fathers and mothers compare the ratings of their children, this activity takes on an importance that goes far beyond chess ability and technique. Parents glow when talking about their kid's recent wins and fast-ascending rating. It is as if numbers on a bimonthly rating sheet reflected the very essence and value of the child.

"The reason why parents put so much into chess has to do with its myth as an intellectual game," says Sunil Weeramantry, who has coached more scholastic national champions during the past six years than any other teacher in the United States. "In this country there is no payoff for chess talent, as there is for, say, tennis, but some parents are still willing to go to extremes to support the play of their kids. They do it because they're in love with the idea that they've spawned a genius. But in point of fact chess aptitude does not necessarily translate into general intelligence." Indeed, there have been grandmasters who were illiterate, and many masters have no more than average intelligence. There are examples of learning-disabled and even retarded people who play chess proficiently. Both Weeramantry and Bruce Pandolfini assert that any adult with normal intelligence can become a chess master over time with regular study. Still, in our culture interest and proficiency in chess connote superior intelligence, and the parents of enthusiastic little players are infatuated with this idea.

Some parents of scholastic champions insist that their kids do little studying on their own. Their kids are well-rounded and busy, they say; the child simply doesn't have much time to practice or take lessons; it's just that he or she has such a knack for the game that it doesn't seem to matter. They would have you believe that their child was born with a precise understanding of rook-and-pawn endgame technique and an encyclopedic knowledge of the openings. Conversely, those children with a reputation for study are denigrated for their lack of raw aptitude, although all the top players take regular lessons and study a great deal. For all his genius, Bobby Fischer probably studied chess harder than any other player who ever lived.

In this small and intense world, the breakdown of boundaries between parent and child is almost inevitable. An eight- or nine-year-old needs his parents at the tournament to make sure he eats lunch and knows how to set the clock, to see that he's not pestered or intimidated by other parents who are looking for an edge, and to ensure that he is not taken advantage of by a careless tournament director. The parent is more than a fan; while he roots as if each tournament were the finals at Wimbledon, he is also defending the child's interests and attending to details. But in the emotional tumult of wins and losses, a parent may misperceive his importance or be too heavy-handed. Some parents don't believe that their kids can win a game if they are not in attendance. One mother who hasn't the slightest idea of how to play stands by the door of the tournament room with her eyes closed, her lips moving and her fists clenched. For hours she incants a secret mantra that will give her son the strength and concentration to win. After his important victories, she is convinced that she was the difference, and after his losses she blames herself for not trying hard enough. One father, a surgeon, quivers as he agonizes over his son's games. If you speak to him while the child is calculating a move, the man's voice cracks into falsetto, his face white with strain. Part of him strives to be casual and civil, but his body language says, How can you speak to me while my son is thinking?

As a pregame ritual, some parents hassle tournament directors and other parents about every detail. For example, they may argue with all the force and dignity of their professional personae that their child's chess clock should be used for the game instead of his opponent's identical clock, or that their kid's chess pieces should be the ones selected. A few parents become violent under the pressure, and when things don't go their way or when their kids lose, they curse and challenge other parents or tournament directors to fight.

AT THE END of the first round of the 1985 New York City Primary Championship, held at the Manhattan Chess Club, the mother of a seven-year-old was crying. She said that the father of her son's first-grade opponent had whispered moves to his son. Every time her boy took a piece, this father became red in the face and smacked the table with his fist. Her son won the game anyway, but afterward the other boy's mother glared at her with hatred and she didn't know how to respond.

An hour later two other fathers were arguing. One of them wanted to lodge an official protest because a child watching his son's game had made a comment. "What did he say?" the other father inquired.

"It doesn't matter."

"Your son won. It doesn't sound as if you have anything to protest about."

"Don't you dare tell me when I should or shouldn't lodge a protest."

While we were killing time over coffee as our kids played an early round in the primary championship, Kalev Pehme, the father of a brilliant little player, said to me, "I don't mind spending all my free time on Morgan's chess. He has more talent for chess than I have for anything I do." It was a disarming admission. "Did you notice that in the ratings he's the number-one seven-year-old in the country?" Kalev went on. We are both writers, but whenever we get together our conversation invariably turns to scholastic chess, and we brag about the prowess of our seven- and nine-year-old sons like old men celebrating the professional accomplishments of their grown children.

Last year Josh won this tournament, which is generally considered the most important scholastic tournament besides the nationals. He had just turned eight, and for me this first major victory was filled with novelty, charm and promise. It was an event which somehow connected my cuddly baby boy to the young man he would someday be. Now, in 1985, he was one of the older children in the primary division and was seeded first. Parents and children expected him to win the championship a second time, and being the favorite seemed burdensome. "It's much better not to be the number-one-rated player," Josh said; he still had to sweat through his games and win, but the payoff would be less special. Although he was the highest-rated third-grade player in the country and was playing well now, during the past year he had learned that other little kids could beat him and that he was likely to have ups and downs. Once when he was feeling depressed over a lost game I remarked that he was probably playing as well as Fischer had at eight, and he answered glumly, "Well, he must have gotten a lot better very fast."

During the first day of the tournament, children who had finished would come by to watch Josh's game. They would discuss his attacks and wonder how they stacked up against him. "Did you ever lose to a lower-rated player?" one little kid asked him as if he were addressing Dave Winfield.

After the first round, the father of Josh's opponent came over and asked me timidly, "Did Josh say anything about how my son played?"

In passing Josh had mentioned that it had been an easy win. "He said your son played a terrific game," I lied, watching the man hang on my words.

Joshua's reputation had invested him with powers beyond his playing ability. Children were afraid of him; they blundered when playing against him or offered draws when they had strong positions. But only two months before he had wanted to stop playing, and despite his restored enthusiasm, Bonnie and I were keenly aware of his vulnerability.

GOING INTO THE last round Joshua's score was 4–1 and Morgan's was 5–0. If Josh beat Morgan, they would tie for first place. During the last rounds parents were ordered to stay out of the playing room to eliminate accusations of cheating and to allow the kids to play without distraction.

We waited by the door. "You're lucky that you don't get nervous," I joked with Kalev, whose face was white and trembling. Our friendship is one of co-conspirators. Kalev shamelessly plots and plans Morgan's assaults on the chess world; his ambition has no boundaries, and the two of us trade fantasies about how great our kids are going to be. But sometimes Kalev's fantasies make me nervous, because if Morgan, who is younger, were to win everything in sight, there would be nothing left for Josh.

"Hey, Josh, you're losing," I heard one of the kids exclaim behind the closed door, and I could see Kalev try to restrain a smile.

At primary tournaments, little kids milling in and out of the playing room give news flashes to desperate parents: "Josh is worse through the opening," "Josh is down two pawns" or "Josh has a positional advantage." The rumors are intoxicating and unsettling. Often the parent is depending on the acumen of the weakest players, because the strongest play more complicated games, which take more time. Usually a player will glance at the top board as he leaves the tournament room. Often he counts the pieces wrong; more often he misses the attack and only counts the pieces. Still, a parent has nothing else to go on.

The door swings open and I glimpse Joshua's expression. He looks upset, so I'm sure he's losing. I see a blur of pieces and am instantly convinced that he has fewer on the board. He must have lost his queen; that's why his blur looks smaller than the other kid's. How could he lose his queen to that fish? Irrationality overwhelms me, and even if the tournament director were to come out and report the position as one favorable to my son, I would still feel the defeat in my bones.

"Don't believe him. Josh will pull it out," Kalev said in response to the latest rumor flashing past on its way to the Coke machine. Kalev always says this when Josh is losing; it's like knocking on wood. Even when my son is playing children other than Morgan, Kalev is conflicted. He wants Josh to win because we are friends, but he also roots for him to lose; he would like Morgan to have the higher rating. I feel similarly ambivalent when his son plays.

"No, he's down material, he's gonna lose," I said, using the same tactic against him. I've held a crying Morgan on my knee, kissed his salty face and at the same time felt relieved that he lost. It would be agonizing for Josh to have his younger friend leapfrog ahead of him on the rating list.

After our kids had been playing for about thirty minutes, Morgan had to go to the bathroom. He waited for a few minutes outside the door with his father but someone was inside. A tiny, cherubic child who at that time could have passed for five, Morgan was becoming upset; his clock was ticking. Finally Bonnie took him by the hand to a bathroom on the next floor.

A few minutes after they returned, a woman, a regular at the Manhattan Chess Club, came over and whispered in my ear. "Fred, did you watch Morgan when he went to the bathroom?"

"Why would I? Of course not."

"You have to be careful," she said in a singsong voice. "One of the fathers told me that Kalev will take any opportunity to give moves to Morgan." I was too nervous and abstracted to focus on this remark until afterward. I knew that Kalev would never cheat against Joshua or anyone else. Some parents routinely start rumors about cheating by children and parents as a tactic. At the very least, such an accusation compromises the win or the spirit of one because it is difficult to disprove. Or perhaps it is not a tactic, but merely the raw manifestation of a parent's conviction that his child simply cannot be bettered by another kid.

Eventually Joshua won the game, but Morgan won the city championship on a tiebreak, meaning that his opponents in the earlier rounds had better results in the tournament than Joshua's.

DURING SEVERAL TOURNAMENTS in 1985, I observed one father, who was about six foot six and had the overweight build of a retired defensive lineman, stationing himself squarely in front of his son's opponent and staring at him throughout the game like Vladimir Zoukhar, the Russian parapsychologist who used to glare at opponents for Anatoly Karpov. His son, a year older than Joshua, was an exceptionally good player and would have won most of his games regardless of where his father stood. The man was devoted to his son's chess, took him to the best teachers and traveled with him on weekends to tournaments. It was his dream that his boy would win the Aspis Award for the best player in the country under thirteen.

During the lunch break in one tournament that fall, Joshua was still playing, and this zealous father came over to Bonnie and offered to bring back a sandwich for him. Bonnie gladly accepted; unfortunately, in her preoccupation with the game, she forgot to pay the man. That afternoon, when our two children began to play each other, he stormed over to her and demanded his money, and later, when his son's position deteriorated, he walked from parent to parent, describing how Bonnie had tried to avoid paying him for Joshua's lunch.

That tunafish sandwich was the beginning of a big problem for my family. A few months later our kids played again in a tournament at the Manhattan Chess Club, and the father began impugning our family character to anyone who would listen by describing the tunafish sandwich episode. It was a long, tough game. Bruce happened to be working in his office, and at one point he walked into the tournament room for a few minutes to check the positions of the more interesting games. That evening I received many phone calls from parents and officials at the club who relayed the assertion by this father that Pandolfini had signaled the winning moves to Josh by an elaborate system of ear-pulls and winks. For weeks he insisted to people that Joshua could not have beaten his son without Pandolfini's covert assistance, and again recounted the sandwich incident as proof of the corrupt moral fiber of the Waitzkin family. I recalled Russian grandmaster Boris Gulko's helpless rage when former world champion Tigran Petrosian claimed in *Izvestia* that Gulko's exceptional results in 1975 must have been the result of cheating by his friends.

My relationship with this parent continued to deteriorate. The next time our kids played he grabbed me by the arm, pushed me against the wall and said that we should go outside and fight. By now Josh had become reluctant to play his son, fearing what would happen to me during the game. That winter, many parents and tournament directors were confronted by this father. During one tournament he spat at the well-mannered mother of a strong sixth grader, a rival of his son for the Aspis Award. From his behavior, one might conclude that this man is deranged; yet I've been told by several people who know him outside the chess environment that he is a decent and civilized human being.

THE VOYAGE OF vicarious glory is a risky one for parents. "We have absolutely no social life," said the hardworking parents of a brilliant young player, who travel to tournaments every weekend and on most vacations with their talented son. Some of these events are three-day affairs, and these parents, who hardly know how to move the pieces, spend seventy-two hours holed up in a stuffy hotel. Everywhere there are games, the analysis of games, the tension of games, the anticipation of more games. There are games on every sofa and easy chair, games over hamburgers and french fries, games behind every pillar in the lobby. Such an event is hallucinogenic and relentless. While their child plays, the parents move listlessly, like fish in an aquarium, from table to table. They feel out of place and so tense that they can barely speak to each other. They are intelligent people, embarrassed about their avarice, but when their kid is winning, intoxication washes aside reservations. They've decided that it makes their son too nervous when they watch him play, so to pass the hours they look at the games of other talented kids, smiling supportively and feeling guilty about rooting against them.

If you ask these parents about their aspirations for their child, they answer swiftly, "Are you crazy? We don't want him to grow up to be a chess player." It is hard to believe them; why else are they devoting body and soul to his development? Yet their zealous support may ensure his choice of some other occupation. For some fathers and mothers, passion for their child's success has become so gargantuan that the kid's own predilections have been subsumed by their need. Some of the best young players go to tournaments with their wildly supportive parents to satisfy Mom and Dad rather than for love of the game, and as teenagers they will probably give it up when they discover other interests.

ROMAN

The day Grandmaster Roman Dzindzichashvili took up residence in the southwest corner of Washington Square Park everything seemed to change. Players walked differently—more stiffly or with a self-conscious shuffle or with a list in his direction. While appraising complicated positions, they assumed various affectations: a wink, a shrill laugh or a melancholic expression. One young player, a shy psychotic who spent much of his day mumbling quietly beneath the trees, began to flaunt his madness. Within eyeshot of the great grandmaster he would fall to his knees and make obscene sexual gestures at every woman who walked through the park. Another player, who for years had felt it necessary to incant the most vulgar language imaginable in order to play his best, suddenly assumed an attitude of understatement and urbane politeness; he moved his pawns with an uplifted pinky as if he were toasting royalty with an elegant wine. Some players stopped playing altogether, preferring to crowd around Dzindzi's (pronounced Gin Gi's) games. "For a glimpse of genius," they would say, but perhaps their abstinence was more an act of shame, so that this grandmaster, recognized throughout the world for his brilliancies, would not notice their fumbling play and wasted lives in the park. But others were redeemed by Dzindzi's presence; it was proof that their way of life was valid, even noble. One thin black man about forty, with knife scars crisscrossing his face, pronounced the name Roman with the familiarity of a dear, lifelong friend, but I don't believe that they ever spoke.

He was a timid man and a weak player who lost most of his games. Year after year, during the outdoor months, he played with a brave little smile, though his game seemed to decline steadily. One afternoon, while Roman played blitz at an adjacent table, I asked the black man what he would do in the winter, when it was too cold to play in the park.

"I'll stay in my room studying," he answered with a fierce pride that I hadn't noticed before. He didn't have the money to go to the chess shop in the cold weather, so he would study in preparation for the following spring. In effect he was saying, "Bobby Fischer used to play here. Now Roman does, and so do I."

AT THE TIME, Roman Dzindzichashvili had the third- or fourth-highest rating in the United States, and most grandmasters would readily have admitted that he was the most talented active player in the country. Before emigrating to the United States in the late 1970s he had been a powerful grandmaster in the Soviet Union. Boris Gulko said that if Dzindzi had been born with the dedication to match his immense talent he might one day have challenged for the world championship. But now he was fed up with tournament chess in the United States, he would explain obliquely; others speculated that lately his gambling proclivities had made him unattractive to organizers, who may have stopped offering him accommodations or waiving his entrance fees in order to induce him to attend their tournaments. Whatever the reasons, in the summer of 1986 Dzindzi was a fixture of the chess corner of Washington Square, and every player was affected by his presence much in the same way that those in a small community are touched by that of a world-famous neighbor.

Dzindzi is a swarthy, portly man with an affable manner. Week after week he wore the same black short-sleeved shirt and scuffed black shoes. He was in the park all the time. At seven in the morning, when all the other tables were deserted, his heavy, unshaven face smeared with sleep or sleeplessness, he could be found playing chess or backgammon with some wretched soul who looked as if he hadn't eaten in a month. At midnight, beneath a dim park light, he would be playing blitz, gin rummy or poker with a cadre of regulars until the police drove them out. His life was a continuum of games; he passed relentlessly from one to the next and hardly seemed to notice what or with whom he was playing. It was clear that Dzindzi couldn't exist without playing something. If there was a pause, a half hour without a game, his brow would furrow in concern, and he would begin to feel the first unpleasant edge of agitation. He would start pacing from table to table until someone called him over with a gambling proposition. While he played there was rarely any expression on his face—certainly no joy, only a tired smile occasionally in return for a compliment or for a five-dollar bill after a checkmate.

Despite his incontestable genius, Dzindzi frequently lost; he was such a powerful player that in order to get opponents he had to offer staggering odds. He was a terrible gambler and everyone knew it. Whatever he offered, his opponent would shake his head; "No, no, not enough. I'm a patzer and you play as well as Korchnoi." Then Dzindzi would give a weary nod; it was true, he did play as well as Korchnoi and had once been Kasparov's teacher, but what did it matter now; let's get on with the game. His opponents knew that he had to play, in the same way that a shark must swim; he would always give better odds rather than risk losing the action. He gave competent players rook odds, sometimes even queen odds, and would offer international masters a five-minute to two-minute time advantage. Or he would play them equally and offer five-to-one game odds, meaning he had to win five games in a row in order to collect the bet. But if that wasn't enough, he'd give seven-to-one game odds, or even nine-to-one, against players with an international reputation, and when the match finally began his face would sink heavily in relief. His games were filled with magic— intriguing complexities, astounding sacrifices—sparkling games that contrasted oddly with his bored countenance and half-closed eyes.

In the afternoons aficionados who were strangers to the park began coming to watch Dzindzi play. In good weather forty or fifty people jammed around his table, jostling one another for a better glimpse. They cheered his sacrifices and rustled with excitement at his puzzling constructions. Then, after four wins in a row, he would titillate his admirers with yet another outrageous sacrifice, but this one wouldn't quite work, and he would lose the game and his bet. Within a few weeks he didn't have a nickel and owed half the people in the park. But losing didn't seem to bother him, and it made the park regulars feel special to lend him money so that he could play on.

During Dzindzi's months in Washington Square he was shadowed everywhere by a thirty-year-old man from California, a weak master who craved chess genius more than anything else in life and had latched onto Dzindzi in a move of desperation. If he could be around Dzindzi twenty-four hours a day, watch each game he played, listen to his chess ideas and his philosophy of life, beg him for tidbits of advice, observe the way he walked and breathed, his eating and even his sleeping habits, then maybe he too could become a great player. He knew that it was his last chance; it is rare for a thirty-year-old master suddenly to become much stronger.

This man was forever at Dzindzi's side. While the grandmaster played blitz against a patzer, the Californian scrutinized the games as if Alekhine were playing Capablanca for the world championship. When Dzindzi was hungry, the man followed him to a sandwich shop. When Dzindzi slept on a park bench, his head on a folded newspaper, his devoted acquaintance sat nearby studying a book and waiting for the grandmaster to wake up. The Californian was an extremely intelligent man and a keen observer. One morning, while Dzindzi slept, he spoke about the ruined lives in this corner of Washington Square and speculated like a sociologist on the social environment that allowed such degradation. "What a waste," he said sadly, flicking his hand in the direction of the grandmaster.

In Los Angeles the weak master was a law student, and he said that soon he would be returning there to finish his degree. Almost gaily, he referred to his time in the park as a final hedonistic fling before his real work in life began. He talked with warmth and nostalgia about his close-knit family and about the beauty of the mountains and the Pacific near his home.

A few minutes later Dzindzi roused himself like a sleeping bear, and instantly the Californian stood up and stretched. As Dzindzi blinked his eyes and scratched his tousled black hair, the weak master smiled broadly, as if he had been touched by the vibrant potential of a new day. In a few minutes the two men were preparing themselves for an eight A.M. poker game.

Whenever we chatted subsequently the Californian made it a point to say that he was planning to leave within a few days. As the weeks passed and the weather turned cooler, we stopped speaking, but whenever I paused on my way through the park to look at one of Dzindzi's games, the Californian smiled at me and shook his head with a certain irony.

THE MOST SHOCKING event to take place on the day of Dzindzi's arrival in Washington Square was the departure of Israel Zilber. From the moment Zilber had first slumped at a table, ready to play all comers for a dollar, it was clear that he was far and away the best player there. From time to time all the regulars tried to unseat him, but no one had ever offered a serious challenge. Zilber would usually win, even against strong masters, all the while arguing raucously with his private voices or trying to soothe them with soft Latvian lullabies. Wearing a large sheriff's badge on his grungy vest, he truly perceived himself to be the best chess player in the world and occasionally spoke incoherently about his victories over Karpov and Kasparov. Had Zilber remained sane and in Russia, these games might have actually taken place. But even if he weren't beset with raging voices and hallucinations, his megalomania might be explained by the park itself, because in time, the park gets into the blood of all its players and becomes the world.

When Dzindzichashvili arrived, Zilber's voices apparently spoke to him about self-preservation and the need at certain vulnerable times in a man's life for a stressfree environment. The cruel logic of chess was too powerful even for schizophrenia. Evidently Dzindzi was too strong an opponent for the Sheriff, who had known the grandmaster decades before in Russia, and must have recognized him as from another life. Zilber packed his chipped army of pieces, clutched his bulging suitcase of rags, hunting knives and girlie magazines in one hand, his outsized billy club in the other, and tottered away from Washington Square. It must have been like searching for a new frontier, and one might have supposed that Zilber was bitter at having to leave, except that in his new home, a tiny strip of park with several chess tables eight blocks south on Sixth Avenue, he chatted just as before to the trees overhead and looked happy enough. His new location was very close to our apartment, and Josh and I passed him several times a day. Except for an occasional scouting trip to Washington Square, Zilber was always at this new place, his pieces set up, exchanging remarks with his voices while waiting for a challenge. With the exception of half a dozen games with Josh, I never saw anyone stop to play a game with him for all the months he was there. Heaven knows where he found the money to survive.

IN THE AUTUMN, Dzindzichashvili left Washington Square, and life quickly returned to normal. The player who had respectfully given up his vulgar language began to curse again; the twenty-year-old psychotic quieted down and stopped harassing women. In the chill of fall the play at the tables seemed crisper than in the summer, and while the regulars waited for a game they talked about their winter plans. Some were looking for part-time work; others would try to survive on welfare. When they could afford it, they would meet at the chess shop on Thompson Street.

As soon as Dzindzi left, Zilber returned to his old table, and his game was as sharp as on the day he had departed.

SEARCHING
FOR
BOBBY
FISCHER

In the fall of 1986, I flew to California to find Bobby Fischer. During my interviews with his friends and travels to his old haunts, it occurred to me that if it weren't for Fischer, Josh probably wouldn't be a serious player today; in fact, many of our best young talents wouldn't be studying and competing. In the seventies, Fischer elevated the game to national importance and convinced the world that being a chess player was respectable, even romantic; he captured many more imaginations than he did enemy kings. Today, parents of talented players are enthralled when their kid plays well and someone observes reverently, "Maybe he's the next Fischer." They encourage him, and prod him when he doesn't feel like studying. They tell him about Fischer's dedication to the game when he was eight and what it was like that summer watching him beat Spassky on television. As the child's rating soars, his parents begin daydreaming about world championships. They spend whole weekends standing in narrow aisles between rows of chess players watching their child weigh the relative value of pawn to e4 or bishop to f3. When Josh engineers a lovely combination or sacrifices his rook for mate, the electric excitement that runs through me and the pride that lingers is somehow justifiable in this practical and fiercely materialistic era largely because of Fischer.

AFTER WINNING THE world championship in 1972, Bobby Fischer became an American folk hero, like Daniel Boone or John Wayne.

He had bragged to the world that he was going to beat the Russians and he had delivered. He had become the ultimate chess genius in a land inimical to talented young players. While for the most part he had educated himself as a player, Spassky and other Russians had been provided a systematic chess education by the state. While Fischer accomplished his victory working alone, the Russian champion was backed by a vast machine of sports doctors, therapists and scores of grandmasters to analyze during the match, a national effort much like a contemporary America's Cup assault.

At the time, George Steiner wrote of Fischer: "He has made world headlines and popular features of a totally abstract, esoteric, terribly narrow cerebral hobby. He has boosted ten- and twentyfold the financial rewards at the summit. . . . He has generated a chess fever across the United States. . . . These are staggering achievements for a twenty-nine-year-old loner whose bad manners and indifferences to customary social behavior and to the personal feelings of others verge on the transcendent."*

According to those closest to him in the early seventies, Fischer was a hugely unattractive person. Consider this description by Brad Darrach, a *Life* journalist who wrote frequently about him:

> Bobby is tall and broad-shouldered; his face is clean-cut, masculine, attractive. But on second glance this impression dislocates into a number of odd parts. His head, for instance. That amazing brain is lodged in a small oval skull that doesn't reach very far above the ears. His low forehead makes his jaw look large, at certain angles almost Neanderthal. When he feels weak or uncertain he resembles the dopey kid Jerry Lewis used to portray. Yet there is a sense of danger about Bobby. When he is angry or confident his face is alert but unthinking, the face of a big wild animal that hunts for a living. His eyes are like a tiger's, with the same yellow-green serenity and frightening emptiness. When he laughs, his wide, full-lipped mouth opens into a happy cave filled with white teeth. Most of his facial expressions are rudimentary displays of fear, hunger, anger, pleasure, pain, suspicion, interest—all the emotions a man or animal can have without feeling close to any other man or animal. I have rarely seen him register sympathy, invitation, acknowledgment, humor, tenderness, playfulness. And never love.

* George Steiner, *Fields of Force* (New York: Viking Press, 1972), p. 28.

Bobby wears a business suit about as naturally as a python wears a necktie. He stands six one, weighs close to 190, and a padded jacket makes his shoulders seem so wide his head looks "like a pea sitting on a ruler," somebody said. His torso is flaccid, his arms girlishly soft. But his hips and thighs are powerful and his movements vigorous. Sometimes they are comically awkward. Bobby walks twice as fast as the average hiker, but he walks the way a hen runs—and this hen fills a doorway. He comes on head forward, feet wide apart and toes turned in, shoulders lurching side to side, elbows stuck out, fingers flipping. Fastening his eyes on a point about four miles distant and slightly above everybody else's head, he charges toward it through the densest crowds.

Bobby functions like Frankenstein's creature, a man made of fragments connected by wires and animated by a monstrous will. When the will collapses or the wires cross, Bobby cannot execute the simplest acts. When he loses interest in a line of thought, his legs may simply give out, and he will shuffle off to bed like an old man. Once, when I asked him a question while he was eating, his circuits got so befuddled that he jabbed his fork into his cheek.

Bobby seems to keep only one thought in his mind at once, and a simple thought at that. He talks in simple sentences that lead him where he is going like steppingstones, and his voice is flat, monotonous, the color of asphalt—the voice of man pretending to be a machine so people won't be able to hurt him. But Bobby is too vital to play dead successfully. Energy again and again escapes in a binge of anger. Every night, all night, it escapes into chess. When he sits at the board, a big dangerous cat slips into his skin. His chest swells, his green eyes glow. All the life in his body flows and he looks wild and beautiful. Sprawled with lazy power, eyes half closed, he listens to the imaginary rustle of moving pieces as a tiger lies and listens to the murmur of moving reeds.*

Using tactics many considered offensive or crazy, Fischer navigated himself through life to gain his loftiest objectives. During the match against Spassky, his antics were well documented in newspaper and magazine articles. In the days before the event he had the whole world wondering whether he would show up. From hour to hour he changed his mind about playing. To his friends, some of whom were convinced that he was afraid to play, he argued that he didn't need to go to Iceland because everyone already knew

* Brad Darrach, *Bobby Fischer vs. the Rest of the World* (New York: Stein and Day, 1974), pp. 13–15.

that he was the best. For several days, his friends reserved space for him on flights to Reykjavik and pleaded with him to go. Plane after plane, loaded with passengers, waited on the runway while Fischer took walks and naps or ate sandwiches with his frenzied, exhausted companions, musing like a hyped-up Prufrock over the merits of playing or not. Henry Kissinger called and asked him to go for his country's honor, but still Bobby wouldn't commit himself. While the urbane and melancholic Spassky waited in Reykjavik, playing tennis and going to the ballet, Fischer hid out in New York, demanding more and more money. He drove the organizers of the tournament to despair and showed up in Iceland only after he had convinced everyone, including Spassky, that he wouldn't come.

Before the match Fischer had offended Icelanders by calling their country inadequate because of its lack of movie theaters and bowling alleys. He complained that Reykjavik was too far from his millions of fans. He wanted television coverage, but when a television deal was arranged and the match was about to begin he refused to play in front of the cameras, claiming that they were too distracting. He forfeited a game and threatened to leave unless Spassky agreed to play in a small room with no audience and no cameras. He argued about the choice of chess table, about his hotel room, about the noise in the auditorium, about the proximity of the audience to the players and about the lighting. He demanded that the organizers lend him a Mercedes with an automatic transmission and arrange for the private use of a swimming pool. He came late to each game and kept threatening to pull out of the match if his demands weren't met.

None of this had anything to do with chess—and yet perhaps it did. How could Spassky feel like a world champion when his opponent blithely forfeited games, saying, in effect, "I can spot you and still win easily"—and then played the games themselves almost as afterthoughts, following furious bouts of bickering, bitching, accusing, haggling and threatening? How could the Russian not be distracted by this mad whirlwind who almost incidentally made brilliant moves? Perhaps Fischer dismayed Spassky as much by calculated mayhem as by his skill over the board. But more likely he was following his instincts, psyching himself by his outrageous excesses, as John McEnroe does when he curses at referees. Throughout his career, Bobby had infuriated tournament directors with his financial demands and conditions for playing, had pulled out of tournaments when these weren't met, had psyched many world-class opponents by not acknowledging their existence and had played the game as if he were playing against himself.

In sharp contrast to the gaucheness of his antics, his contradictory demands and insults, was Fischer's deceptively simple, pure style of play. He was the monster of the chess world but the priest of play, an unrelenting chess moralist, appalled by fanciness and flair for its own sake, by moves that were inferior, even if they won.

Frank Brady's biography of Fischer describes Bobby as a player:

> Fischer's force of spirit at the board is unnerving. He rarely leaves the table and when he does, unlike other players, he has virtually no interest in the games around him. His game, his struggle, his creation, consumes him. . . . [He] is mysteriously silent. . . . He *empathizes* with the position of the moment with such intensity that one feels that a defect in his game, such as a backward Pawn or an ill-placed Knight, causes him almost physical, and certainly psychical, pain. . . .
>
> The simplistic beauty of his game is the element that confuses those he plays and produces paradoxical comments like Petrosian's: ". . . he did not play that well," referring to Fischer's magnificent victory at Palma. . . . While his opponents are clamoring for grand schemes and intricate themes, Fischer gives them precision and clarity in an almost mathematical purity.*

After the Spassky match, the public did not focus attention on Fischer's playing style or, for that matter, on his personality. His quirkiness, crassness and offensive materialism were quickly forgotten as he achieved the celebrity of a rock superstar. He had become a larger figure in his sport than any other sports figure in history. Before Fischer, professional chess in the United States was ignored by the public and played for low stakes by impoverished men who usually had to work at other jobs to exist. Despite the obscurity of his sport, he could now command the same money as

* Frank Brady, *Profile of a Prodigy* (New York: David McKay, 1974), pp. 180–81.

a heavyweight boxing champion. He was pursued by the media and feted by statesmen, kings and despots around the world. Chess organizers stood smiling and ready to bend rules to accommodate his whims, and they began to plan tournaments that would command vast international audiences.

Then Fischer made a wholly original and unexpected move by refusing to defend his title against Anatoly Karpov. Turning his back on millions of dollars, he retired into the protective fold of the Worldwide Church of God in Pasadena, a fundamentalist Christian sect that observes Saturday as the Sabbath and believes in the Second Coming. He gave the organization most of his prize money and became a recluse. No one knows precisely why.

AS I LEARNED more about Bobby Fischer's underground life, I began to wonder if he had made a kind of existential mistake, a whimsical decision that had taken on unexpected power and permanence. Perhaps over the years since his disappearance he has gradually forgotten who he once was, or else the memory has become shaky, less relevant than the forlorn life around him. Earlier in his career, he had disappeared from the chess world, once for eighteen months. It was a gambit he occasionally played, part of the larger game plan of his life. At these times, when he refused to play in tournaments and dropped out of public view, people predicted that he would never play again. He seemed to need these periods out of the public eye to replenish his fire, and he enjoyed teasing the chess world, making them beg, before surprising everyone again with the magnitude of his genius. Always he returned smoldering with fury and armed with greater strength than before. He couldn't bear to be taken for granted, to be merely the best of the lot; he needed to know that without him the game was barely surviving.

Indeed, after the Spassky match Fischer told friends that he was going to keep the championship for thirty years, and while the public slowly awakened to the fact of his disappearance, chess in the United States languished; sponsors weren't interested in putting up money for tournaments without his magical lure. Fischer had made chess and he had taken it away.

* * *

FOR MORE THAN fifteen years Fischer has walked the streets of Los Angeles in various disguises. Often he has a mangy red beard, but sometimes he is clean-shaven, like the charismatic young man on the cover of national magazines in 1972—except that now his hair has receded and the warts on his face have grown large. He won't allow a doctor to remove them; he doesn't trust doctors. Many days he rides buses, listening to talk shows through the headset of a transistor radio, gathering evidence for his political theories. Many afternoons he goes to the library to read political science and history books and to work on position papers. Late at night he works on chess.

Friends say that Fischer has tried to become more well-rounded. Sometimes he plays softball. He likes to look at the mountains and to breathe clean air. He loves Chinese food just as much as when he was the world champion, and his appetite remains astonishing. When he has the money, he goes to Mexico to practice his Spanish, but more often than not he has been broke—sometimes so broke he can't pay for coffee. His trousers and coat have become stained and baggy, and he frequently wears the shoes he bought just before his crushing match against Tigran Petrosian in 1971.

IN NEW YORK I had occasionally met with old friends of Fischer's who said they had received letters and phone calls from him. One of them proudly brandished a crumpled letter he claimed was from Bobby, showing the wrinkled sheets to friends as proof of his own celebrity, but not letting anyone read it. A woman who said that Fischer spoke to her regularly on the phone claimed that he had become infatuated with her after studying her games that had been published in *Chess Life*. She said that during their conversations he frequently tore into Kasparov's games, referring to him derisively as "Weinstein, the Jew," which she found odd, considering that his mother was Jewish. Softly, careful not to make him angry, she sometimes reasoned with him about his hostility to Jews or urged him to play again, but for the most part their relationship was a love affair through chess—an exchange of moves and positions that left her feeling light-headed and filled with yearning. When she discovered that Fischer had had a brief affair with another woman, she was deeply hurt and considered flying to California to confront him.

According to his New York friends, Fischer would talk periodically about making a comeback—perhaps even allowing one of them to make some inquiries—and then would change his mind: "I've been thinking . . ." he would begin when he was about to veto a deal. Always there was a problem: not enough money, or the organizer was Jewish and was going to make too much profit, or the playing site was too public, or he wanted a television deal— or he didn't want a television deal.

One South American grandmaster, a friend of Bobby's for more than twenty years, has spent considerable time and money trying to arrange a match in Mexico between himself and Fischer. This confrontation would be the high point of the grandmaster's life, and seeing it come to fruition has become an obsession. He has traveled across the country dozens of times to talk with Bobby, has spent months in Mexico making arrangements and has ignored his own chess career and personal life to set up this match that Fischer quibbles about and rejects time after time.

Fischer has been changing his mind and vetoing plans since 1972. It is interesting that even while he volleys back lucrative options, his friends keep trying, beseeching and humoring him, starting all over time after time to find new ways to please him. These contacts with Fischer at this phase of his life—now so tragically stunted, repetitive and predictable—are for his friends the most compelling part of their own lives. Their little secrets are so precious that I have never been sure whether they are real or totally fabricated. But their need to say what they know about him, to broadcast their friendship, is more revealing than the tidbits they whisper about his life.

The same might even be said of Boris Spassky, the former world champion, a highly cultured man. "Of course Bobby was the stronger player," he says without the slightest trace of jealousy. Year after year, he tells the same Fischer anecdotes and refers to a brief phone conversation they had as though it were a major moment in his life. Spassky has accepted his place in history as the man who lost to Bobby Fischer. Despite all of his accomplishments, it is as if his life finally achieved greatness as Fischer's foil, and that something went out of him after Bobby disappeared.

I FLEW TO California with the phone numbers of Fischer's old West Coast friends, who I hoped would put me in touch with him. For years he has refused to talk to writers; he won't read a letter unless he is paid five thousand dollars, and even then the chances are that he won't answer it; friends say he has turned down fifty thousand dollars for an interview. Still, I had the naïve idea that I would be able to find him in Pasadena or L.A., and that he would agree to talk with me. Sometimes, I reasoned to myself, a stranger can help you see things from another angle when friends screaming in your ear can't get through. I had spoken to players in both the United States and the Soviet Union who were confident that Fischer could still beat Kasparov. I had talked to businessmen and organizers in New York who said that Fischer could make millions if he would play again. Why not try? I would ask him. Is this musty little room so special? Would money and adulation be so terrible? I knew that before his disappearance he'd had differences with FIDE over the structuring of the world championship format, but Bobby and I are the same age and I also know that at forty-three I don't find the issues that consumed me at twenty-nine as important. I would suggest that it was time to change his life and that it was easier than he might think. A casual yes, and the labyrinthine arguments and obstacles that had entombed him for years would give way to some of the greatest chess creations of all time.

Sometimes it only takes a little nudge. I would tell him about Josh and the other little kids who study chess in order to be like him. You're an inspiration for some of the most talented little players in the world, I'd tell him. I could just see Josh, Bobby Fischer and me walking into Svetozar Jovanovic's chess class at Dalton.

LINA GRUMETTE'S HOME in West Hollywood is a chess salon, dark in the afternoon because of the tall shady trees that surround the two-story house that she calls a shrine to Bobby Fischer. On the walls are pictures and newspaper cartoons of him during his playing days. Often games are going on in one or more of the rooms, which are silent except for the creak of a chair and the occasional moving of a piece. Lina wanders from one game to the next to see how they are going. Here, as in chess enclaves everywhere—Jack Collins's apartment in New York, the Franklin-Mercantile Chess Club in Philadelphia, Harold Bugner's house in Alhambra or Sokolniki Park in Moscow—one feels the importance of this intense, brooding activity without being able to say exactly why. In such places men, and occasionally women, spend considerable amounts of their lives within a game. In the darkening light of late afternoon the players in Lina's house have solemn faces, and as they nod their heads over puzzling combinations, they might be davening in shul.

Lina Grumette is in her late sixties and has the frail beauty of an aging Tennessee Williams spinster. When she talks about Bobby she becomes uneasy, filtering her words, apparently concerned about what he would think if he were listening. She calls herself his chess mother. "We were very close. I worried about him," she says in a way that makes it clear that their past intimacy is still a factor in her life.

Lina described her private dinner with Bobby in Reykjavik in 1972, on a night when officials were convinced that he would pull out of the match against Spassky and return to New York the next morning. "What I said to him wasn't anything startling, but it interested him very much. It was about the Church of God, and after I'd spoken to him, he decided to play." I asked her what it was that she had said to change the course of chess history, but she only smiled and turned her head. No, she would never tell; she had promised him that she wouldn't. There are infidelities and then there are infidelities.

"After the match I got a lot of publicity without wanting it," Lina said. "I told Bobby that there were some people who wanted to interview me and that I wouldn't say anything he wouldn't like, just a few harmless sentences because I was tired of driving them all away. Bobby said, 'No. Don't talk to newspaper people.' But I was being bombarded on all sides not only by the press but by television programs, so I appeared on one, and then he wouldn't talk to me for two years. After that we talked on the phone but I only saw him once."

From Fischer's point of view Lina had been unfaithful. He has told all his friends that their associations with him must be entirely private. It is basic to his life plan. When Lina described the breakup to me she was both sad and indignant. She had been responsible for the championship match's continuing, so in a way she felt she owned a small piece of his success. Since he was a teenager, when he played in West Coast tournaments and sometimes during periods of estrangement from his mother, Bobby had lived in her house. She had covered for him a hundred times, fending off interviewers and people who came over to meet him, while he was alone upstairs studying. She felt that she had a right to a little piece of recognition, but to Fischer this was like stealing part of his genius.

ACCORDING TO HIS West Coast friends, since his break with Lina Grumette Bobby has lived for much of the past sixteen years in downtown Los Angeles, near the Union Depot. It is the seediest part of the city, Skid Row, and he has moved from one grungy hotel to the next, usually registering as "Mr. James." A couple of days after I arrived in Los Angeles, Victor Frias and I walked along Main and Hill streets, past boarded-up hotels, porno shops, the Cum Again Theater, past junkies and drunks in doorways, broken glass under our feet. Frias was spending a month in California playing in tournaments and had some time between events to take me to Fischer's old neighborhoods and to visit some of his friends. Victor was on a hot streak, coming in first or second in each of his California tournaments. His wife was pregnant, and he was hopeful that his prize money would cover his expenses for the trip. During the past several months, he had been playing as well as any player in the country, but he knew that he couldn't make it financially in the United States as a professional player and was planning to take a full-time job when he returned to New York after this last tournament binge.

One of Bobby's friends used to drop him off in the evening in front of one of the sleazy hotels in this area after they'd spent the day together looking at girls on the beach, going to bookstores or analyzing chess. Bobby rarely invited his friend up to his room, and he would step out of the car and walk past the drunks, pushers and whores without noticing them. The neighborhood was a war zone of misery, but he was living in a different orbit. According to friends, usually he rode the buses or walked around the city when he woke up in the afternoon; then, late at night, he would go over chess games on the worn pocket set he had gotten in Argentina in 1960. Now, as Victor and I walked along Hill Street, Bobby was probably no more than a few blocks away, sleeping late in a shabby little room.

I looked at my watch and remembered that Josh had played in a scholastic tournament that morning at Hunter College Elementary School, and the thought of it made my neck stiffen. It was the first time he had ever played in a tournament without my watching over his shoulder or standing vigil outside a closed door. I began to imagine that he had done poorly. Lately, Pandolfini had been telling him that he was playing the opening too mechanically; in the beginning of the game, he'd just throw his pieces out as if he didn't consider this stage a legitimate part of chess. Josh never really clicked into gear until he was a little behind. Then the fear would get to him and he'd start to see patterns and begin calculating like a computer in order to ward off disaster. Against kids he could get away with this, but he would have to start concentrating on the openings, memorizing thousands of variations, if he ever was going to be good against strong adults. Did I want him to spend the rest of his childhood memorizing variations? Would such concentration on chess leave him isolated and disfigured like Bobby? The old questions kept cropping up. Maybe Josh resisted learning the openings because he knew in his heart that he didn't want to be a player, and I wasn't listening. If he lost his games against Marc Berman, Matthew Goldman and David Arnett, I'd feel terrible and wouldn't care much about finding Bobby Fischer.

WHEN BOBBY COULD afford it, he sometimes lived in a nicer neighborhood on the corner of Wilshire and Fairfax, an area like much of Miami Beach, with small residential hotels, populated by old people sitting on porches or looking blankly out their windows. It didn't seem to matter to him where he lived or who his neighbors were. He was on the run, hiding out from reporters and old friends, but mostly making it as hard as possible for the KGB to track him down and kill him. He was certain that the Russians were afraid of him because he was the only one who could take their championship away.

Or sometimes he lived in Pasadena. In the spring of 1981, he was spotted by the district police wandering along a highway like a derelict, and when he couldn't or wouldn't tell them his address, he was jailed for vagrancy. Fischer wrote a pamphlet about the incident, entitled "I Was Tortured in the Pasadena Jailhouse," which was a best seller in chess clubs even though it never says a word about chess.

Despite all his demands for big purses and appearance fees—he consistently campaigned for material rewards for players—Bobby never really cared much about money or what it could buy. After pressing for bigger and bigger guarantees, at one point before the Spassky match he offered to play for nothing, which panicked his financial advisors. Once when he was going to play a big exhibition he was given the largest and most elegant suite at a hotel but turned it down because the view was too engaging; he wanted a little room with no view so that he could study. Fancy rooms, views and cultural sideshows like school, poetry and concerts are contemptible distractions when you are trying to accomplish more than anyone else in the history of your art.

In this respect, Fischer's life hasn't changed at all. He still studies many hours a day, so what does it matter if his window looks onto an alley and there are roaches crawling in the sink? What people tend to forget about him is that his genius was buttressed with more knowledge than that of any other player in the history of chess; no one has ever memorized as many opening variations and whole games as Bobby. He ate chess day and night and had been doing so since he was a kid. In high school he studied chess books while his teachers lectured on other subjects, and when they told him to put away his books he studied games in his head. He dropped out of school at sixteen in order to have more time to study. Later, after the break with his mother—his father had left the family when Bobby was two—he would spend most of the day and night inside his room studying. He'd analyze until two in the morning, then sleep late, and when he woke up he often went out to find more chess books.

There must have been an undercurrent of despair in this singular and fanatical dedication. Perhaps at times Fischer felt the frustration of a young mystic straining to make objects levitate, to make the squares talk to him. The stakes were high and the culture was against him. In the early fifties, a child chess prodigy was perceived as odd rather than gifted. It would have been easier for him if his genius had been for an admired endeavor like mathematics or playing the piano; in devoting his life to chess from the age of eight, he typecast himself as a weirdo and outcast. He must have felt tremendous pressure from his mother, from his teachers, who said he was wasting his life on a game, and from his schoolmates, who were learning about girls, Shakespeare and football. All this must have driven him further and deeper, and made him greater.

FISCHER FIRST BECAME interested in the Church of God in 1961. During a visit to a friend's home in Reno, he locked himself in his room for most of the night analyzing, sometimes taking a break to study the Bible. Once in a while he'd come out and talk about his ideas on religion, then return to his room. Other chess players there who hung around watching television—Bobby was convinced that the set emitted deadly rays—thought that his involvement with the Church of God would come to no good, that he was being taken in by the smooth speaking style of Ted Armstrong and that his ideas about religion and the world at large were childish or misguided. Still, no one criticized him; "We didn't want to crush his point of view," said one of them, "because he was such a great genius."

When Bobby was a teenager, people said that he might be the greatest chess player who ever lived; certainly he thought so himself, and he was the champion of his country at the age of fourteen, a unique achievement. But perhaps there's a price to be paid for such precocity. When a man is the best at what he does for his entire life, there is little room for self-questioning or doubt. Cultivated by unprecedented success, with virtually no outside editing, Fischer's ideas grew wild. Well-meaning friends who argued with him were usually dropped. Others accepted his strangeness as an aspect of genius and were on guard not to contradict him. When he was a teenager, little was said about his affection for a color photograph of Adolf Hitler. Friends reasoned that politically he was naïve; he was the ultimate prodigy with a limitless future; what did it matter that he had a few strange ideas? It was more important that his game was developing so rapidly. During a trip to the Soviet Union when he was fifteen he won a number of blitz games from the great Tigran Petrosian but was disappointed that the world champion, Vassily Smyslov, wouldn't play him.

When I asked Lina Grumette about Fischer's attraction to Nazism she instinctively brought a finger to her mouth: "Sssshhh." Then in a hushed voice she said, "You know, he thought that Hitler was a great man." She had no idea why Bobby idolized the dictator and despised Jews. When he was seventeen, she recalled, he had made anti-Semitic remarks. "But I thought that he just didn't understand. I didn't think it was serious until much later."

I asked a number of Fischer's old friends to try to explain why Nazism appealed to him, but the question made them nervous and none of them had a plausible theory. After their break with Bobby these people seemed to feel a little guilty about having listened to so much filth.

Although he has never met Bobby, clinical psychologist Lou Cassotta, a Fischer fan since the early seventies, is willing to speculate about the origins of this peculiar second and all-consuming love affair in Fischer's life.

"For most of his life, Fischer has worked in opposition to the rest of the world. If you ask him to behave in a socially acceptable manner, he instinctively says no. He has to; he must resist any attempt to be socialized. That's how he knows himself, by defining himself in opposition to others. That's why he doesn't commit himself to a woman, why he rejects the people who are closest to him. He is afraid of intimacy. His friends know how fragile he is, and so they pander to him. Anybody who says anything to him

that doesn't suit him, he writes off. In this way he has created a
world that reflects back to him whatever he wants. If he consciously
wanted to make himself as unlike everybody else in the world as
possible, he probably couldn't have done a better job. But he does
it instinctively. He knows himself to be a person who takes the
path that no one else will take. He has done this his whole life.
Even in quitting at the pinnacle he was doing it. A normal person
in his shoes would take advantage of his position by defending his
title, writing books, making all the money he could. Instead,
Fischer chose the life of an impoverished recluse. There is something admirable about his way; it captures the imagination.

"My guess is that it all started with a control issue early in his
life. Perhaps a battle with his mother. Possibly he had to act in
opposition to her power, intelligence and appetite for the arts, her
Judaism, in order to hold on to his own identity and not be subsumed by her. Then he discovers chess, which is respected neither
in society nor in his home. But he is so fantastic a player that he
makes it respectable, even fashionable. It's an unbelievable achievement, but in looking at the history of his life, it seems almost
inevitable that he'd choose something that wasn't accepted and go
out and try to make it work. That alone was a large part of his
triumph.

"So when he's finally on top, and the game is recognized, why
does he leave it? Maybe for the same reason. Now everybody
thinks it's fine to be a chess player, and he can't stand that. His game
is now mainstream and it makes him uncomfortable. So he in-
volves himself in something—Nazism—which every decent, normal American thinks is horrible, and he's going to try to make *it*
respectable. He must believe that he'll triumph again, just as he
did before. He must be convinced that he has become involved in
something that is more important than chess, that he will be the
one who finally exposes the Jews.

"Of course the difference is that as a chess player Bobby was a
genius and that as a political thinker he's a schmuck. But anti-
Semitism is perfect for him because it is built on opposition. Nazis
are the bad boys of the world. Fischer identifies with that; he was
a bad boy who never did what he was told."

*   *   *

ONE CHILLY AFTERNOON Victor Frias and I went to McArthur Park, within walking distance of Bobby's downtown L.A. neighborhood. It is big, with winding paths and a nice lake where kids fish and a few brown ducks swim around. There used to be a larger population of ducks, but five or six years ago they began to disappear. Hungry Vietnamese who lived nearby were fishing for them at night with hook and line.

McArthur Park sits between two worlds. One side is the western perimeter of L.A.'s thriving industry and affluence—expensive condominiums, art galleries and tall, modern office buildings in the distance. But to the east and south the park is bordered by a poor, predominantly Latin neighborhood with delis, bars blaring Rancheras music and cheap Mexican restaurants. Sandwiched between the bars and restaurants are what seem like dozens of health clinics, enough for an entire city, each with a big sign advertising the end to your physical woes.

In the southwest corner of the park fifteen or twenty down-and-out men played chess. As we approached them, I whispered to Victor that since no one here knew him it might be fun to get into a money game. Victor didn't reply but within a few seconds I realized how preposterous my suggestion was. The first player who looked up broke into a broad smile. Victor Frias, international master from Chile, was a celebrity in McArthur Park, and he was quickly surrounded by a dozen men slapping him on the back, asking about where and whom he had been playing and about the successes of other Latin American masters.

Twenty feet away, a stout man hunched over one of the tables. He didn't seem to notice us, and for a time Victor ignored his game, which was the only one still going on. But as Frias joked with old friends and the man moved his pieces and hit his clock, you could feel that the lack of contact between them was filled with tension. After a time they nodded at each other. Without saying a word, they had agreed to play.

The heavyset man was the star of McArthur Park. He commanded respect among the players there in the same way that Israel Zilber is the acknowledged "Sheriff" of Washington Square and Valentin Arbakov is known throughout the Soviet Union as the king of Sokolniki Park in Moscow, where he spends much of the day drinking vodka and taking on all comers for kopecks. The chess world is remarkably tight, and though these men often sit and sleep in the cold waiting for a game and work their craft for nickels and dimes, they have reputations that cross oceans. Susan Polgar of Hungary had known about Zilber in Washington Square and made it a point to go there to play blitz with him when she came to New York. Arbakov has beaten many top grandmasters who come to Sokolniki Park to test themselves against him. The stout man in McArthur Park has also beaten many grandmasters, but what makes his success more surprising is that until recently he was merely an expert and now his rating is only that of a weak master; as a tournament player he is not in the same class as Zilber and Arbakov, who both play at the grandmaster level.

Without asking, Victor Frias knew the rules of the game they would be playing, and he looked a little unhappy. Normally in blitz each player gets five minutes on his clock, and for a player unfamiliar with speed chess, the action is too fast to follow. But the stout man in McArthur Park had made his reputation as a one-minute player; each man began with sixty seconds on his clock, and unless someone was checkmated, the one who first used up his minute lost, regardless of his position.

Frias is tough-looking, with a thick black beard and the build of Roberto Duran when he fought as a middleweight. Sitting at a chessboard, he smolders with intensity. He is a great five-minute player, one of the best in the United States, but from the beginning it was clear that against the fat man he was at a decided disadvantage. His opponent had an incredibly fast and powerful right hand built up from years of practice; it moved like Ali's jab, and in one flowing cobra stroke he grabbed a piece and smacked the clock. He played only a few openings, but he had practiced the sequences of moves for rhythm and speed. In only three or four seconds he moved through the opening fifteen or twenty moves of each game, hand flashing from piece to clock, and invariably by the time they were in the middle game, Frias was eleven or twelve seconds behind.

In one-minute chess there is no time to pause and consider; it is absolutely instantaneous and instinctive, and watching the action is like seeing the film of a prizefight that has been put on fast forward. There is no following its logic. It is hard to discern whose hand is moving what piece; chessmen fly in the air and fall to the ground. The fat man had memorized thousands of one- and two-move traps, the kinds of moves good players scorn as cheap shots and that don't work in slower games. But this man had no time for depth or art; he had devoted much of his life to learning the best shortcuts in a game that doesn't allow its participants time to think. He was a grandmaster of cheap shots.

As the two of them played they breathed heavily, as if they were running; sweat dripped from their faces. The fat man would never agree to begin the next game until he had fully caught his breath. He knew precisely the energy he needed for the next sprint. His clock had dents and gouges from the force with which he pounded it with his thick fingers. Even more remarkable than his hand speed were his eyes. While Victor occasionally cost himself a second to glance at the clock, his opponent smacked it without looking. He knew the precise angle from rook to clock, from queen to clock, and uncannily, at the exact instant when Frias ran out of time, without looking away from the position, the man would announce, "You lose."

Again and again Victor had won positions, a few moves away from mating his overweight but speedy opponent, but would lose on time, and after an hour, when they decided to quit, he was several games behind. Before leaving the table, he slyly offered to triple the stakes if the fat man would agree to play with seventy-five seconds on each clock instead of sixty, but he knew that his opponent would refuse. The fat man had worked at his game for years, was brilliant within its crazy dynamic and had gained a reputation that gave his life meaning. He knew that even the great Fischer, rumored to eat sometimes in the Mexican restaurants nearby, might lack the hand speed and coordination to beat him in one-minute chess. If he gave Frias another fifteen seconds there would be moments in which he could think, the game would inch a little closer to real chess, and he wouldn't have a chance in hell.

*   *   *

RON GROSS WAS Fischer's best friend in California from 1972 until their friendship ended in 1984, when he talked about Bobby in an interview with a reporter. They had been friends since Fischer was twelve years old. When they first met in New York, they spent their time playing, searching for chess books and studying the game together.

Gross recalls an afternoon with his fourteen-year-old friend at the Manhattan Chess Club. "We were playing and I noticed the great cellist Gregor Piatigorsky standing nearby watching. He had made an appointment with Bobby; he wanted to see the 'game of the century' that Fischer had played recently against Donald Byrne. I said, 'There's Piatigorsky, you ought to talk to him,' but Bobby refused; he didn't want to stop playing. He had me in an off-balanced position, down the exchange but up a pawn. With Piatigorsky waiting, Bobby got nervous and made a mistake, and suddenly he had the worst of it. This made him even more stubborn. We weren't playing with a clock, and with Piatigorsky standing there Fischer thought about his position for almost an hour. I finally won the game, and afterwards Bobby got up from the table and started screaming at Piatigorsky, 'Who are you that I have to show you my game?' He blamed this world-famous artist because he'd lost a game to me, and after making Piatigorsky wait all that time, Bobby wouldn't play out the game for him. By anyone's standards he'd been outrageously rude, but that's the way he was."

In recent years, according to Gross, Fischer was still studying as much as when he first met him, but the books had changed. A couple of years after the Spassky match he began to distrust Ted Armstrong and broke with the Church of God. Now, instead of hunting down religious tracts or collections of chess games, he coveted books like *The Protocols of the Elders of Zion* and *The Myth of Six Million Dead*. He was convinced that the Jews were controlling the country and that the Holocaust was a self-serving fantasy created by Zionists. He'd call up Gross at one or two in the morning to ask if his friend had read a new article about world control by the Jews. Usually Gross would lie and say he'd read it or would promise to do so soon. He didn't want to upset Fischer and hoped he would forget this crazy preoccupation and return to chess.

Perhaps if he met a girl it would help. Bobby had always been attracted to women but had little to do with them because he felt that they took his mind off work. It was rumored that his poor performance in Buenos Aires in 1960, when he was seventeen years old, was due to his passionate involvement with a prostitute during the tournament, and he had vowed never to let this happen again. After his retirement, friends often tried to get him dates. In his late thirties and early forties he was eager to meet girls, but these associations were like his recurrent fantasy of making a chess comeback; his pattern was to encourage friends to set up dates and then to reject the women—his relationships rarely got past the talking stage. Once Gross fixed him up with a buxom blonde. "They got on very well," recalled Gross. "They spent the evening talking about blacks. Neither of them liked blacks much.

"There's an anti-Semitic bookstore near Inglewood," Gross said. "We'd go in there to find an article or book he wanted to read, and it reminded me of going to chess bookstores in New York when we were kids. Once we drove to this Inglewood bookstore, but Bobby didn't want to go inside because he didn't want the owner to see him, so I had to go in and buy the books for him. He had a special discount at this store, and before I went in he reminded me to ask for his discount. Then when I brought out the books he got all excited. Bobby has great enthusiasm for whatever interests him. It was just like the old days, except that the subject was different. I'd talk to him about his ideas, but I had to be tactful because I didn't want to tell him that he was out of his mind."

Despite a shared passion for chess, the two men couldn't be less alike. Gross is a gentle, well-mannered, neatly dressed real-estate salesman who taught junior high school until recently and lives in a pleasant middle-class home in Cerritos. He is an affectionate, doting father to his adolescent daughter and an affable man who watches pro football on Sunday afternoons. It's hard to imagine Bobby coming over on weekends, sitting on the sofa in his filthy clothes, shoes falling apart, spewing his newest ideas about Hitler and the Jewish global conspiracy or chortling about an anti-Semitic

Spanish comic book he'd found in Tijuana. It was embarrassing to be around him, Gross recalls, "because when he got started on the Jews, whether he was in the house or at a restaurant, he'd bang the table and curse."

Bobby made Gross's wife and daughter uncomfortable, and Gross seems to be relieved that the relationship is over. Nevertheless, he genuinely liked Fischer and enjoyed his boyish enthusiasm for the outdoors and for physical fitness. Mostly, however, he was captivated by Fischer's chess. For hours after he had tired of describing Bobby's quirks, he and Frias analyzed games that Gross had played against Fischer. For each of them it was a special time, and they behaved like two writers looking through a cache of unpublished manuscripts by Tolstoy. Gross seemed to remember every game he had ever played against Fischer, even positions from speed games played more than thirty years before. "I'd have prepared a line to play against him, something he couldn't have seen," Gross said, "because I always knew what chess periodicals he was reading, but he'd find moves you'd never see in a book."

Chess players around the world, from Kasparov to rank beginners, are curious to know how the present-day Fischer compares in playing strength to the one who defeated Spassky in 1972, and how he would stack up against Karpov or Kasparov now. Grandmaster Peter Biyiasas claims that Fischer is a much stronger player today. Over the course of several weeks in 1981 Fischer lived with Biyiasas and his wife, Ruth Haring, in their home in San Francisco, and the two grandmasters played well over a hundred speed games. "If anything, Bobby's gotten better," said Biyiasas. "He's like a machine. There was a feeling of inevitability about those games. Fischer saw too much and was too fast. While he played, he made comments and joked, as if he were playing against an amateur. I didn't win a single game."

Even more impressive to Biyiasas was Fischer's ability to analyze chess positions. "We looked at Karpov-Kasparov games and he'd say, 'But look at these blunders. Karpov could have drawn this game, but he lost it.' They didn't look like blunders to me, but when Bobby took the time to explain, I saw that he was right every time. There's no doubt in my mind that he's still the best in the world."

Listening to Biyiasas, one has the impression that Fischer has been incubating for years, growing stronger and stronger, spiraling off into his own chess universe. According to several Fischer friends, former world champion Boris Spassky arrived at the same conclusion after losing the vast majority of speed games he played against Fischer in a secret meeting in 1987.

Ron Gross, who is a strong master, has a more measured opinion. He played forty or fifty speed games against Fischer in 1984 and lost them all save for one win and two draws. He described the games with loving detail. "One day Bobby won seventeen in a row, and then I drew a game in which he allowed a perpetual check. I had played the Hennig-Schara and I was killing him on the queenside. I had a check over there, and he allowed it, and I couldn't figure out why. Afterwards he said, 'Why didn't you win the piece? You had a won game.' I'd been so overjoyed to get a draw that I hadn't looked for a win."

According to Gross, Bobby doesn't study as much chess as he used to and has declined in strength slightly from his 2780 rating in 1972, but he is certain that Fischer is still strong enough to beat Karpov, and perhaps Kasparov. "His anti-Semitism gets in the way of his chess," Gross said. "Whatever we talked about, chess or physical fitness or history, he would eventually guide the conversation back to the Jews. He believes that the Russian Revolution was engineered by some old rabbis, and that the Bolsheviks were Jews. He won't read *Chess Life* because he believes that it's run by Jews. He's certain that the U.S. Chess Federation and FIDE are controlled by Jews. This way he can believe that the Jews have cut him off from playing or from making money at chess."

While we talked, Gross's pretty daughter, who sometimes participates in scholastic tournaments around Los Angeles, came into his study to speak to her father. I asked her about the top young players in the area and learned that she has competed against Yvonne Krawiec and her brother Daniel, kids Joshua has also run across in national events. Somehow this indirect connection seemed intimate, as if I had happened upon a California friend of Joshua's. In the chess world it seems that talented players know about one another regardless of where they live or how young they may be. Nine-year-olds in California stay abreast of the careers of their contemporaries in New York; there are pockets of children all around the country studying and competing, kids whose parents were turned on by Fischer and want their children to be great players. I began to describe a game Josh had played against Yvonne at the nationals in 1985, when he blundered an exchange but still managed to win in the endgame. In the telling I was at least as wrapped up in this contest between two eight-year-olds as Gross had been while demonstrating a brilliant Fischer game.

I described the children's chess world in New York to Gross and mentioned my theory that many of these kids, including my own, might not be playing today if it were not for Fischer. "I don't think Bobby had much awareness of his role in chess and the impact he had on other people," Gross responded. "It didn't seem to matter to him. People are always telling me how great it would be for American chess if Fischer played again. That's true, but it doesn't mean anything to him. What he did for the game doesn't interest him at all, and he doesn't like anyone who helped him along the way. He fired all his lawyers; he fired his mother. No one could do enough to please him. All he cares about is his place in chess history. Once I realized that, I knew he'd never risk playing again."

Gross asked his daughter if she had done her chess homework. She answered in a way that made it perfectly clear that on a beautiful sunny afternoon chess was the last thing she would choose to do. Gross desperately wants her to be a player, but she resists him. She wrinkles her nose and shakes her head fetchingly; who wants to study openings? Apparently this has been going on for some time, and by now Gross's ambition for her chess is tinged with realism. "She's into other things," he said with a sigh.

Maybe I will be like Gross in three or four years, when Josh has drifted out of the children's chess wars, thinking nostalgically of all the talent he had, of all the great games he wasn't playing, of how far he might have gone if only he had kept at it.

I NEVER DID meet Bobby, of course. No one knows of anyone who has run into him for more than a year, and he is referred to as "the ghost of Pasadena." More and more, rumors have replaced verifiable fact. There are stories about his handing out political pamphlets on street corners, attending chess tournaments in disguise, traveling to New York to make a quick visit to the Manhattan Chess Club, living in a swanky hotel in Mexico for six months, flying to India to arrange a match with a grandmaster, spending an hour discussing chess with a truck driver and playing a private match with Spassky, but nothing is known for certain.

In 1987 the woman in New York who claimed to speak to Bobby regularly on the phone flew to California to meet him for the first time. "He's so fast," she said, referring to the games they played against one another in her hotel room. "He's better than ever. No one could beat him." But she is so intoxicated with her relationship with Fischer, her face rapturous as she talks about him, that one can't help wondering if it is all a fantasy. "He's so pure, like Jesus," she said to me.

IT IS SAID that Bobby has Nazi friends in San Francisco. But one of his old acquaintances assured me that Fischer's anti-Semitism is nothing serious. Some say his chess is phenomenal and others claim he rarely plays anymore. He has become shifting sand. He is whatever people want him to be. Apparently Fischer has created his disappearance with as much care and depth as his most complicated chess positions. For a time after the Spassky match, he wasn't hiding so much as living a private life. His circle of friends was large, and people could contact him quite easily. Important players like Karpov, for example, traveling to California, would meet with Bobby and discuss the possibility of a match with him. But over time he narrowed his circle and became more difficult to track down. Old acquaintances who had bragged publicly or had agreed to be interviewed about their relationship with him received one last phone call with the curt message that their friendship was over. During the last several years, his life seems to have become devoted to hiding. He has put passion and cunning into living invisibly, and private investigators hired by magazines have been unable to track him down.

CLAUDIA MACAROW, WHO many believe now takes care of Fischer, is reputed to work two full-time jobs in order to support him. Lina

Grumette was a friend of Macarow's for several years, and I asked her why Claudia worked so hard to finance Bobby's invisible life. "No reason," said Lina. "She has nothing to gain except that she likes the idea of being around him." In many ways Macarow has replaced Lina. "I found out that she looks through all of his mail before showing it to him," Lina complained. "She used to take his messages, and I've always suspected that she never gave him the ones she didn't want him to see. She manipulated him." Despite her soft speaking voice, Lina was upset and perhaps a little jealous. These days Claudia's phone is disconnected, and it is rumored that she has moved out of state. If so, who is taking care of Bobby?

TOWARD THE END of their friendship, Gross and Fischer traveled together to Mexico. "He looked terrible," Gross recalls, "clothes all baggy, wearing old beat-up shoes. We went down to Ensenada to go fishing. I remember that out on the boat one afternoon Bobby was green with seasickness. I tried to get him to take a pill but he wouldn't consider it. But though he was sick, he was in good spirits. Everyone was catching rock cod, dolphins were swimming under the boat and we saw whales and flying fish. He was as excited as a little kid at seeing these things. He was fun to be around sometimes, because he had such enthusiasm. Then I noticed that he was favoring his mouth, and he told me that he'd had some work done on his teeth; he'd had a dentist take all the fillings out of his mouth.

"I said, 'Bobby, that's going to ruin your teeth. Did you have him put plastic in the holes?' And he said, 'I didn't have anything put in. I don't want anything artificial in my head.' He'd read about a guy wounded in World War II who had a metal plate in his head that was always picking up vibrations, maybe even radio transmissions. He said the same thing could happen from metal in your teeth.

"I thought about what he'd done for a while, and a month or so later when we were at a spa, I asked him, 'What are you gonna do when you lose your teeth?' And Bobby said, 'I'll gum it. If I have to, I'll gum it.'"

THE
NATIONALS

In the opinion of many experts, the United States today has the strongest group of preteen players of any country in the world, including the Soviet Union. Among them are approximately a dozen children between the ages of seven and twelve who have the potential to be world-class grandmasters. These kids have approximately the same playing strength as did such world champions as Anatoly Karpov, Gary Kasparov and Bobby Fischer when they were the same ages. Another dozen children play only slightly below this lofty standard.

Social and cultural realities dictate that in the future most of these young players will devote their energies to pursuits other than chess, but if one of them were someday to become a world champion, this period of competing prodigies may be remembered as the most curious remnant of the Fischer legacy. While American chess professionals suffer from lack of respect and an inability to make a living, the children's chess world thrives, and each year more and more parents who once rooted for Bobby Fischer as fervently as they cheered the Beatles are captivated by the idea of their kids' becoming chess champions, or at least *young* chess champions.

Each spring, the emotional odyssey of the chess parent comes to a head at the time of the National Scholastic Chess Championship. If a child is one of the highest-rated players, with a realistic chance of winning his division, the pressure on him and his parents during the weeks prior to the event can be horrible. Parents keep trying to reassure themselves and their kids that winning doesn't matter, that chess must be kept in perspective, that life will quickly return to normal; the summer is coming up, after all, with camp, baseball and lots of other distractions. But an inner voice blasts these arguments apart with the crazy but unshakable moral conviction of Vince Lombardi, who proclaimed, "Winning is the only thing." Despite love for the artistry of chess and the hundreds of little pleasures and pains during the preceding year of study and play, in the weeks before the nationals all the effort that has been expended over the previous year is weighed against the child's performance during this single two-day event.

IN JOSHUA'S CASE, the upcoming 1986 primary championship was shadowed by the memory of losing in the seventh round the previous year. One poorly played chess game had changed him; he would never again be the same cocky little boy who was convinced that no child on earth could beat him. By his ninth year, he had studied the game more intensely than most people ever study a subject before attending college, but ironically, in becoming so accomplished so young he had been forced to scrutinize the limits of his potential. Already he had seemed to learn what many of us artfully avoid realizing for another twenty or thirty years: that wanting to be Tolstoy or Einstein or Sandy Koufax doesn't make it so. During the past year, even when he was loving the game and was playing his best chess, he would sometimes refer to himself derisively as a patzer, and whenever he played in Washington Square and ogling bystanders made a fatuous comparison to Bobby Fischer he would wince visibly. Early success had made it more difficult for him to be a dreamer, and his rigorous, caustic self-assessments made me feel terrible. What's wrong with imagining yourself a world champion when you're only eight years old? I had. I was going to be an NBA All-Star, bringing the ball up the court like Bob Cousy. I was going to catch a bigger marlin than the one in *The Old Man and the Sea*.

That spring I was afraid for Josh. At least once a day I would say to him nervously, "It doesn't matter if you don't win. You're improving all the time. You'll win another year in another division."

For a while he nodded patiently when I went through this ritual, but one afternoon he said to me pointedly, "If I finish second I'll feel like a failure. Only first place means anything." It was a lonely time for him. He took his chess lessons with a grim, pursed mouth, memorized openings dutifully on the floor in his bedroom with the door closed, and at night lay in bed worrying about losing. Maybe we were putting him in a position that he couldn't handle. He had the highest national rating of any primary player, and as the number-one seed he would be burdened by the sense that everyone was gunning for him. He would play his games on board one, in front of a television camera, and according to the rules of the Swiss system, as long as he kept winning, his pairings for the tournament would theoretically be more difficult than those of any other player.

Bonnie, Bruce and I tried to adopt an easygoing attitude. In the weeks preceding the tournament, most other kids practiced by playing in scholastic or adult tournaments; instead we decided that Josh should play in Washington Square. During the past year he had learned a lot about positional chess and had developed sophisticated technique and feel for the endgame; lately, however, his games had become flat and he had stopped attacking, instead waiting for his opponent to make an error. Perhaps too much theory and technique were getting in the way of creative play.

In the warm weather of April, Josh was back in Washington Square playing seven-minute speed games against hustlers who broke away from book openings after five or six moves. The games were all improvisation, sacrifices and flashy tactics—intuitive, gut-level chess, just what he needed.

Josh's friend Poe, who often reeked of cheap cigars, played the white pieces against Josh's Dragon Sicilian and showed him that if he didn't get his pawns rolling on the queenside he was going to get beat. Poe mated him often until Josh started playing aggressively with his pawns. Everyone wanted to help. Hustlers who were usually close-mouthed about their tricks, failed masters who floated to the marble tables high on grass—all of them had something to show him: a Levenfish attack, a crafty little opening trap in the Benoni. Wouldn't it be something if the little kid who'd started here when he was six won the national championship?

After two weeks in the park Joshua's game had come alive. He was sacrificing pieces for an attack, finding combinations, playing for mate instead of trying to pick off a pawn. Pandolfini had taught him where his pieces ought to be, and the guys in the park were reminding him what to do with them. It was a wonderful ragtag group that sparred with Josh every day after his classes at Dalton. By common consent, they didn't smoke grass, drink from a bottle or take a leak behind a tree when he was around.

By two weeks before the nationals, Josh was playing his best chess ever, but he was also a bundle of raw nerves. He had always been a calm and confident player. Often other kids' hands would tremble when they played him, and frequently they would cry when he beat them. Josh never showed signs of nervousness and never cried in public. Even when he beat adults as a six-year-old he had showed little excitement; it was as if he had expected to win. But in the weeks preceding the tournament he would sometimes look up from a game in the park with an expression of alarm, and afterwards, when I asked what was wrong, he would say that he felt as if walls were closing in on him and he had become frightened. Sometimes when people spoke, their voices sounded unbearably loud in his head. I asked a psychologist friend about these symptoms, and his disquieting reply was that unlike adults, kids haven't developed methods to handle pressured situations. I didn't feel good about his answer, or about the fact that my mother screamed at me that I was a terrible parent for allowing my son to go through such torture. At night Josh called out moves in his sleep. The week before the tournament, I noticed that he was pulling the hair out of the front of his head as he contemplated a position, making a little bald spot. When I pointed this out to him, he became angry and accused me of interfering with his concentration.

Josh was out there all on his own.

WE TRAVELED TO Charlotte, North Carolina, with Bruce and with Morgan and Kalev Pehme. Morgan was a year and a half younger than Josh but had the vocabulary and wit of a smart fourteen-year-old, and he was already one of the three or four strongest chess players in the country in the third grade and under. He and Josh were close friends, and I was relieved that as members of the Dalton team they wouldn't have to play each other in the nationals, as they had in New York events. Often before playing each other in tournaments, they bristled competitively like young tomcats, but while we went sightseeing in Charlotte, they traded baseball cards and gossiped about the other top players. Without caginess, Kalev and I both admitted to feeling nervous, though with a cigarette trembling in his hand he insisted that I was in worse shape.

Morgan and his father had been training for the nationals as if it were a holy crusade, and whenever the conversation turned to miniature golf, baseball or old James Bond movies—all of them Morgan's passions—Kalev deflected it back to chess, reminding his son of offbeat openings that they had been preparing. Since Morgan knew more openings than Joshua, these conversations were unnerving to both of us, carrying the message that Josh had studied the wrong variations or had not prepared nearly enough.

For the last few days I had been trying to keep Joshua's mind off chess. I had read an essay by Mikhail Botvinnik in which the former world champion suggested that before a major tournament a player should put chess out of his mind and take long walks in the country for a week or ten days to build up the necessary energy for the struggle ahead. We had arrived in Charlotte a day early, and I immediately inquired at the hotel desk about the best place for long walks. Josh was disgusted; he wanted to play baseball and didn't care about Botvinnik's advice. Kalev pointed out that the Russian probably didn't have seven- and nine-year-old kids in mind, but I prevailed, and so Kalev was forced to read aloud to Morgan from his Russian encyclopedia of chess openings as we walked beneath shady trees and along a winding trout stream.

Besides Josh and Morgan there were half a dozen children who had a realistic chance to win first place in the primary division, the strongest of whom was Jeff Sarwer, the little boy who studied chess full time instead of going to school. "Jeff is the only one I'm afraid of," Josh confided. "But why should you be afraid of him?" I said. "The last time you played him you won easily."

"Not so easily," Josh answered. I was annoyed that he was afraid of another kid; I wanted him to feel impregnable, to assure me that he couldn't lose. I said something about Bobby Fischer's never being afraid of anyone and immediately regretted it. Josh was only being honest.

As it turned out, there was a possibility that Jeff would not be allowed to play. A number of parents had complained that since he didn't go to school, he had no right to participate in this national scholastic event. Kalev argued that keeping Jeff and Julia out of school to pursue full-time chess careers was criminal. "What if things don't work out for them or if they sour on chess?" he said. "How will they support themselves? They're living a warped life."

Certainly it was a monomaniacal life. Little Jeff studied and played chess from morning until night. He was insatiable about the game, happy when he was moving pieces and restless when there was no opponent to crush. "Kill, kill, kill," he sometimes said with an impish grin as he launched his attacks.

Jeff's father demanded perfection from his kids. In an interview he once described how he had taught Jeff not to have nightmares. Instead of comforting the child, Mike Sarwer would tell him to go back to sleep and bring his dream back, but this time he had to overcome the conflict that had terrified him. Mike claimed that both his children had learned to do this. On occasions when little Jeff didn't come up to the mark, his father would order him to stand facing the wall for hours reflecting on his ways. But whether because of his father's training or because of a natural fighting spirit, spindle-legged, bald-headed little Jeff perceived himself to be a chess superman. On the Shelby Lyman show, where he later appeared as an analyst during the Karpov-Kasparov matches, he ridiculed Kasparov's play as if the contender were an amateur. He boasted that he would be the youngest world champion of all time, and some experts who observed his ingenious attacking style and natural feel for the endgame thought that he might be right.

Jeff dismissed all other chess children as dull and stupid. He hated them for being pretenders at his game and way of life. He was different from any other chess kid I had ever met. His passion for the game was hotter, and his arrogance at eight was so disarming that it was easy to forget that he was a little boy.

But sometimes the veneer cracked. A couple of weeks before the nationals Jeff had ventured into Washington Square and played a few speed games against one of the guys with whom Josh practiced regularly.

"You ought to play my man Josh," the black man said while he moved the pieces.

"Josh is a putz," Jeff answered.

"I think Josh'd beat you" was the home-field response. Other Josh supporters chimed in, and soon Jeff began to cry and left the park. These bantering remarks had tipped his world. In his mind he had no equals, and these were the terms by which he played the game.

Kalev argued with me and Josh that if people took a stand against the Sarwer kids' playing, maybe Jeff's father would come to his senses and send them to school.

"It would be terrible to keep Jeff out," Josh answered firmly. "How could they do that to him? No one loves chess as much as he does. It's his whole life."

Despite their tense relationship, Josh respected Jeff and deferred to his greater passion. If Josh happened to win the national championship after Jeff was excluded, it wouldn't feel right. I also suspect that if Josh had suddenly withdrawn from the tournament, Jeff would have been disappointed.

JOSH SAYS THAT no sport makes him sweat as much as chess. He is referring to the hours of straining to peer ever more deeply into the position in front of him, to the flood of energy needed to develop an attack, and to the dread he experiences trying to fend off an assault which seems directed at his soul more than at his pieces. In the nationals, children play four games the first day and three the last. Each game can last as long as three and a half hours; the longer it takes, the more intense the emotional experience and the more difficult it is to gather energy for the next one. The last game of the first day might not end until ten at night. There's hardly time for the child to eat and get a good night's rest before tomorrow's eight A.M. game. Haggard parents demand instant sleep from their little warriors, but after an intense fourth game on Saturday night, eight-year-olds are so wound up that they can't relax. They toss and turn in bed searching for checkmate, and on Sunday morning, the day they have been training for all year, they may be nervous and drained. Coaches of the best players dread long games in the early rounds and hope that the other contenders are softened up by such efforts before their kid plays them.

Josh played his games in a large banquet room on the second floor of the Quality Inn. Most players sat beside one another at long cafeteria tables, but since he was ranked first, he and his opponent sat alone at a smaller table in front of a television camera mounted on a tripod. It felt eerie to Josh to play in front of this unattended camera.

Except for a cough or the snap of a chess clock, the room was quiet while the children played. A dozen men were posted throughout to answer procedural questions and to accompany a child to the bathroom, so that there would be no temptation to speak to a parent or coach in the hall. While the kids played, these men looked as grave and ceremonial as palace guards, and they appeared to be very large, no doubt because their wards were so small.

Along with fifty or sixty other parents, Bonnie and I watched Josh on a large television set in the lobby of the hotel. Some of the onlookers didn't understand the game and reacted to the televised moves with a dumb respect, as if listening to the theoretical musings of a molecular biologist, but others were sophisticated about chess and followed the action with lively interest. I was constantly on guard. When I wasn't worrying about a kingside attack or Joshua's weak pawns, I concentrated on keeping my face composed, so that it was neither manically happy nor gray with pallor. I wanted to be calm under fire, but I could feel the truth seep out in twitches, grimaces and grins. Often the parents of Joshua's opponent were sitting hip to hip with us on the sofa, pleading audibly for little Tommy to pull off the big win, and it was hard not to hate them. I tried to be careful that my rooting didn't transgress the limits of propriety, but sometimes I couldn't restrain myself and would bound off the sofa with a whoop when the other kid hung his rook or failed to notice the threat of mate in three. The parent beside me would wince or clench his jaw, and

once a father said "Damn" with such raw bitterness that I felt
ashamed. Watching your little boy play for the national championship is a roller coaster of hopes and dashed dreams.

IN THE FIRST round, Josh was paired against the eighty-second-
ranked player. We expected the game to be easy and quick; afterwards, he and I would have a catch outside for twenty minutes,
and then he'd have a sandwich and rest in his room for half an
hour before the second round.

But it didn't work out that way. The boy considered his moves
thoughtfully, like a seasoned player. He shadowed Josh through a
difficult opening without making a mistake. I sat watching the
monitor beside the boy's father, who mentioned that they had
driven up from New Mexico for the tournament. I began to sense
that they wouldn't have traveled all the way from New Mexico to
North Carolina if the son weren't very good. After an hour and a
half, not a single pawn had been exchanged and the position was
murky with tension and multiple threats. Most of the other children
had already finished playing their games and were jumping into
the outdoor pool adjacent to the lobby or racing into the video-
game room. Intermittently the stronger players walked over to
check Joshua's position; they were surprised that he was having
such a difficult time in the first round.

The father was a nice man, and I tried to be congenial. After a
while he mentioned that his son didn't have a high rating because
there weren't many scholastic tournaments in New Mexico, but
that in the local chess club he frequently beat players with a rating
of 1600 or 1700. This information cracked whatever was left of my
calm. Wasn't there something vaguely illegal about this? In the
very first round we had been paired against a ringer. A couple of
months earlier, I had watched with amusement and contempt as
a frantic father complained to a tournament director each time his
boy's position became difficult that other parents and coaches were
conspiring against his son. Crazy though it was, I wanted to do the
same thing. We could easily lose this game.

After two hours neither player had an advantage, and the other
father said pleasantly, "This is a no-lose situation for us. If he wins

it would be spectacular, but if he loses, it's to be expected. After all, he's playing the number-one seed." By now every other game was finished, but on the first board the position was completely closed down; only a couple of pawns had been taken, and for both players all avenues for attack seemed blocked. By now dozens of kids were eating sandwiches in front of the set, assessing the position. Josh was playing solidly, but so was the other boy. The father smiled at me and asked questions about my son's chess education. He remarked that there weren't any good chess teachers in New Mexico, which at this moment seemed to invest his son with monumental powers; the boy had learned on his own! I tried to respond but found it difficult to make conversation. Even if Josh managed a victory, the game was taking too long; he wouldn't have the strength to win three more games today.

The boy's father was happy and growing more confident and chatty. After hours of watching the game I couldn't focus on the pieces, which seemed to drift and blur like a heat mirage. Pawns and bishops were impossible to distinguish on the monitor, which caught the reflection of children splashing in the pool outside. Was that a knight hiding in the shadow of a queen? Then there was a quiet exchange, one of the few in the two-and-a-half-hour game, and afterwards Josh seemed to be up a pawn, but no one could tell for sure. Two moves later, the boy from New Mexico pushed a piece, and immediately Josh took an unprotected pawn with his bishop; the boy had made a blunder, and half a minute later he knocked over his king. There was still plenty of play in the position, but losing the second pawn had unnerved him. It was strange. The game had been even for so long, and then in a minute it was over. The boy's father was still smiling. "My son has never played better in his life," he said. The father didn't even seem disappointed, except maybe a little at the corners of his mouth. He is a different type than I am.

The next round began immediately. Josh played a girl with a respectable rating but beat her using less than five minutes on his clock. Under different circumstances, playing so quickly would have been an indication that he wasn't concentrating, but after that first game he needed to prove to himself that he could win easily, and he knew he couldn't play another slow, close game and have anything left for the evening rounds. By the seventh or eighth move the girl was rattled by the quickness of his responses, as if he had planned the whole game before they even sat down. He attacked her directly, with no positional subtleties, going for the neck. On the screen she looked defeated, holding her head between her hands, and she was checkmated in eighteen moves.

Josh shook her hand, turned and walked out of the room. When I met him in the hall, his eyes were hollow and bloodshot, and he said that he wanted to take a nap. There were nearly two and a half hours before the next round.

The third game was against a talented young player from Charlotte who played through an intricate modern opening but faltered in the middle game. The fourth game was against the highest-rated player on the Hunter College Elementary School chess team, Dalton's arch-rival. He made a mistake, and it was an easy win for Josh.

After the first day, half a dozen children had 4–0 records, including Josh and Jeff Sarwer, but Morgan had drawn his fourth-round game, which in all likelihood put him out of the running. At dinner his round face was gray and droopy, and he didn't have a smile in him. A simple oversight had cost him a rook, and he had been lucky to draw the game. Kalev dealt with his own disappointment by analyzing the game again and again, as if logic and identifying Morgan's tactical error might change the result. It was difficult for me to be excited about Joshua's chances for winning and at the same time to express regret for Morgan, and it was hard for Kalev to be enthusiastic for Josh. At the nationals heavy emotions frequently clang against one another. I said to Kalev that if Morgan won his last games, he still had a chance to tie. "That won't happen," Kalev said flatly. "Someone will win all seven."

SEVERAL OF JOSHUA's friends from his previous school, The Little Red School House, had come to Charlotte with their fathers. None of these kids had studied chess seriously, but they were excited about playing in the nationals and hanging out with Josh. Although they had known him since he was a toddler, they had little feel for his chess life. Occasionally they had watched him beat their fathers at chess, which always seemed like an aberration, and they knew that sometimes he couldn't attend weekend baseball games because he was playing in a tournament. For kids, such unseen events don't have much significance; they hardly seemed to notice his shelves of trophies. But here was their friend seeded first among this rapacious army of chess children and methodically winning his games. Still, when Jevon, Ben or Jeffery asked him between rounds to play baseball or video games or to go swimming and he refused, they were puzzled. Why? Josh had always been up for anything. "I'm playing a chess tournament," he pointed out with a certain edge to his voice.

Josh was rationing himself more like a man than like a nine-year-old. He knew he had to rest between rounds and to review his openings; he knew that chlorine in the pool would irritate his eyes. When it was nine o'clock and his friends were clamoring around the video machines, he was climbing into bed without any urging from his parents. Win or lose, he was giving this tournament his best shot.

BETWEEN ROUNDS, PANDOLFINI was calming and encouraging to Josh, reminding him of key ideas in his openings and traps to watch out for, but during the games he was distant and apparently uninterested. While his pupil played, Bruce occasionally walked through the lobby, glanced at the position on the screen, chatted with a few parents and then returned to his room to work on a manuscript. Sometimes he didn't come back for an hour. He was unanimated when Josh was winning and smiled faintly when he was struggling. Despite the fact that they had worked together for three years, this was the first time Bruce had ever come to one of Josh's tournaments, and it was no accident.

On Saturday night we talked until three A.M., and in his gentle manner Bruce explained that he was put off by much of what he saw here: the single-minded emphasis on winning, the tacky one-upmanship of parents, the pain endured by young losers. Watching the nationals had brought back what he hadn't liked about being a tournament player; simply put, that one's self-worth as a human being became linked to winning or losing, and that friendships were frequently strained by competition over the board. He was also uncomfortable with the role of coach. Teaching Josh rook-and-pawn endings in our living room was one thing, but plotting the demise of another player, particularly a young one, was something else. He spoke elliptically of opening an institute for creative thinking, using chess as a tool to stimulate the problem-solving potential of children. While he spoke I recalled his fantasy of playing tournaments in elaborate disguises, without personal risk.

But at this moment I found Bruce's distaste and feigned neutrality annoying, even though I realized that he was bracing himself for disappointment and also carving a way out both for himself and for Josh. Of course it was true that my son would be miserable if he did poorly, and that Bruce would worry about where he had gone wrong as a teacher, but tomorrow we had a chance to win. Like it or not, such an event has its bloody side. There cannot be ecstatic winners without miserable losers, but this weekend wasn't the time for agonizing about it. Josh and I wouldn't have been in Charlotte if it hadn't been for Pandolfini's artful lessons and his insistence over the past three years that my son could be a great player. Bruce had made Josh, and now he could only bear to peek through one eye.

In the first two rounds on Sunday, Josh played against Gottfried from New York and Goloboy from Massachusetts, each among the strongest for his age in the country, and won both games without much difficulty. Still, in the game against Goloboy, a sleepy-looking little kid with phenomenal talent (the following spring, at the age of eight, he became the youngest player in U.S. history to win an official tournament game against a master), Josh made a strategic mistake, abandoning a potential mating attack for an endgame with a pawn advantage. In the past, when feeling nervous or playing poorly, he had used the endgame as a crutch. He had such confidence in this phase of play that even with inferior positions he would trade off pieces, playing to win in the endgame. He was like a tennis player trying to cover three quarters of the court with his forehand. Against strong players this was a surefire recipe for losing, and Bruce had hoped that he had broken Josh of the habit.

*   *   *

JEFF SARWER HAD also won his sixth-round game. He and Josh had the only perfect scores and would play each other in the final round. Morgan had won his fifth- and sixth-round games, and if Josh and Jeff drew their game and Morgan won, there would be a three-way tie for the championship. Having calculated the tie-breaks, however, I knew that Josh, who was higher-seeded than either of them, would win the first-place trophy if he drew Jeff. Josh had also figured this out, although I knew he would be playing to win.

For months, Pandolfini had said that if they met, Jeff would be Joshua's toughest competition. They had similar attacking styles, and both played the endgame with a sophistication rare even among chess prodigies. Bruce had said that if Josh played Jeff it would be like playing against himself.

Who would have the psychological edge? Jeff believed that no other child was in his class. Josh believed in himself but had learned that losing was part of the game. Jeff had humiliated Josh in the fall, Josh had returned the favor in the early winter, and the kids hadn't played again in the intervening five months.

Five hundred and fifty kids had come to Charlotte for this tournament and had slept in nice beds, but according to several parents, Jeff and his sister and father slept in their car. There was something spartan and foreboding about their habits; Jeff and his dad shaved their heads and wore sandals on outrageously dirty bare feet. No one ever saw them eat; *did* they eat?

When Jeff wasn't playing chess, he sat on the ground against a wall beside his sister and father, hugging his grimy legs. He rarely spoke, and never to the other chess children, whom he enjoyed describing as "ugly putzes." If Josh said hello, Jeff would nod once without a trace of a smile. "I'm not like other children," he had once told me.

The Sarwers had come to Charlotte to win, but Jeff's older sister Julia, a beautiful girl with delicate features, long, curly brown hair and a gypsy style of dressing, had lost one of her early-round games, and her father had shouted at her in front of parents and children, "You have no talent. You don't deserve to be a chess player. Why do I bother with you?" While Julia cried, he continued to berate her.

It was easy to judge the Sarwers, but perhaps not altogether fair. The majority of parents at the tournament were affluent, and their children weren't really dedicated to the game. Many of them would leave Charlotte saying that too much importance was placed on chess, there was too much tension and other things in life were more important. Quickly, the sedatives for loss would take the shape of middle-class alternatives, at least until the tournaments began again in September. The kids would return to school and to their video games, play sports, take piano lessons and go to summer camps, but the Sarwers would be back at the Manhattan Chess Club ten or twelve hours a day, practicing opening variations and getting ready for Maya Chiburdanidze (the women's world champion) and Gary Kasparov. For better or worse, chess was their life; how could the heavens not be on their side? While I walked with Josh to the tournament room for the seventh round, these thoughts plagued me. The gods above were buzzing back and forth, having already made the decision. I wasn't at all happy about this storybook ending. Maybe my mother and Pandolfini were right: kids shouldn't have to endure such tensions. Neither should their fathers.

"Daddy, I'm scared," Josh said at the door. He had never said this to me before a chess game. "My stomach hurts. I don't feel like playing." I handed him his blue pencil, the same one he had used to score the moves in each of his first six games, the magic pencil. "Your stomachache will go away when you start to play," I said, my voice sounding hollow, and I gave him a kiss on the cheek. I wasn't sure that it would go away; I knew mine wouldn't.

One of the tournament directors closed the door. I had forgotten to remind Josh that Jeff is a great attacking player, and not to get into an endgame without a significant advantage because Jeff played the endgame as well as he did. Of course, Josh had been told all this before, but not having reminded him at the door made me feel useless. At least I had sharpened his blue pencil.

Downstairs a hundred people were crowded in front of the television as if for the kickoff of the Super Bowl. Bonnie was sitting cross-legged on the floor in front of the monitor, cradling our daughter on her knees. In the group were the fathers of the other children whom Josh had beaten, as well as the parents of Josh's neighborhood friends. Jeff Sarwer's father nodded stiffly once, just like his son. Pandolfini was nowhere to be seen.

Everyone seemed to be looking forward to this moment, but to me it was a leap into chaos. This game between two children was about fatherhood, life choices, happiness and failure. It had become too large, no longer just chess; I had allowed it to become too large. If we lost, everyone would say, "Forget it, it's only a game," which would make me feel crazy. If it was only a game, why had we done all this work? Chess players have never been good at explaining why they have spent their lives moving pieces. For the last couple of years Josh and I had been struggling to climb a mountain which only grew higher. The better he played, the better he needed to play. Sometimes I'd pull him along kicking; other times I'd feel disgusted with myself and hold back, and then he'd begin to pull me. Why? After three years of living this life with him, I still didn't know why. Maybe I never would. If Josh lost this last game, I hoped that I would be able to control myself and be a decent daddy.

JEFF HAD THE white pieces, which is normally an advantage because white moves first, but more so now, because Josh had done considerable opening preparation with white for the nationals, and not nearly as much with black. Jeff played the f4 variation of the King's Indian, a line that Josh had never seen before. It was a sharp opening, with four of Jeff's central pawns moving forward like a phalanx. If Josh made a mistake, the game would be over before it began. Jeff was moving as fast as my son had moved against the girl in the second round. His face was cocky; he was sending messages.

"It's very complicated," said FIDE Master John Litvinchuk, who was analyzing for the parents. Three or four other masters in the room seemed to agree without speaking. After a dozen moves, the position was riddled with ambiguities and potential advantages, but the kids were playing too fast for the analysts to be certain who was ahead. It was Jeff who was pushing the pace, playing as if he had rehearsed this game a hundred times; Josh was riding a runaway horse, trying to think his way through unfamiliar terrain but gradually becoming drawn into a blitz game that didn't allow time for reflection. Maybe it was nine-year-old machismo, to show that he could play just as fast; more likely, he was too flustered by Jeff's cocksure moves to take his time. When he had played this way in the seventh round the previous year, he had snatched a pawn without considering the consequences and had been forced to resign seven moves later.

There was nothing so dramatic now, but it was becoming clear that Jeff's position was better. His advancing pawns had forced Josh to pull his knight back to its original square. Jeff was fashioning little attacks and Josh was dodging and retreating. His position looked cramped, while Jeff's pieces were moving ahead. In each of the first six games of the tournament, it was my son who had been the aggressor, but now he was defending; his opponent's speed and confidence were intimidating, and Josh began to slump a little at the board. He wasn't making large mistakes, but Jeff's moves were just a little better, and they were adding up, just the way Steinitz had taught in *The Modern Chess Instructor*. He was beating Josh positionally, pushing him back, taking space, placing his pieces in the right squares from which to attack. Twenty moves into the game he was able to pry two of Josh's pawns apart so that they could no longer defend each other. My son's face looked strained, and he began to bite on the neck of his T-shirt. Now his isolated pawns had to be defended by other pieces, which was a considerable disadvantage. They would be vulnerable later, and the pieces defending them would be unable to attack. Then Josh attempted a maneuver that might give him an open file, a little room in which to operate, and if Jeff defended inaccurately he would lose a bishop. But the plan was unsound, and after several pieces were exchanged, Josh was down a pawn.

For a minute or two I couldn't quite believe it; Josh was losing. Instead of speculation about who was going to win, the talk around me had suddenly switched to my son's possibilities of drawing the game.

Now Josh forced an exchange of queens. A big mistake. As a rule, when you are down material without a compensating attack, you should never exchange pieces. Next he exchanged rooks. It was as if in this stressful moment he was seeking the endgame like an old friend. Litvinchuk and the other masters were shaking their heads; the game was lost.

I had been dreading this moment for a year. I felt disconcerted, naked. It was awful that so many people in the room were watching. "It's okay," Bonnie said quietly, and I shuddered. Finished with their games by now, Joshua's neighborhood friends and their fathers were studying the screen quietly. They seemed to be embarrassed, but perhaps it was only I who was embarrassed.

Jeff's father and sister were smiling and exchanging casual remarks. I noticed Pandolfini standing at the back of the crowd looking at the screen with a serious expression. Too late. I was angry at him, which was ridiculous; it wasn't Bruce who had lost. I wished I could take the defeat coolly, and that Josh didn't have to endure the end of it. I couldn't bear to look at the screen anymore. The game had reached the stage that frequently occurs when the position is lost and the players go through the obvious forced exchanges until the inevitable resignation.

Some of the kids began chatting with their fathers about the flight home, school and other matters. It was a relief to hear about a world beyond this game. I began to think about how much I loved my son. If he never played another chess game it would be okay. After it was over, I would meet him at the door and give him an enormous hug.

JOSH GOT UP from the board to go to the bathroom and began to cry there. For two years in a row he had lost the championship in the seventh round. He washed his face with cold water but couldn't stop crying. He tried to envision the endgame position in his head. He loved the endgame, when most of the pieces are gone and the position seems as clear as a few big trees in a field, the answer apparently obvious. But there are tricks everywhere, transformations one wouldn't think possible: knights more powerful than queens and rooks, knights able to fend off two bishops. Sometimes when it looks easy, the answer comes only when you calculate so deeply that your mind feels it will burst. Often Bruce had forced

Josh to calculate fifteen or twenty moves ahead. Josh had discovered that on a good day he could see as deeply as his teacher, even occasionally finding wins that Pandolfini had overlooked. Sometimes when there were only a few pieces left, it was easier to find the answer in your head than by looking at the board. But as he stood there in the bathroom, no matter how he envisioned his knight and five pawns against Jeff's bishop and six pawns, he was lost.

Finally Josh returned to the playing room and looked at the position again. It was still a loss; in fact there was hardly a move left for black by which he wouldn't lose another pawn immediately. He tried to control himself; he didn't want Jeff to see him crying. He moved his king one square. It was just a move. Jeff answered by pushing a pawn to the fifth rank, which looked reasonable. He had a three-to-two advantage on the queenside; the object was to make a queen and win. But in that instant Joshua's body stiffened, and he began to calculate with his hands shielding his eyes.

"That was a mistake," Pandolfini said. For the past half hour, since he had entered the lobby, he hadn't said a word about the game. He had watched with a strange little smile and explained to everyone who asked him about the position that he couldn't distinguish the pieces on the monitor. This wasn't true; it was simply that he didn't want to talk about it. He would have much preferred to be back in New York, writing in his little studio and looking forward to my phone call in the evening giving Joshua's results. Bruce was a chess player who hated playing chess, and this was much worse than playing.

"Jeff should have moved his bishop. That would have increased the pressure," Pandolfini went on.

"The position is still lost. There's no saving it," answered Litvinchuk, who was rated higher than Bruce and was one of the strongest teenage masters in the United States.

"There is a chance for a draw," Bruce said, speaking evenly and still looking directly at the screen, "if Josh moves his knight to the opposite side of the board to h1, apparently out of play, and allows Jeff to pick off his remaining pawns with his king. It might work."

Bruce seemed to be straining to make something out of nothing.

According to his unlikely scenario Josh could save the game by taking his one remaining knight out of action, temporarily sacrificing another pawn, which would put him in precisely the necessary position to win all his material back. Even if it were theoretically possible, Josh wouldn't think of it. Perhaps a strong master would think of it, and maybe he wouldn't. Litvinchuk began to analyze. The entire maneuver would take fifteen or sixteen moves. Litvinchuk said he wasn't sure; it was very complicated.

Josh sat rigidly for ten minutes, began to make a move and then drew back his hand and thought again. Then he moved his knight to h1. Downstairs in the lobby parents and children gasped.

"Now when Jeff takes the rook pawn with his king, Josh pushes his g-pawn, using it as a decoy to lure the bishop away from a defense of the queenside," Bruce explained.

Jeff took the rook pawn. "Push the g-pawn, Josh," said Pandolfini.

"Push the g-pawn, push the g-pawn," the kids and parents watching the game urged. They had no sense of the value of the move; they had simply fallen in step behind Pandolfini. When Josh pushed the g-pawn, people cheered.

Jeff thought that his opponent had given up and was surrendering his material without a fight. But Bruce and Josh were sharing the same vision as surely as if they were talking to each other through the monitor. As Pandolfini calmly laid out his fanciful idea, Josh made the moves. He didn't even seem excited; it was like one more afternoon in the living room analyzing an endgame position with his teacher.

"If Jeff doesn't take the second pawn, bring your knight back to the queenside and start winning them back," said Pandolfini. By now John Litvinchuk was beginning to be convinced, and as Bruce called out the moves, he nodded while, like a chorus, parents and kids urged Josh on.

Now all Josh had to do was to play knight takes bishop. Then Jeff would take Josh's last pawn with his king, but Josh would be able to pick off Jeff's last two pawns before he could bring his king back to defend. A hundred voices were screaming, "Take the bishop, take the bishop," including mine, even though I was too overwrought to understand the position. Bruce was still calmly talking to Josh as if he could hear, while all around us people were shouting Bruce's instructions.

But instead of taking the bishop, Josh stood up and offered Jeff his hand. For one awful moment no one could figure out why; was Josh confused and resigning because he was down two pawns?

"It's a draw," Josh later told me he had said to Jeff.

"I don't agree," Jeff had answered in his formal manner.

My son sat down again. "Take the bishop," people pleaded in the lobby, but Josh paused and wrote down the move he was about to make on his score sheet the way he had been taught. "No need to hurry, Tiger," Bruce had always said. "Take your time. Play like a big boy. Be sure." My son put down his pencil and looked at the position again for another few seconds, relishing the ending as if it were a favorite dessert he couldn't quite bear to finish, then took the bishop. Soon the last two pawns came off the board, exactly the way Pandolfini had predicted sixteen moves earlier, and there were just two kings left on the board separated by one square.

IN THE LOBBY, kids and parents were cheering, men slapped me on the back, a man Bonnie didn't know hugged her. A woman placed my baby daughter in my arms; while we had been yelling and staring at the television, Katya had toddled out the front door. A group of people checking into the hotel for a business convention walked over to the monitor filled with a nearly bare chessboard and looked at one another in bewilderment.

When Josh came out of the tournament room his face was flushed white and red. "Could you believe I pulled that out?" he said absently, as if he were still in a distant world.

John Litvinchuk grabbed him by the shoulder. "How did you *do* that? How did you *do* that?" he screamed. Then he wanted to discuss a mistake that Josh had made on the twentieth move. My son blinked and said he couldn't remember.

Later Josh would recall winning the national championship as the greatest experience of his life, but at this moment he seemed to be in a trance, not so much excited by winning as relieved not to have lost, and still caught up in the game. I gave him a hug and suggested that he ought to see his mother, Bruce and his friends, who were waiting for him downstairs, but just then Morgan came out of the door to the tournament room in tears. He had lost his game. If he had won, his score would have been six wins and a draw, tying Josh's and Jeff's. Kalev approached his son but Morgan put up his little hand and his father stopped in his tracks. At this moment Morgan couldn't accept his father's consolation and regret.

Josh put his arm around Morgan's shoulder and whispered something; then the two of them walked through the crowded hall, past all the little players and their parents, to a large parking lot outside. Josh was only eighteen months older than Morgan but he looked much bigger and older; he was growing up. In a few more years people wouldn't make such a big deal of it when he beat grown-ups in Washington Square. Maybe by then he would be embarrassed to have his father hovering over his games like a protective hen. What would I do with my Saturday afternoons?

A few people called out congratulations to Josh as he walked by, but he paid no attention. He knew what Morgan was feeling; it had happened to him last year. For a few minutes, the two of them embraced while Morgan cried on his friend's shoulder. Then they walked around the parking lot for half an hour. At one point seven-year-old Morgan confided to Josh his fear that for the rest of his life he would be remembered as someone who couldn't win the big game. As if his own prodigy days were decades in the past, Josh replied, "Morgan, I'm going to tell you a secret: you're a much stronger player than I was at your age."

EPILOGUE

The final scene in this book took place in May 1986. It is now two years later, and during the intervening months I have often wondered if the book should have ended where it did. Characters I've written about have experienced triumphs and suffered personal tragedies. Josh and I have wandered into so many intriguing stories that I find myself yearning to write these contemporary tales into my chapters. But finally I resolved that despite the attraction this game has for me, particularly when my son is moving the pieces, I had better get on with something else in my professional life before more years passed, and that perhaps I also needed to move on for Josh's sake. Still, the reader might be interested in a few recent histories and observations.

In December 1985, following another hunger strike and several public protests, Boris Gulko and his family received visas to emigrate to Israel. He believes that they were allowed to leave the Soviet Union because of articles written by Western journalists about his plight and demonstrations for him in the West. After a month in Israel, the Gulkos decided to settle permanently in the United States, and at present they live in Boston. Gulko is now one of our top players and was recently appointed grandmaster in residence at Harvard, a newly created chair. His wife, Anna Akhsharumova, won the 1987 United States women's championship, achieving a perfect score of 9–0. Their greatest concern is whether they will be able to support themselves adequately as chess players in America.

* * *

AFTER WE LEFT Moscow in 1984 Volodja Pimonov became increasingly involved in the fight for human rights. He met regularly with political activists and participated in demonstrations for refuseniks. In one demonstration he was beaten and seriously injured by KGB agents. At the hospital he was asked to sign documents denouncing his political views; when he refused, the KGB would not allow the hospital staff to treat his injuries. At great personal risk a Jewish doctor cared for Pimonov until he recovered.

Since 1985 Pimonov had repeatedly applied for emigration to join his wife and baby daughter in Denmark and was repeatedly turned down. At one point he was informed that his application would not be considered until the year 2002. He suffered periods of profound depression but continued to write free-lance articles for Western publications describing what he called the charade of glasnost. In interviews with Western journalists he spoke passionately about the lives of thousands who have been denied permission to emigrate, and of hundreds detained in labor camps and psychiatric hospitals because of the expression of their religious and political beliefs. In January 1988 he was convinced that his own incarceration in a labor camp was imminent; instead, for reasons that he still does not understand, he received a visa to leave the Soviet Union. On February 5, 1988, Pimonov joined his wife and two-year-old daughter in Copenhagen.

IT IS STILL nearly impossible for even a top grandmaster to support himself by participating solely in United States tournaments, and most of our best players spend considerable time in Europe, where they can count on making a living. Chess parents continue to worry about the wisdom of cultivating wonderful little players who will almost inevitably turn to more respected and lucrative professions just when they are arriving at the peak of their creative powers. The economics of chess will remain bleak in this country until a larger general public begins to appreciate the beauty and excitement of the game, and until major corporations begin to sponsor events as they do in other parts of the world. Perhaps for chess to capture the national imagination again we will need a new Bobby

Fischer—though, it is to be hoped, without the bizarre trappings of the old one. By now most chess players have given up dreaming that Bobby will ever challenge for the world championship again, although Fischer's friends claim that he is currently planning his latest comeback, this time in South Africa.

Nevertheless, the general health of chess in the United States is on the upswing. Each year since 1983, when I first began exploring the chess world with Josh, there has been a modest increase in the prize funds of major tournaments, and more tournaments are being played in attractive hotels, rather than dingy rooms like the Bar Point, which no longer exists. Each year the scholastic chess world has grown in size and enthusiasm, and in 1988 the National Elementary Championship in Detroit will have nearly one thousand children competing, almost twice the turnout of five years ago. This July the United States Chess Federation will send a team of eight boys and girls between the ages of nine and sixteen to Timisoara, Rumania, to compete in the world youth championship, and our team, at least on paper, is as strong as any in the world, including the Soviet Union's.

JOSH IS NOW eleven. Currently his rating is 2101, the highest for his age in the United States, and this summer he will be the U.S. representative in the under-twelve division of the world youth championship. Ever since he received his invitation to compete in Rumania I have been distracted by daydreams of his crushing the best kids from Bulgaria, Hungary, Yugoslavia, Poland, Rumania and Russia. Whenever I bring up the possibility of his winning the world championship, Josh dutifully says, "Awesome," but I can tell that he dreams of other things.

Each week Josh studies chess openings with International Master Victor Frias and endings with Bruce Pandolfini. A few days ago Bruce told me that our son had grown too strong for him to teach further, and that next fall it would be best for him to begin studying the endgame with a grandmaster. When I mentioned this to Josh, he cried, insisting that Bruce was wrong.

Several weeks ago Josh played in a simultaneous exhibition in the Bronx against world champion Gary Kasparov, along with fifty-eight other children. For the past few weeks he had been playing without passion or concentration, but against Kasparov it was as if his honor were at stake. For two hours he was oblivious to television crews and flashing cameras; with pink-flushed cheeks and hands shielding his eyes, he stared relentlessly at the game. The world champion raced from board to board, hardly pausing to consider his moves, but time and again he would stop at my son's game for two or three minutes, scratch his short black hair, grimace, calculate, rock back on his heels and then smile at Josh, shake his head and think some more. Josh was so focused on the game that he didn't seem to notice Kasparov's special attention until after the twenty-eighth move, when the world champion offered his hand and said, "Draw." Then Josh pumped the air once with his fist, just as he does on the playground in pickup games with his buddies after scoring the winning basket.

Josh was one of two who achieved a draw against Kasparov, the other being fourteen-year-old K. K. Karanja. Afterward chess masters speculated whether an eleven-year-old had ever drawn with a world champion in a simultaneous exhibition. Someone said that when Botvinnik was twelve, he beat Capablanca. Ten minutes later I was still trembling with excitement and Josh was being interviewed by one of the TV networks. When the reporter asked my son about his career aspirations, I overheard Josh answer that he hoped someday to play second base for the New York Mets.

ABOUT THE AUTHOR

FRED WAITZKIN was born in Massachusetts in 1943 and graduated from Kenyon College. His work has appeared in *Esquire, New York* magazine and the *New York Times Sunday Magazine,* among other publications. He lives in New York City with his wife and two children.